CONTEMPORARY
POLITICAL SOCIOLOGY
GLOBALIZATION, POLITICS, AND POWER

Kate Nash

Blackwell
Publishing

© 2000 by Kate Nash

BLACKWELL PUBLISHING
350 Main Street, Malden, MA 02148-5020, USA
108 Cowley Road, Oxford OX4 1JF, UK
550 Swanston Street, Carlton, Victoria 3053, Australia

The right of Kate Nash to be identified as the Author of this Work has been asserted in accordance with the UK Copyright, Designs, and Patents Act 1988.

First published 2000
Reprinted 2002, 2005

Library of Congress Cataloging-in-Publication Data

Nash, Kate, 1958–
    Contemporary political sociology : globalization, politics, and power / Kate Nash
        p.   cm.
    Includes bibliographical references and index.
    ISBN 0–631–20660–4 (hb : alk. paper) — ISBN 0–631–20661–2 (pb. : alk. paper)
    1. Political sociology.   I. Title.
JA76.N32   1999
306.2 — dc21   99-16133
                                                            CIP

A catalogue record for this title is available from the British Library.

Set in 11 on 13pt Sabon
by Best-set Typesetter Ltd, Hong Kong
Printed and bound in the United Kingdom
by TJ International, Padstow, Cornwall

The publisher's policy is to use permanent paper from mills that operate a sustainable forestry policy, and which has been manufactured from pulp processed using acid-free and elementary chlorine-free practices. Furthermore, the publisher ensures that the text paper and cover board used have met acceptable environmental accreditation standards.

For further information on
Blackwell Publishing, visit our website:
www.blackwellpublishing.com

JA 76 NAS

CONTEMPORARY POLITICAL SOCIOLOGY

To Minky

CONTENTS

ACKNOWLEDGMENTS

I would like to thank Alan Scott and Neil Washbourne for their help with this book, especially for reading some parts of the draft more than once. Colleagues at the University of East Anglia read chapters in draft and I would like to thank them for their helpful comments, especially Sigrid Baringhörst, Barbara Goodwin, John Street, and John Zvesper. David Owen made some useful suggestions on several chapters. Thanks also to Anne-Marie Fortier, Fran Tonkiss, Monica Greco, Maryam Najand, Zoé Nash and Roberta Sassatelli for ideas, support, and encouragement throughout the project.

CHAPTER 1

Introduction: Changing Definitions of Politics and Power in Political Sociology

Political sociology has never been easily distinguishable as a field of research from others in the discipline of sociology. In general terms, however, it has been seen as concerned, above all, with relations between state and society. Most practitioners would probably agree with Orum's broad definition: political sociology directs attention toward "the social circumstances of politics, that is, to how politics both is shaped by and shapes other events in societies. Instead of treating the political arena and its actors as independent from other happenings in a society, [political sociology] treats that arena as intimately related to all social institutions" (Orum, 1983: 1).

In principle, given the wide range of this definition, it might be expected that political sociologists would be interested in power as at least a potentiality in all social relations, and to have elaborated a conception of politics as an activity conducted across a range of social institutions. In practice, however, although they have some-times gestured toward such an approach, the focus of political sociology has been politics at the level of the nation-state. It has shared what may be seen as the prejudice of modern sociology for taking "society" as the unit of analysis and treating it as a distinct, internally coherent and self-regulating entity, organized around the nation-state. The most influential definition of power in sociology is that of Max Weber: power is "the chance of a man or a number of men to realize their own will in a communal action even against the resistance of others who are participating in the action" (Weber, 1948a: 180).[1] On this definition, power could be a dimension of any social relation and politics need not be seen as a highly specialized activity, exercised only in relation to a specific institution. In fact, however, Weber, like others, focused his attention on the state as a special kind of institution that successfully possesses a monopoly of the legitimate use of force within a given territory (Weber, 1948b: 78). As Dowse and Hughes argue in their introduction to political sociology, although there seems to be no compelling *analytic* argument why the discipline should have focused its attention on state institutions, *as a matter of fact*, political sociologists have concerned themselves principally with the ways in which society has affected the state (Dowse and Hughes, 1972: 7).[2]

From the point of view of the new political sociology, such an approach is fundamentally flawed. Economic, political, and cultural globalization means that the nation-state now has greatly reduced power with respect to certain issues, having been over-ridden or by-passed by other institutions and processes. At the same time, the class formations around which national politics were organized have become fragmented and the political concerns associated with class-based political parties problematized. In part this has arisen from changes in the structure of the workforce and the fragmentation and dislocation of stable, secure working lives with economic insecurity and the institutionalization of "post-Fordist" working practices. The fragmentation and pluralization of values and life-styles, with the growth of the mass media and consumerism and the decline of stable occupations and communities, all mean that previously taken-for-granted social identities have become politicized. In this context, the rise of social movements and networks organized differently from parties, and representing non-class identities such as gender, ethnicity, and sexuality, have changed both the form and the content of politics. Wider definitions of power and politics are needed to encompass the formation, contestation, and transformation of identities and institutions across the social field, if fluid, fragmented, and fast-changing contemporary social relations are to be understood.

Empirical changes would not be sufficient, however, to create a new approach to political sociology if there were not also new theoretical tools with which to make sense of them. There has been "a paradigm shift" in political sociology, away from state-centered, class-based models of political participation, or non-participation, toward an understanding of politics as potential in all social experiences. New political sociology is above all concerned with cultural politics, understood in the broadest possible sense as the contestation and transformation of social identities and structures.

In theoretical terms, this paradigm shift is related to a more general change of orientation in sociology, the "postmodern turn." In some respects, this phrase is misleading. It is true that post-structuralists have been among the most adventurous of those who have attempted to re-think politics (and there are no self-identified postmodernists in sociology for whom the term might be more appropriate). The "postmodern turn" followed the eruption of new social movements and student politics in the 1960s, which was nowhere more dramatic than in France, where post-structuralism developed. During *les événements* of May 1968 students and workers occupied universities, factories, and offices, practically paralysing the French state. Class politics did figure in these movements, but more important were the attempts to imagine new ways of life and discussions about how to end conformity to "the system" summed up in such slogans as, *Soyez réaliste, demandez l'impossible* ("Be realistic, demand the impossible.") The uprising ended with the relatively powerful Communist Party accepting better pay and conditions for workers. This was seen as capitulation by the students, who wanted nothing less than revolution, and it led to intellectual disaffection from traditional left-wing politics and a period of questioning established ways of thinking in universities. It is directly from such conditions that the post-structuralist interest in politics as the reconstruction of identities and everyday social life emerges.

In other respects, however, the "postmodern turn" in sociology is a misconception. Post-structuralism has actually been developed more in philosophy than in sociology or political theory, and its abstractions have not always been easy to relate to these, more empirical, disciplines. Furthermore, schools within sociology itself, which are sometimes hostile to post-structuralism, have also contributed to the paradigm shift. This is true, for example, of the "sociology of reflexivity" associated with Anthony Giddens and Ulrich Beck. In some ways it would be better to think in terms of the "cultural turn" rather than the "postmodern turn" for these reasons.

Nevertheless, it is undoubtedly the case that the most far-reaching and systematic reconsideration of politics in relation to culture has come from post-structuralism and post-Marxism. It is for this reason that the "postmodern turn" will be used to describe the paradigm shift in political sociology with which we are concerned in this book. It aims to show how a model of cultural politics derived from post-structuralism can be used to illuminate processes which are increasingly of interest to sociologists.

We will begin in the following two sections by briefly examining the terms of the political sociology developed from the theories of the "founding fathers," Marx and Weber. We will then go on to consider those of the new political sociology in the post-structuralist "analytics of power" elaborated by Michel Foucault, and the post-Marxism of Ernesto Laclau and Chantal Mouffe. On this basis, a model of cultural politics is constructed which will help to link post-structuralism to the work of contemporary sociologists on politics through an understanding of the "postmodern turn." Finally, there will be an outline of the chapters to follow, indicating how each one deals with a particular empirical topic in the new political sociology.

1.1   THE MARXIST TRADITION OF POLITICAL SOCIOLOGY

In many respects it is far from evident that the state should have a central place in Marxist analyses of capitalism given their over-whelming theoretical commitment to the view that it is economic relations which ultimately determine all social and political life. Marx himself, concerned primarily as he was with capitalism as a mode of production, concentrated on the economic level and had rel-atively underdeveloped and tentative views on the state. In fact, Adam Przeworski goes so far as to suggest that, given his theory of capitalism as a self-perpetuating economic system of production and exchange, there was no room in it for theorizing the state as con-tributing to its reproduction (Przeworski, 1990: 69–70). Although this is an extreme view, based on Marx's later work, it is true that it has proved very difficult for neo-Marxists to give due weight to ideology and politics without giving up the central theoretical Marxist commitment to economic class struggle as the motor of history.

The roots of later Marxist theorizations of political power as a translation of economic power concentrated in the modern state are there already in Marx's writings. Although Marx had no fully developed theory of the state, he did discuss it in various ways throughout his writings. Here we shall follow Dunleavy and O'Leary's (1987) classification of Marx's analyses of the state into three distinct, and somewhat contradictory, positions on how it contributes to the reproduction of the capitalist system and the economic power of the bourgeoisie. All of them have been followed up in different ways by neo-Marxist theorists (Dunleavy and O'Leary, 1987: 209). First, on the instrumental model, the coercive aspect of the state is emphasized; it is seen above all as repressive of working-class resistance to exploitation. The "executive of the modern state" is "but a committee for managing the affairs of the whole bourgeoisie" (Marx, 1977: 223). On this model, economic power is quite simply translated into political power, by means of which the dominant bourgeoisie rules over subordinate classes through the liberal state. Secondly, in his later, more empirical writings, Marx suggested a different model of the state – the arbiter model (Dunleavy and O'Leary, 1987: 210). In "The Eighteenth Brumaire of Louis Bonaparte" he sketches the modern state in such a way as to suggest its relative autonomy from the interests of the bourgeoisie. The modern state has grown so strong that in exceptional moments, when the bourgeoisie cannot completely dominate the other classes against which it must struggle, it may become an arena for competing interests, an ostensible mediator, and may even act independently to limit the power of the bourgeoisie (Marx, 1992). However, "state power does not hover in mid-air;" it is only class interests that are represented at the political level and ultimately economic power will determine how state power is to be used (Marx, 1992: 237). Despite the relative autonomy of the modern state, then, economic power is translated into political power since it needs the material support of the historically ascendant class, and it therefore works ultimately to ensure the economic advantage of the bourgeoisie. Thirdly, in his mature economic work, Marx suggested a third model of the state: the functionalist version. On this view, developed in *Capital*, volume 3, the state is "superstructural," determined entirely by changes in the economic "base" of society. The state apparatus, government, and legal forms operate in order to optimize the conditions for capital accumulation, regardless of how directly the bourgeoisie manages state institutions and irrespective of the balance of forces in society (Dunleavy and O'Leary, 1987: 210–11). On this understanding of the state, political power is irrelevant; the state is but an epiphenomenon of the economic logic of the capitalist system which reproduces itself in every social and political institution to the advantage of the dominant economic class.

For some time after Marx's death, this economistic model of capitalist reproduction was Marxist orthodoxy. Although early Marxists gave some consideration to the role of the state in sustaining capitalism, theorists such as Kautsky and Plekhanov, concerned above all to establish Marxism as a rigorous science, worked to discover the historical laws by which the economy developed. They therefore reduced the superstructure – the political, ideological and, cultural – to emanations of the economic base (Taylor, 1995: 249–52). It is the neo-Marxist rejection of this simplistic economism which in recent years has led theorists to consider political power at the level of the state as relatively autonomous of economic power.

Neo-Marxism

The most important neo-Marxists for our purposes here are Antonio Gramsci and Louis Althusser because of their influence on post-Marxism. Writing in the 1920s, Gramsci was the first Marxist to theorize the ideological and political superstructures as relatively autonomous of the economic base. As such, he was a major influence on neo-Marxists such as Althusser, and later on post-Marxists. The key term for Gramsci is "hegemony," which means the way in which the dominant class gains consent for its rule through compromises and alliances with some class fractions and the disorganization of others, and also the way in which it maintains that rule in a stable social formation (Gramsci, 1971; Simon, 1982). In terms of Dunleavy and O'Leary's typology, Gramsci's is an arbiter theory of the state: the state is formed by the balance of forces achieved in the struggle for hegemony. For Gramsci, a class does not take state power, it becomes the state (Laclau and Mouffe, 1985: 69). However, Gramsci is innovative in Marxism in not thinking of the state as the institution in which politics takes place. According to Gramsci, hegemony is gained in the first place in civil society where ideology is embodied in communal forms of life in such a way that it becomes the taken-for-granted common sense of the people. All relations of civil society involve issues of power and struggle, not just class relations. Gramsci is actually the first theorist of cultural politics, since he sees politics, not as confined to the level of the state, but as taking place in all social relations, representations, and institutions. Politics is more a cultural sensibility than an institutional activity.

Gramsci's thought in this respect was limited, however, by his commitment to a residual economism. Gramsci, like Althusser, saw ideology as practices which form subjects; for both thinkers, our experience and our relationship to the world are mediated through ideology. In Gramsci's view, however, subjects are not necessarily class subjects, but rather collective political wills which are formed by articulating ideas and values in different combinations in order to draw different groups into the hegemonic project. However, as a Marxist, Gramsci was committed to the belief that ideological struggle was grounded in class struggle; he therefore argued that there must always be a single unifying principle in every hegemonic formation and that this can only be given by a fundamental economic class. As Laclau and Mouffe (1985: 69) point out, this is not just to say that, ultimately, the economy determines politics, but also to see the economy itself as outside hegemony, as somehow naturally given and non-political. As they argue, this is economistic in so far as there is nothing for Marxists to do but identify the direction in which the economy is heading; there is no possibility of political intervention, nor even of effective class struggle, in the domain that really matters to Marxists, the economy. In their view, Gramsci limited the scope of politics in that it should be seen as fundamental to the founding, and contestation, of any social order whatsoever. Gramsci's model is also limited in that, seeing politics as ultimately rooted in class struggle, it cannot give sufficient weight to social movements organized around gender, race, sexual politics, the environment, and so on. However, to reject economic determinism and the centrality of the class struggle is to go beyond Marxism altogether.

Similar issues arise in the work of Louis Althusser, also an important influence on post-Marxists. Although Althusser's project was to rescue Marxism from economism, in so far as it remains within the Marxist framework, economism cannot be avoided. Althusser maintained that the state should be seen as relatively autonomous of the economic base. However, his theory of the state is better described as "functionalist," rather than in terms of Dunleavy and O'Leary's arbiter model. Although he insists that political structures have their own laws of development, there is no discussion of class conflict at this level; the state is fully implicated in the logic of capitalism where it functions to reproduce the mode of production (Dunleavy and O'Leary, 1987: 255). As Althusser sees it, the state is relatively autonomous of the economic base because, although the economy determines "in the last instance," it does so by determining another level of the mode of production as dominant according to the specificity of the mode of production: in feudalism, religion is dominant; in capitalism, the state. Furthermore, since the capitalist mode of production requires the state to reproduce its conditions of existence, there is a reciprocal determination between the economic and political levels; the last instance of economic determination never arrives since the economy is itself formed by the political (Althusser, 1971).

In so far as Althusser's theory of the state is functionalist, it has been criticized as involving a sophisticated form of economic reductionism. The problem is that, if the economy is determining in the last instance, then whatever the form and dynamic of contingent, actually existing capitalist states, ultimately they are irrelevant in relation to the necessity of the reproduction of capitalism itself. In fact, the term "relative autonomy" is oxymoronic: if autonomy is relative, then ultimately it is not autonomy at all. As Paul Hirst argues, Althusser is trapped by his own question – "how is it possible for capitalist social relations to exist?" – since there is no general answer to this question which would not involve him in the teleological logic of functionalist explanations. Althusser is searching for the causes of an existing state of affairs which the explanation then takes to be necessary for their existence: in effect, the consequences make the causes necessary (Hirst, 1979: 43–5). The conclusion that Hirst draws from this is that, if the relative autonomy of the state is to be taken seriously, there can be no reduction of the political to the economic: the form of social classes produced as effects of politics must be analyzed as such. As we will see, post-Marxists have subsequently taken the issue of the autonomy of the political much further than this.

In fact, the most influential aspect of Althusser's work has been the importance he gave to issues of ideology and subjectivity.

Althusser saw the state as working through the repressive institutions of the police and the army, but also through ideology embedded in state institutions – for him, a mixture of public and private institutions, including those of education, the family, trade unions, and religion. Althusser saw society as a complex of structures, each with its own dynamic, linked into a totality by the ultimate determination of the economy. The function of ideology is to make individuals into subjects who will fit the positions provided by those structures. Although it is described as consisting of "representations" – "images, myths, ideas or concepts" – ideology does not work through the conscious mind, but in an unconscious relation to the world which is lived in social practices, such as religious rituals, political meetings, and so on (Althusser, 1971: 39–44). Althusser's theory of ideology avoids the pitfalls of the Marxist notion of "false consciousness," in which people are seen as dupes of the capitalist system, since he does not see ideology as consciousness at all; in his view, ideology is itself material, involving experiences lived in real social practices. However, ideology does involve a degree of mystification in that subjects necessarily live an imaginary relation to their real conditions of existence (Barrett, 1991: ch. 5).

Althusser's lasting influence lies in the way in which he situated ideology as a matter of practices rather than conscious ideas and beliefs and the emphasis he gave to subjectivity as a means of social control. However, the Marxist epistemology which gave him the assurance to assert that subjects systematically misrepresent reality has been rejected. Althusser maintained that Marxism is scientific because it is "open" and "counter-intuitive" where ideology is "closed," and that it draws its problems from politics and practice rather than from critical theory (Benton, 1994: 45–9). This is problematic since Marxism has invariably seemed extremely dogmatic to non-believers, and at the same time it has been riven by factional disputes. Furthermore, it is difficult to draw a distinction between science and ideology according to the "openness" of science given that, following Thomas Kuhn's (1970) extremely influential work on science, even the natural sciences are less concerned with genuinely testing theories than with confirming them. Rejection of a sharp distinction between "true" knowledge and "false" ideology, or indeed knowledge and rhetoric, or knowledge and opinion, is an important feature of the "postmodern turn" which we will look at in more detail below (pp. 32–43).

1.2 THE WEBERIAN TRADITION OF POLITICAL SOCIOLOGY

The autonomy of the political at the level of the state is central to Weber's political sociology. In fact, Weber's work stands at the beginning of a tradition of thought which is explicitly anti-Marxist on just this issue of the autonomy of the state and the importance of liberal democratic politics. As a liberal committed to the defence of individual freedom, which he saw threatened in modernity, Weber opposed his work to Marx's economic determinism. He took the concentration of the means of administration in the nation-state to be as important as the concentration of the means of production in capitalism theorized by Marx (Bottomore, 1993: 10–11).

As we saw above, Weber defined power in such a way as to suggest that it may be present in all social relations, so that politics need not be seen as confined to the single arena of the state. In fact, his definition of politics is also very broad: "[it] comprises any kind of *independent* leadership in action" (Weber, 1948a: 77).[3] Despite these definitions, however, Weber immediately narrowed the field of his analysis to the power and politics of the nation-state. He saw the state as the most powerful institution in modern society since it has gained the legitimate monopoly of force over a given territory, and therefore took politics to involve "striving to share power or striving to influence the distribution of power, either among states or among groups within a state" (Weber, 1948a: 78). As David Held (1987: 150) points out, Weber's emphasis on territoriality is crucial; the modern state is a nation-state in competitive relation to other nation-states, rather than with armed segments of its own population. Weberian sociology therefore explicitly shares the propensity of sociology in general, and including Marxism in the ways we have discussed, for taking total societies organized around nation-states as the object of its analysis.

Weber describes the state as gaining its power in modernity by concentrating the means of administration in the hands of an absolute monarch, expropriating the "ownership of the means of administration," in a way similar to that described by Marx in the case of workers who are deprived of control of the means of production (Weber, 1948b: 81–2). Officials in modern, rational bureaucracies have little or no control over what they do since the rules and procedures of bureaucracies take on a life of their own, restricting the activities and decisions of those who work in them to the functions of the offices they fill. In this way, bureaucracy forms a "steel-hard housing" within which most individuals in modern societies must live and work, since its effects are felt not only by those who work in administration, but also by those who are administered.[4] According to Weber, this form of life is the price that must be paid for living in a highly complex and technically advanced society. Bureaucratic administration is the only rational way of managing economically and politically differentiated societies since economic enterprises need predictability above all; without it, they cannot calculate in order to ensure profitability. This is why the socialist dream that the state will wither away once the dominant class has been deprived of its power in the ownership of the means of production is more like a nightmare for Weber: to abolish private property would increase the power of the state since there would be no countervailing power of the market, and management of the economy would come entirely under the control of bureaucrats (Held, 1987: 150–4).

Although Weber saw himself as a neutral social scientist, his political sociology has a normative dimension. He is concerned to analyze representative democracy as it actually works in modern societies, arguing that the ideal of participatory democracy cannot be practiced in large-scale, complex societies. On the other hand, however, he is also concerned that democracy may be the only way in which the "steel-hard housing" of modern bureaucratic power can be broken. Clearly, the elite administration that must run modern societies cannot be directly accountable to the masses; this would make for inefficiency and unpredictability, especially given what Weber sees as the irrationality and ignorance of the general population. Democracy is important, nevertheless, primarily because elections provide testing grounds for charismatic leaders who are then given the mandate of the people and who can establish the goals the bureaucrats are to realize. Such leaders offer the only chance of overriding the bureaucratic machinery (Giddens, 1972: 38–9). More conventionally, democracy is important because, even if it only offers the opportunity to dismiss the ineffective from office, it thereby provides a certain degree of protection for the people (Held, 1987: 154–60). In Weber's view, democracy is less the rule of the people than the rule of an elite which combines exceptional leaders and bureaucratic experts.

Political sociologists have been inspired by Weber's view of liberal democratic politics. Elite theorists tend to see democracy as working along the lines proposed by Weber (Marsh, 1995: 285); and, although the history of its intellectual development has not been thoroughly traced, there are affinities between pluralist theories and Weber's view that there are many sources of power, not just the economy, and that elites do not rule supreme but can be challenged by organized groups in the political process (Held, 1987: 187). A sympathy with pluralism also runs though the new political sociology. However, it has been re-thought in ways which represent a break with this Weberian tradition. Ironically, this is because new political sociologists take seriously Weber's own view that power is extensive across the social and extend this to analyze politics beyond the nation-state.

However, it may be that Weber's view of power and politics is problematic in terms of his own sociological theory. Despite his belief in democracy as a way of mitigating the power of bureaucracy, Weber was generally pessimistic, seeing the "polar night of icy darkness" in which individual freedom is highly constrained by impersonal administration as a likely outcome of the development of modern societies (Weber, 1948a: 128). But this pessimism is linked to his view that the majority of the population is uninterested in, and ignorant of, political matters. It is certainly the case that there is widespread apathy concerning party political matters; the proportion of the population in Western liberal democracies who use their vote is in steady decline. On the other hand, the growth of social movements means that, if one looks at politics in the wider sense, members of society may be involved in political struggles where they see issues as having a direct impact on their lives. While we should not ignore the tendencies toward organizational atrophy that Weber identified, if we take the wider view of politics we must see individuals as much more actively engaged in re-making the social than he was able to discern from within the terms of the political sociology he founded.

Elite theorists

Elite theorists are concerned with the question of how and why it is that a minority must always rule over a majority, a fact which they see as inevitable in any society. Political elite theorists are above all concerned with the decision-makers in society, those they see as holding power as a cohesive, relatively self-conscious group (Parry, 1969: 13–14). Modern elite theorists have been extremely influential in political sociology. Joseph Schumpeter, in particular, has been an important figure as a popularizer of Michels's ideas on political parties and Weber's theory of democracy. He influenced the generation of sociologists and political scientists involved in the professionalization of the discipline in the 1950s, especially in the United States. According to Bottomore (1993: 28), so great was this influence that, for some time afterwards, political scientists in particular took electoral politics and voting behavior as the only worthwhile topic of study to the exclusion of the substance of political conflicts.

Michels took the concentration of power in the hands of an elite to be a necessary outcome of complex organizations. He is responsible for the emphasis in empirical political sociology on analyzing the dynamics of party politics. His famous "iron law of oligarchy" states that, in modern societies, parties need to be highly organized and so inevitably become oligarchic, being hierarchically run by party leaders and bureaucracy such that the bulk of members are excluded from decision-making (Michels, 1962). Michels was critical of this process, although he saw it as tragically inevitable. As a socialist, he was disappointed that socialist parties would be unable to realize their democratic ideals, unlike Weber and Schumpeter for whom bureaucratic and hierarchical parties are the only means by which political leadership in large-scale societies can emerge (Scott, 1996a: 317–18).

Developing Michels's thesis, Schumpeter saw democracy as nothing but competition between political parties whose elite members deal in votes, just as businessmen deal in commodities. It does not, and should not, mean rule by the people; it is rather a method for arriving at political decisions by means of a competitive struggle for the people's vote. Once elected, professional politicians must be allowed to rule, assisted by a strong independent bureaucracy of expert administrators, since the stability of the political system requires respect for the judgment of elected representatives (Schumpeter, 1943).

A radical version of Weberian elite theory is the institutional elite theory proposed by C. W. Mills. In Mills's view, the elitism of the US in the twentieth century is a serious hindrance to democracy rather than the factor that makes it possible and viable. As he sees it, power has become concentrated and unified in the elites of three institutions in the US: the military, the corporate, and the political; the connections between them having been strengthened by the growth of a permanent war establishment in a privatized incorporated economy since World War II. This concentration, combined with the one-way communication of the mass media as it is organized by elites, makes the ordinary citizens ignorant and rather complacent, although fitfully miserable, about the extent to which they lack control over their lives (Mills, 1956).

Mills's argument is similar to that of Marxist elite theorists, notably Ralph Milliband, for whom the capitalist class assures its reproduction by means of the close links it enjoys with the leaders of such powerful institutions as political parties, the civil service, the media, and the military (Miliband, 1969). They differ, however, in that Mills refuses to see the power elite as necessarily unified by virtue of its economic class position and social background, arguing that the shared interests and perspective of its members are the contingent product of particular historical developments. Marxists, of course, explain the unity of the elite in terms of the interests of capitalism (Bottomore, 1964: 34). However, a comparison of Miliband's and Mills's studies clearly reveals the convergence of Weberians and Marxists on the issue of the relative autonomy of the state. For Miliband, like other neo-Marxists, the state must be able to separate itself from the immediate interests of ruling-class factions if it is to be effective in ensuring the interests of capitalism in the long run (Held, 1987: 207); while for Mills, as for other Weberians, however much it is conditioned by elite decisions taken elsewhere, the political elite of the state has its own effectivity.

New political sociologists share with elite theorists an interest in how certain groups are excluded from the political process. In common with critical elite theorists, they see this exclusion as a problem which prevents the realization of the ideals of democracy, rather than, like Schumpeter and Weber, a solution to the difficulties of democratic political participation in modern societies. However, once the problem is framed in different terms, it is possible to be somewhat more optimistic about the possibilities of making the political process more inclusive. Re-thinking the scope of politics also makes it possible to re-think the terms of democracy.

Unlike elite theory, new political sociology tends not to be so concerned with the division between executive and administrative leaders and rank-and-file members of organizations and institutions. In a fragmented and pluralistic society, divided along lines of gender, ethnicity, sexuality, and so on, it cannot be supposed that it is solely, or even mainly, a result of an elite's monopolization of the machinery of decision-making that social groups are excluded from power. In the terms Michels puts forward, for example, it might be the case that in a political party both the elite and the ordinary members share an interest in excluding women from decision-making. How an organization or institution is structured in terms of exclusion depends on the perspective from which it is examined, the specific historical moment, the contexts within which decisions are made, and the particular constructions of interest in play at that particular time and in that particular place. It is important for political sociologists to look at all these aspects, and the way in which different lines of exclusion interact with and over-determine each other, rather than assuming in advance that differences in decision-making power are the sole, or even the main, dimension of exclusion.

As Dowse and Hughes point out, it is implicit in all elite theory that the real interests of members of organizations and institutions are opposed to those of the elite. If both groups have common interests, it is not evident that an elite would be anything more than a number of individuals holding the top positions in society (Dowse and Hughes, 1972: 152). From a post-structuralist perspective, "interests" are always socially constructed; there is no possible appeal to "the way things are" which is not already steeped in assumptions, values, and beliefs. This does not mean, as Terry Eagleton (1991) mistakenly argues, that no possible claims can be made on behalf of an oppressed group. It means only that such claims cannot be grounded in an appeal to "reality," that interests are only "real" from a particular political perspective. On this understanding, any claim based on "real interests" is part of a political project; it cannot be seen as based on a neutral, scientific theory, in touch with the objective social world. In terms of elite theory, this means that there is no necessary objective opposition of interests between elite and rank and file. There may well be a division between them, but it is contingent on the construction of interests within the organization or institution, not the "real" interests of its members. Furthermore, how that opposition is constructed will also depend on the perspective from which the analysis was carried out, and its representation of those interests must itself be analyzed as political.

Elite theory has tended to approach studies of democratic processes from a conservative perspective, radical and Marxist elite theorists notwithstanding. Schumpeter's work has not only focused attention on electoral politics as if they were politics *tout court*, it has also led to "actually existing" democracy being taken as a more or less perfect instrument of rule, with scope for only minor technical improvements (Bottomore, 1993: 28). In effect, for empirical political sociologists – the charge is less valid in the case of more conceptual and normative work (Held, 1987: 178–85) – a limited view of what politics involves has been strongly linked to a limited view of what democracy must be if it is to be practicable and to allow for stable government. The state-centric view of power and politics held by elite theorists is linked to their understanding of mass society consisting of a passive, ignorant and apathetic population, technically incompetent to participate fully in politics, according to competitive elitists, and continually deceived as to its real interests, according to more critical versions. Once politics is seen as a matter of everyday life, however, the emphasis changes completely. New political sociologists see society itself as cut across with inequities of power, any of which may be politicized and therefore become the focus of contestation. Far from being passive, social agents are seen as engaged in remaking their own identities and the institutions of their everyday lives.

Pluralism

Unlike elite theory, pluralism tends to see citizens as actively involved in politics. This brings it closer to the concerns of new political sociology. In fact, post-structuralist political sociology has been compared to pluralism as if the two were indistinguishable (Dunleavy and O'Leary, 1987: 255–6). It is undoubtedly the case that they have a good deal in common. Nevertheless, pluralism also shares certain features of mainstream sociology, including, ultimately, a commitment to a state-centric view of politics.[5]

As pluralists see it, politics is a matter of competing interest groups, none of which can dominate completely over any of the others since all have access to resources of different kinds. Furthermore, they see the state itself as a set of competing and conflicting institutions, rather than a monolithic entity which exerts its power over the rest of society (Smith, 1995: 211). For this reason they avoid the term, preferring to think in terms of government. Similarly, the "people" in a democracy is not a unified whole with a single will to be exerted, far less an apathetic, incompetent mass which needs to be ruled by an elite. Democratic politics involves endless bargaining in order to influence government policy, which is nothing more than a compromise between the differing interest groups involved in the political process (Dowse and Hughes, 1972: 135).

In response to their critics, pluralists have revised what has been taken as an excessively naïve view of the openness of liberal democratic politics. Neo-pluralists see elites, and especially corporate elites, as having a greater degree of influence than other groups on government policy; they take it that this may not be openly and visibly exerted in the political process and that it may constrain the effective influence of other interest groups (Held, 1987: 202). In this respect, in neo-pluralism there is a convergence between neo-Marxism, pluralism and radical elite theory (Marsh, 1995). However, neo-pluralists do not fully endorse the presuppositions of elite theory; instead, they argue that the elite is not unified, nor is it capable of manipulating and deceiving the citizens into accepting elite rule. On the pluralist view, elites must be seen as existing only in so far as they are genuinely responsive to the interest groups they purport to serve (Dowse and Hughes, 1972: 138). Neo-pluralists also depart from the assumptions of neo-Marxists: although business may on occasion subvert the democratic process, this is a contingent matter; politics at the level of the state is primary and so it cannot be the case that the state is ultimately driven by the interests of any particular group, including the capitalist class.

Those political sociologists who participate in the "postmodern turn" share with pluralists an understanding of politics as central to social life and as independent of the state. Society is seen as made up of a multiplicity of self-defining groups who do not owe their existence, nor their identity and power, to the political process at the level of the state. Furthermore, for post-structuralists in particular, there is no natural essence to these groups: they are seen as constructed in alliances and conflicts with others, not as based on intrinsically shared "real" interests or characteristics. In fact, there are "cross-cutting solidarities" between groups, as individuals belong to more than one depending on how they experience their political identity in different social contexts. Finally, both pluralists and post-structuralists argue against totalizing conceptions of a unified society with sovereignty residing in the nation-state: the lines of division, the over-determination of political identities, and the mobilization of power and resources across the social cannot simply be added together into one unified domain with a single sovereign center (McClure, 1992).

However, ultimately, pluralists share the definition of politics held by other mainstream political sociologists to which political sociologists informed by the "postmodern turn" are opposed. Pluralists are interested in the plurality of interest groups which form and re-form in the social only in so far as they orient their demands to governmental institutions. Although the state is seen as little more than the arena in which social groups engage in political conflict, it is only in so far as these conflicts take place at the level of the state that they are treated *as* political (McClure, 1992: 118–19). By definition, for pluralists there is no politics outside the state.

This limited pluralist definition of politics is linked to a restricted definition of power which, although wider than that of other schools in traditional political sociology, nevertheless makes it impossible to see the construction and contestation of social identities as political. Famously, Dahl (1956: 13) defines power as "a realistic . . . relationship, such as A's capacity for acting in such a manner as to control B's responses." This presupposes an already constituted social actor who is in possession of power such that he or she is able to control the effects produced. As critics of pluralism have pointed out, the emphasis on observable effects means that they neglect ideas and the way in which the political agenda may be shaped in such a way that direct manipulation of the outcome of the political process is unnecessary (Lukes, 1974). Post-structuralists would go still further to argue that the formation of the identities, capacities, and concerns of social groups must itself be seen as an effect of power.

This is a much more fundamental way in which the social and political is structured than by decisions taken in a centralized bureaucracy.

Although pluralists do not take the interests of the social groups they study as given, their definitions of power and politics prevent them from seeing the formation and contestation of political identities in the social field as political and lead them to focus only on the way in which individuals try to maximize their interests at the level of government. In this respect the pluralist perspective remains within the framework of the old political sociology. A theory of politics of this kind cannot begin to grasp the asymmetries of power between classes, races, and men and women which have been politicized by the activities of new social movements since the 1960s; pluralists were, in fact, extremely surprised by this development (Held, 1987: 199–200).

1.3   DISCOURSE THEORY, POWER, AND POLITICS

The single most important theoretical contribution to the new political sociology is undoubtedly Foucault's definition of power. Foucault himself has rather a paradoxical relationship to the new political sociology: although he is the theorist whose work has been most influential in its development, and although he was actively engaged in various political activities, including campaigns for prisoner's rights and gay activism, he professed himself to be much more interested in ethics than in politics (Foucault, 1984a). This preference for ethics, which he saw as a matter of self-creation rather than of principles of right and wrong, is related to his distaste for systematic theorizing. Foucault refused to provide us with a map of social and political institutions with which to understand contemporary politics, but his work can be used to analyze the working of power in unexpected places and unexpected ways. On this basis, it is possible to re-think politics as a possibility for resisting power and transforming social practices outside the dominant institutions of the state.

We will first look at an outline of Foucault's "analytics of power," and then at the development of a more systematic theory of power and politics in the work of Laclau and Mouffe. As post-Marxists influenced by Foucault and by Gramsci, they have developed a theory of cultural politics which is very useful as a more general statement for the understanding of cultural politics at the heart of new political sociology.

Foucault's analytics of power

Foucault explicitly denies that he has constructed a *theory* of power, arguing that power must be analyzed in its operations and effects and cannot be captured in a systematic set of related concepts conceived in advance of its application (Foucault, 1984b: 82). He prefers, therefore, to think in terms of an "analytics of power" in which power is identified only in the instances of its exercise. It is, nevertheless, possible to make some general points about this "analytics."

Power for Foucault is, above all, productive. His analyses are opposed to what he calls the "juridico-discursive" model in which power is seen as possessed by the state, especially the law, and is used to impose order on society. According to this theory, power involves legitimate prohibition modeled on the legal contract, according to liberals, or repressive legislation and policing to preserve class domination, according to radicals. It is, at any rate, essentially negative, restrictive, and inhibitory (Foucault, 1980a). According to Foucault, to think of power in this way is to miss how it works in institutions and discourses across the social field. Foucault is concerned to analyze power in the details of social practices, at the points at which it produces effects, as a fluid, reversible, and invisible "microphysics" of power. In Foucault's model, power is productive in the sense that it is constitutive, working to produce particular types of bodies and minds in practices which remain invisible from the point of view of the older model of power as sovereignty. Power is pluralist: it is exercised from innumerable points, rather than from a single political center, as the possession of an elite or the logic of bureaucratic institutions, and it is not governed by a single over-arching project. However, it is not that to see power as productive is to see it as good. On the contrary, in most of his work at least, Foucault's use of the term "power" implies a critical perspective on social practices. It is productive of regulated and disciplined social relations and identities which are to be resisted.

The most general sense in which power is productive for Foucault is through knowledge. Knowledge, especially that of the social sciences, is closely implicated in the production of docile bodies and subjected minds. "Discourses" is the term Foucault uses for these systems of quasi-scientific knowledge. Knowledge as discourse is not knowledge of the "real" world as it exists prior to that knowledge. Although it presents itself as *representing* objective reality, in fact, discourses *construct* and make "real" the objects of knowledge they "represent." Knowledge is distinguished from other ways of apprehending the world and considered to be "knowledge" of the objective world because it is supported by practices of power. As Foucault sees it, it involves statements uttered in institutional sites in which knowledge is gained according to certain rules and procedures, by speakers who are authorized to say what counts as "truth" in that particular context. For Foucault, the analysis of discourse requires the determination of how new objects of knowledge emerge, under what discursive and non-discursive conditions, and especially, what effects of power they produce. As he puts it, "Truth is linked in a circular relation with systems of power which produce and sustain it, and to effects of power which it induces and which extend it" (Foucault, 1980b: 133).

Foucault's analysis of knowledge as constitutive and implicated in power breaks, then, with the "official" view the social sciences would like to have of themselves as disinterested, neutral, and, as such, contributing to human progress. It also breaks with the radical view that knowledge produced in elite institutions is inherently mystificatory, concealing real relations of power. As Foucault sees it, it is not so much that discourses conceal power, but rather that they contribute to its exercise in the production of social relations of authority and conformity.

Power produces individuals both as objects and as subjects. In *Discipline and Punish*, Foucault describes how docile bodies are produced by organizing individuals in practices of surveillance which train comportment according to classifications of normal and abnormal. This takes place in different ways in different institutions across the social field, including the military, factories, schools, hospitals, and so on (Foucault, 1979). In *The History of Sexuality*, volume I, he analyzes the production of sexualized bodies in practices of confession (Foucault, 1984b). According to Foucault's analysis, far from being natural, "sexuality" has been developed over a long historical period. We in the West have learned to experience ourselves as desiring in particular ways, initially through the Christian confession and now, in contemporary society, in settings which use therapeutic techniques – in psychotherapy proper, but also in counseling, social work, education, even "phone-ins" about personal problems, confessional TV shows, and so on. In Foucault's view, the body is imprinted in history; its capacities are historically specific and produced in practices of power.

It is in terms of the construction of subjectivity, however, that Foucault has been most influential in the new political sociology. His work has displaced the humanist idea that the subject is the source of intentional meaning, self-reflexive, unified, and rational which has been dominant in modern Western thought (McNay, 1994: 4). For Foucault, subjects are always *subjected*, produced in discourses and practices of power which position them as speakers in possession of self-consciousness and, most importantly in the twentieth century, an unconscious that determines desire. In *The History of Sexuality*, volume I, he discusses at length the irony that in trying to liberate him or herself in therapy, the analysand is actually subjecting him or herself to a strategy of normalization which *produces* the very subject who should free him or herself in this way (Foucault, 1984a). In positioning oneself as the "I," the subject of speech in the discourse of psychoanalysis, one is produced, and experiences oneself, as an individual with secret desires which must be uncovered in analysis if one is to be free and healthy. The self of psychoanalysis is *produced*, not *discovered*. Furthermore, the production takes place in a relationship of power in so far as the analysand's speech, thoughts, and dreams must be interpreted by the analyst, positioned as an authority by the discourse of psychoanalysis. What the case of psychoanalysis illustrates, according to Foucault, is that subjectivity itself, the very possibility of having a self of which one is aware, of saying "I" with some degree of self-knowledge, is conditional on the exercise of power.

It is clear that Foucault could not have identified the effects of power on the body and on subjectivity using a totalizing theory of power. His analysis depends on examining the precise details of historically specific knowledges and practices as they operate differently in different institutions to produce constraining and subordinate identities. Nevertheless, his studies have been quite extensively criticized as tending to fall back into the negative view of power to which he is opposed, portraying it as a monolithic, unmitigated force of domination. Certainly, as previously noted, his use of the term "power" suggests a critical perspective on existing practices of subjection and objectification. In this respect, it has undoubtedly been highly effective in denaturalizing reified social constructions. However, critics argue that if *all* social relations and identities are the product of power, this critical perspective is actually redundant. There are two related points here. First, it is argued that the concept of power suggests that something is overcome, or dominated, in its exercise. If, however, all human capacities are produced in power, why call it power at all? If power is productive rather than repressive, Foucault could have said that everything is socially constructed rather than that everything is produced in relations of power without losing the sense of his analysis (Fraser, 1989). Secondly, it is argued that, if power is productive of all capacities, it follows that individuals are nothing more than "place-fillers," without resources to resist it: they have no capacities for autonomous self-creation or the generation of meanings and values which they could use against the effects of power (McNay, 1994: 102–4). On this understanding of Foucault's work, far from freeing us from the limitations of seeing power as negative, he actually portrays it as absolutely repressive, allowing no possibility of resistance.

These criticisms do seem to have some bearing on Foucault's early work on power. There does seem to be an inconsistency between his theoretical commitment to an analytics of power as positive and the overwhelmingly negative tone of the historical analyses he carried out. He implies, and sometimes states blankly, that power is every-where, as in this – notorious – statement from *The History of Sexuality*, volume I: "Power is everywhere; not because it embraces everything, but because it comes from everywhere . . . Power is not an institution, nor a structure, not a possession. It is the name we give to a complex strategic situation" (Foucault, 1984b: 93). Critics are undoubtedly right to point out that if power is everywhere, it becomes a metaphysical principle and loses all normative and explanatory content. As Peter Dews (1984: 21) puts it, "only if we can produce a counterfactual, specifying how a situation would change if an operation of power were cancelled . . . can [this] concept be empirically applied."

In his later work, however, Foucault's ideas about power developed in ways which meet these objections. The most significant developments in this respect are his ideas on domination, power, and resistance and the lectures he gave on governmentality before he died. The question of whether these new ideas mean that he actually breaks with his previous ideas is controversial. There are those who see this work as a radical new departure, or at least a change of direction (McNay, 1994; Hindess, 1996: 19), while others argue that Foucault's work is "at root *ad hoc*, fragmentary and incomplete" and should not be interpreted as developing according to an ideal of unity at all (Gutting, 1994: 2). It is indisputable, however, that his later thoughts on power are a good deal more complex than those used in the earlier analyses.

In "The Subject and Power," Foucault discusses the relationship between power, domination, and resistance in contemporary society. He argues that, as a matter of definition, where there is power there must be resistance. He had sketched out this idea in his earlier work, but here he develops it further, arguing that power necessarily works on what he calls "free subjects." It is only where there is the possibility of resistance, where subjects are not fully determined but may realize different possibilities from the range with which they are faced, that it is meaningful to think in terms of power. Slavery does not involve a relationship of power where the slave is in chains, but rather a relation of violence. Apparently in opposition to his previous assertions that "power is everywhere" and that subjects are discursively constructed, Foucault is here committing himself to the view that the "free subject" necessarily exists prior to discourse. However, he retains the view that subjects are constructed in practices of power in so far as he maintains that subjects are *subjected* where they are controlled by others, and also in so far as they are tied to their own identity by conscience or self-knowledge (Foucault, 1982).

Foucault links his analyses of power directly with the antagonistic struggles of social movements, arguing that one of the most important aspects of these struggles in contemporary society is the way in which they challenge subjectification. To some extent, social movements are based on the assertion of existing identities, and so on the acceptance of categorizations of normal/not normal produced in discourses and practices of power. On the other hand, however, they sometimes involve the refusal of existing identities:

on the one hand, they assert the right to be different and they under-
line everything which makes individuals truly individual. On the other
hand, they attack everything which separates the individual, breaks
his links with others, splits up his community life, forces the individual back on himself and ties him to his own identity in a constraining way. (Foucault, 1982: 211–12)

The examples he gives are struggles against the power of men over
women, of parents over children, of psychiatry over the mentally ill,
of medicine over the population and of administration over the ways
in which people live. Foucault makes the point that it is in part a
result of the way in which social movements resist power that it is
possible to analyze it as such. Resistance is necessary to the definition
of power, and it is also methodologically important to the study of
power in that it brings power relations and the methods by which it
is exercised into view.

Foucault also refines his analytics of power with the concepts of
domination and government in his later work. In fact, according to
Barry Hindess (1996), he increasingly uses domination as a term to
analyze what is more commonly thought of as power, replacing the
term power with government. On Hindess's reading, Foucault used
more precise terms in order to distinguish between power as a feature
of all human interactions and domination as a particular structure
of power in which antagonisms are consolidated in hierarchical and
stable relations. Power, then, is not denounced as such, the implication of the critical perspective of Foucault's earlier work. On the contrary, it now represents the potential fluidity of social relations. Since
power only acts on those who may resist, and who may in turn act
on others, there is always the possibility of reversals of power. In
domination, however, those who are dominated have such little room
for maneuver that reversals of power become impracticable, though
they are never strictly speaking impossible (Foucault, 1982; Hindess,
1996). Again, the activities of social movements may be used
methodologically to understand how far a particular set of social
relationships should be seen as domination or as relations of power,
according to the degree of freedom they enable or allow for the
politics of identity.

Foucault defines "government" as "the conduct of conduct," the
attempt to influence the actions of free subjects. He describes it as
lying between the stable and hierarchical relations of domination and

the reversible relations of power (Foucault, 1984c: 19). Foucault uses the term to refer both to the government of the self and of others. Foucault's work on the ethics of the self is much more widely read than his work on governmentality as a social configuration, but the latter is also important, especially for political sociology, because it deals with the relations between society and the state which are its traditional material. Foucault sees governmentality as a modern form of power, arising explicitly in opposition to its competitor, the Machiavellian idea of sovereignty, in early modernity. Machiavellianism was concerned to maintain peace and security through the figure of the sovereign. According to the advice set out in *The Prince*, the principal object of government is the maintenance of the sovereign's rule over the territory and subjects of the state. For its opponents, however, this type of rule is too external to the society, and therefore too fragile, to be successful. The practices of government should rather be immanent to society itself, and exercised over "men and things" in order promote wealth and well-being. According to Foucault, governmentality was increasingly established from the eighteenth century with the development of capitalism, the emergence of the idea of "population," and a range of knowledges and techniques concerned with managing its expansion, health, and productivity (Foucault, 1991). The idea of governmentality thus develops Foucault's earlier critique of the "juridico-discursive" model of power as sovereignty. It is not that the state is irrelevant, but government through state institutions is just one aspect of the strategies of governmentality. The "conduct of conduct" is attempted in different ways in institutions and practices across the social field. In this way, Foucault's ideas on governmentality encompass his previous work on discipline and the production of docile bodies, and on the production of subjects who rely on authorities for confirmation of their "normality."

The influence that Foucault's work has had on the new political sociology cannot be over-estimated. His direct influence is widely acknowledged by those who work on issues in the politics of identity and difference. In particular, the problematic of anti-essentialism outlined by Foucault – the refusal to take socially constructed identities as metaphysical or natural – has been taken up extensively by those working on the social construction of gender, "race," ethnicity, and sexuality (Said, 1979; Weeks, 1989: Butler, 1990). In this way, the politics of identity and difference he saw as characteristic of new social movements has become an aspect of academic work. Social and political theory is seen as a site of cultural politics in so far as it contributes to the disruption or fixity of normalized identities. Indirectly, Foucault's influence has been still more important. His ideas on governmentality, discipline, and the interrelation of knowledge and power have directed attention toward the exercise of power in practices and the formation of identities across the social field. Once we begin to look at the world through the lenses Foucault provides for us, conventional politics at the level of the state is displaced to the periphery of vision and other forms of politics come into focus. Of course, the way in which new political sociology sees power and politics as significant in the organizations and institutions of civil society, in everyday life and interpersonal relations, and in global culture is not solely due to the influence of Foucault's work. Nevertheless, in analyzing power and government beyond the nation-state, Foucault has provided sociology with some of the tools it needs to understand new forms of politics in contemporary society.

Discourse theory and cultural politics

For Foucault, power does not work only through language and symbols: it is extended in discourse, but it is also exercised in institutional practices which he defines as non-linguistic. Foucault distinguishes between the discursive and the non-discursive: the latter includes the institutions, designated personnel and general social conditions which enable the emergence and extension of discourse. Although discourses contribute to the organization of non-discursive institutions, in Foucault's terms the two orders remain analytically distinct (Foucault, 1972: 163–5). Foucault's analyses of power are, then, at least as much oriented toward institutional practices as they are toward language and symbols. However, this is not reflected in the way in which his work has been taken up: his ideas have been much more readily applied to the analysis of the rules and representations of discourse as language than to social practices and institutions. As Michèle Barrett (1992) argues, the tendency has been to take Foucault's theory of discourse more seriously than his substantive historical analyses of institutions, to dispense with "things," and to substitute a concern with "words" as the only means by which reality is constituted, and therefore the only worthwhile object of analysis.

A version of discourse analysis explicitly focused on representations and symbols is to be found in the work of Ernesto Laclau and Chantal Mouffe. For them, Foucault's distinction between discursive and non-discursive is inconsistent and untenable. As Laclau and Mouffe see it, if discourse is constitutive of objects, then every object is constituted in discourse and the distinction between discursive and non-discursive is either meaningless or is itself a differentiation which can only be made within discourse (Laclau and Mouffe, 1985: 107). This does not mean, however, that they thereby reduce everything to language understood simply as words. They argue for a view of language as always embedded in practices such that there is an indissoluble unity between language, actions, and material objects. Discourse, for Laclau and Mouffe, includes both linguistic and non-linguistic elements. To illustrate the materiality of language in discourse they give an example used by Wittgenstein to demonstrate his very similar ideas about "language-games":

> A is building with building stones; there are blocks, pillars, slabs, and beams. B has to pass the stones, and that in the order in which A needs them. For this purpose they use a language consisting of the words "block," "pillar," "slab," "beam." A calls them out; B brings the stone which he has learnt to bring at such and such a call. (quoted in Laclau and Mouffe, 1985: 108)

The terms "block," "pillar," "slab," as used in discourse are not just words or ideas; they *are* the objects themselves as used in this particular discourse, or language-game, of "constructing a building."

Laclau and Mouffe's theory of discourse has been influenced by the structuralist linguist Ferdinand de Saussure. They see meaning in language as produced in a differential play of signs, rather than by representing objects in the world. There is no intrinsic link between objects and words; what joins them is the way in which *words* are linked together in social conventions. In fact, without language we would be unable to identify objects and concepts with any degree of consistency. Language does not simply *name* the world; it makes sense of it and orders it for us. Jonathan Culler gives a good example of Saussure's analysis of language as a "system of differences without positive terms." He asks us to imagine teaching a non-English speaker what the word "brown" means. To show him or her nothing but brown objects would be useless; he or she would have to learn to distinguish brown from other colors. The word "brown" does not simply label objects that are already given; it constructs "brown" things as different from gray, orange, red, and so on (Culler, 1976: 24–6). Furthermore, it is entirely possible to imagine a world in which such "brown" things were not distinguished at all. They are only meaningful for us because we have learned to recognize them in this way.

However, Laclau and Mouffe are *post*-structuralists. They accept Derrida's view that the structure of language Saussure described is not stable and fixed, but is rather decentered and unstable, continually in process. Derrida extends Saussure's understanding of language as a system of differences, arguing that, in so far as meaning depends on the possibility of being different from itself, it can never be finally fixed. He uses the neologism *différance* as one way of naming the instability of meaning. According to Derrida, a word as a mark on paper or a sound means nothing except in relation to what went before and what will come after it, both in space and time. Meaning is always different from itself, and also deferred in time; hence *différance* which means both "to differ" and "to defer" (Derrida, 1982). Because the meaning of a word depends on its difference from and similarity to others, it can never actually be present in the sign itself, whether written or spoken. It is always indeterminate, though the extent of this indeterminacy is itself a political matter (Derrida, 1996).

In Laclau and Mouffe's theory, indeterminacy of meaning is what makes politics both possible and necessary. Politics involves the contestation of meanings which have been relatively fixed in previous political projects, their re-articulation in new chains of meaning, and the attempt to persuade others of their validity, to fix them in relatively determinate meanings in which they become part of the "grammar" of everyday life. To give an example, the term "man" has quite different meanings in the discourses of communists and neo-liberals, radical feminists and born-again Christians, aid organizations and anthropologists. In each case, the meaning depends on its relationship to other signs; for example, "women" or "God." Furthermore, although it can never be established definitively in any case, the success of the discourse depends on the acceptance of the validity of these meanings. Although the term "power" does not feature in Laclau and Mouffe's theory as centrally as it does in Foucault's later work, for them power is the power to define, and to impose this definition in the face of that which denies it (Laclau, 1990: 31–3). It involves the manipulation of symbols, with all that implies according to Laclau and Mouffe's theory of discourse for effects in the material world.

It is evident that politics here is not an activity restricted to the conventional political institutions of the state. On the contrary, the re-drawing of the state's boundaries, scope, tasks, and capacities may itself be seen as an example of politics in this sense. It is, of course, necessary to distinguish politics from social life more generally, if the two are not to be simply conflated. However, Laclau does so, not in terms of different realms of society, but in terms of modes of activity. Politics involves opening up the possibilities repressed in the constitution of taken-for-granted and apparently "objective" social identities and relations (Laclau, 1990: 33–6). In fact, Laclau and Mouffe's ideal of radical democracy involves the continual politicization and re-politicization of the social, as well as the institution of more egalitarian and progressive identities and relations. This is an optimistic, even a naïve ideal (Bertens, 1995: 193). Certainly, the idea of politics as a matter of everyday life is very different from theories of democracy as dependent on an apathetic mass, or Marxist theories of capitalism as tolerated because of the delusion of the workers. As we will see, however, the idea that if it is not quite the case that everything is political, everything is at least potentially political, is central to the new political sociology.

1.4   CULTURAL POLITICS AND NEW POLITICAL SOCIOLOGY

Although Laclau and Mouffe use the term "discourse" rather than culture, their model of politics is best understood as a model of cultural politics. It is cultural where "culture" is understood in the widest possible sense, as "the signifying system through which necessarily (though among other means) a social order is communicated, reproduced, experienced and explored" (Williams, 1981: 13). This definition includes the more commonly used conception of culture as "the works and practices of intellectuals, and especially artistic activity" (Williams, 1976: 80), and also the still narrower understanding of popular and media culture. The advantage of thinking in terms of cultural politics is that Laclau and Mouffe's model may be linked more easily to the developments in political sociology with which we are concerned in this book, which have not all been elaborated in the post-structuralist terms of discourse theory.

Culture in this widest sense may itself be seen in two rather different ways. In the work of Laclau and Mouffe, discourse is implicated in all social practices, institutions, and identities, including those more conventionally demarcated as economic, social, or political. In other words, for Laclau and Mouffe, "everything is cultural" and, since social reality itself is of the order of discourse, it has always been the case that the social order was constructed, contested, and reproduced through culture.

As others see it, however, the significance of culture in this sense is historically specific. This view is particularly associated with the idea that we are now moving into a new era, that of "postmodernity" (see pp. 234–43). Whereas in modernity culture occupied a separate sphere of society as high art, in postmodernity there has been an expansion of culture into other realms of society. At the economic level, there has been a commodification of culture, and, at the same time, the economy itself is increasingly dependent on culture in the form of advertising, leisure and service industries, and niche marketing according to lifestyle. At the political level, politicians perform to their audiences through the media, and, in the social realm, distinctions depend to an even greater extent than before on the display of cultural credentials, rather than on economic or political power. On this basis, Krishan Kumar suggests that sociologists of postmodernity should adopt an anthropological definition of culture as "a whole way of thinking, feeling and acting" (Kumar, 1995: 120). This seems misguided, however, in so far as it suggests that there is a single unified culture when, according to theorists of postmodernity, postmodern culture is better characterized as fragmented, indeterminate, and unstable.

Culture in the widest sense is seen in two alternative ways, then, as the practices constituting social reality itself or as what was previously a separate sphere of society which has now entered every aspect of social life. Whichever view is taken to be correct, whether the divisions sociology made previously between different realms of society are seen as themselves cultural constructions, on a par with other classifications in discourse, or whether the expansion of culture is seen as a new phenomenon which blurs the distinctions between what were previously separate and distinct domains in reality, cultural politics now takes on an unprecedented importance. This importance is reflected in what is now frequently referred to as the "postmodern turn" in sociology.

A postmodern turn in sociology?

The relation between sociology and postmodernism is complicated. In recent years, there have been a great number of books linking social theory and postmodernism, including two with the title *The Postmodern Turn* (Best and Kellner, 1991, 1997; Bauman, 1992; Smart, 1993; Seidman, 1994a; Bertens, 1995; Ashley, 1997; Owen, 1997). It is undoubtedly the case that many of the features linked with postmodernism, and initially developed more fully in philosophy, are now taken up in sociology. In order for this to be possible, however, postmodern themes have had to be reworked in ways which make them more compatible with sociology as a discipline. As a result, sociologists are unlikely to think of themselves as postmodernists, even if their work may be identified with the "postmodern turn." At the same time, sociology itself has changed, becoming more concerned with culture and interpretation, so that it is possible to identify the work of those sociologists who explicitly reject postmodernism with the "postmodern turn." The work of a sociologist like Anthony Giddens has more in common with postmodernism, despite his opposition to it, than with classical positivist sociology.

As a kind of ideal-type, five important themes of the "postmodern turn" in new political sociology may be identified. We have looked at most of these themes already in the work of Foucault and Laclau and Mouffe. Like many of those associated with postmodernism, Foucault and Laclau and Mouffe do not themselves use the term, preferring the label "post-structuralist." Here we will use "post-structuralism" and "postmodernism" interchangeably, bearing in mind, however, that while the former pertains exclusively to thought, the latter also includes wider cultural changes of the type associated with postmodernity as a new social formation (see the

Glossary for definitions). The "postmodern turn" in new political sociology involves the following features:

(1) *Anti-epistemology*: a concern with studying representations as such rather than what they are supposed to refer to; scepticism concerning the ultimate foundations of truth and value; an interest in *how* claims are constructed rather than whether or not they are "true." Discourse theory, as developed in the work of Foucault and Laclau and Mouffe is anti-epistemological. It is not that discourse theorists are unconcerned with knowledge or "truth." It is rather that they are interested in the social construction of knowledge claims and how these are bound up with the exercise of power.

Although there are differences, a similar concern with the social effects of knowledge claims is also a feature of the sociology of reflexivity of Giddens, Beck, and Lash and Urry. In this work, conflicting expert knowledges are seen as opening up spaces for individuals to use knowledge claims to create their own identities and lifestyles. Again, the "truth" of the knowledge is of no importance; the object of study is how knowledge is used socially and politically rather than whether it is true or false. As Zygmunt Bauman argues, sociology is increasingly postmodern in that it is more concerned with "ontology" than "epistemology," with forms of life in which knowledge is effective than in getting behind the appearances of social life to the real causes of belief (Bauman, 1992: 30).

The question of knowledge is also, however, often thought to be one which opens up a chasm between postmodernism and sociology. It is held that, as an empirical discipline, the latter is necessarily concerned with accurately representing the world rather than reflecting on the means by which it is represented, as philosophy, for example, may do. Opponents of postmodernism argue that its anti-representationalism is incompatible with sociology. Certainly, sociology which had no interest in mapping the world would be so radically different as to constitute a new discipline altogether, but anti-epistemology does not necessarily lead to such a conclusion. As we have seen, much of Foucault's work is empirical, tracing discursive constructions from their historical creation to their strategic use in the present day. In fact, he describes his historical methodology in the most mundane, and from this point of view, conventional terms: "Genealogy is gray, meticulous and patiently documentary . . . requires patience and a knowledge of details, and it depends on a vast accumulation of source material" (Foucault, 1984d: 76–7). Foucault's interest is in how bodies and minds are formed through practices in which representations are implicated. He therefore provides accounts of the processes in which this actually takes place.

However, it need not be supposed that analyses of the world involve direct representation of "things," nor epistemology, a theory of how knowledge may ultimately be justified. Anti-epistemologists argue that we should not mistake the reasons proponents of different approaches give as "real" grounds for knowledge. According to Richard Rorty (1991), it is better to see proposals concerning the nature of social life and how to study it as engagement in something like a conversation in which the better justification is likely to be, and should be, accepted by the scholarly community. Alternatively, using more combative imagery, Vincent Descombes suggests that Foucault supports his empirical work through polemical interpretation: "he knows that to back one interpretation is to declare war on another" (Descombes, 1980: 116). Sociology *is* concerned with mapping "real" identities and structures so that those who participate in it have to convince colleagues of the validity of their investigations. It is not necessary, however, to engage in epistemology in order to do so; what is necessary is to accept that there is no "God's eye view" from which the ultimate foundations of knowledge could be ascertained and to give good reasons for accepting a certain understanding of the world. The postmodern validation of knowledge is social, involving the exchange of words, rather than a solitary, scholarly search for the truth of things. It is, however, no less a validation.

(2) *Concern with the indeterminacy of meaning* as a resource for constructing identities and structures. We have already looked at this theme in Laclau and Mouffe's work, as it has been influenced by Jacques Derrida. (Foucault, as we have seen, is less concerned with meaning and more with the use to which discourse is put in disciplinary institutions.) It is perhaps worth emphasizing, however, that although post-structuralists tend to see meaning as fluid and ambiguous, they do not therefore hold the view that everything is unstructured and chaotic. For Derrida, as for Laclau and Mouffe, indeterminacy of meaning provides the conditions of possibility for politics, the attempt to achieve a relative fixity and stability of social life. As Derrida puts it:

All that a deconstructive point of view tries to show is that since conventions, institutions and consensus are stabilizations (sometimes
stabilizations of great duration, sometimes micro-stabilizations), this
means that they are stabilizations of something essentially unstable
and chaotic . . . it is because there is instability that stabilization
becomes necessary; it is because there is chaos that there is a need for
stability. (Derrida, quoted in Smith, 1998: 146).

It is this relative stabilization that is the work of cultural politics.

Interpretative sociology has long been interested in the question
of how social meanings are made and secured in forms of social solidarity. From the 1970s onwards, however, with the work of inter-
actionists and ethnomethodologists like Erving Goffman and Harold
Garfinkel, it became an insistent theme in the discipline. Zygmunt
Bauman actually refers to this type of sociology as "postmodern
sociology;" he sees it as mimicking postmodern culture in its abandoning of objectivity and its attention to "language games" and the
"fragility and brittleness of social reality" (Bauman, 1982: 39–42).
In this respect, sociology may be seen to have taken a "postmodern
turn" as a result of the growing interest of sociologists in culture and
the interpretation of meaning some time before postmodernism was
a term of art in the discipline.

(3) *Decentering society*: a view of social structures as constructed
in ongoing processes taking place in time and space, rather than
causally determined; there is no central institution (for example,
the state), nor meaning (for example, "truth") around which every
aspect of social life is organized in a fixed position.

As we have seen, this is very much a theme of Foucault's work.
Power is seen as working in different ways in different institutions
rather than as concentrated in, or generated by, the state. Derrida
sees structures as produced in ongoing chains of meaning. They
could only be fixed in time and space if there were a central meaning
which itself remained uncontaminated by *différance*; a "transcen-
dental signifier," like "God," which was certain. Structures for
Derrida, as for Laclau and Mouffe, are precariously sustained by the
relative fixity of meaning achieved in particular contexts through the
use of persuasion or force. A fully constituted structure is, however,
an impossibility; a finished totality is never achieved (Derrida, 1978).
In fact, the "structuring of structures" as a process which is always
relative to social context is a theme of post-structuralist theory in

comparison with structuralism. For structuralists like Althusser and
Saussure, structures involve closed totalities in which the relations
between the parts making up the whole are fixed. In Althusser's case,
the complex of structures which make up society are determined as
a totality "in the last instance" by the economy. In Saussure's work,
fixity is more problematic, but ultimately – and against some of
his other pronouncements concerning meaning – he sees it as secured
by the intentions of language-users (Saussure, 1983: 11–15).
For post-structuralists, such a notion of structure is a reified construct, a product of the prejudices of modern reason which dic-
tates that the truth is found by uncovering the essence of a thing
behind the appearance of flux. Influenced by Nietzsche, post-
structuralists see life as never-finished process, always "becoming"
rather than "being."

At the same time, in sociology there has largely been a turning
away from the idea of societies as self-enclosed systems (the
revival of "systems theory" notwithstanding). While structuralist-
functionalists saw society as endlessly reproducing itself, and Marxists saw it as riven with contradictions that would eventually destroy
it, since the 1970s sociologists have increasingly taken the view that
society should be seen rather as consisting of localized structures sustained in face-to-face interaction and always susceptible to disruption and change. Again, Giddens's work, influenced by Goffman and
Garfinkel, is exemplary of this theme. In fact, although Giddens does
not use the term "culture," his extremely influential structuration
theory – the basis of his sociology of reflexivity – posits a model of
social reproduction which is very close to the model of cultural politics articulated in Laclau and Mouffe's work. Structuration theory
is an attempt to overcome the duality of "structure" and "agency"
which Giddens sees as a perennial motif in sociology. He argues that
social reproduction should be seen as stabilizing relationships across
time and space through the knowledgeable use of rules and resources
– "structures" – on the part of social agents (Giddens, 1984). Structures are created, sustained, and re-made in more or less conscious
social action while, at the same time, social action is itself constrained by existing distributions of resources and ways of making
sense of the world. If we see culture as the signifying structures in
which rules are laid down and the distribution of resources normalized and legitimated, for Giddens it is in culture that social life is
reproduced and re-worked. Giddens is opposed to Derrida's post-

structuralism (which he mistakenly categorizes as structuralism), seeing it as over-formal and insufficiently concerned with social action in specific contexts (Giddens, 1979: 33–8). Nevertheless, the way in which Giddens sees social life as reproduced in decentered structures is very similar to the model of cultural politics influenced by Derrida's work.

(4) *Anti-essentialism*: identities and structures are seen as socially constructed and historically contingent. Again, we have already looked at this point in some detail in the work of Foucault and Laclau and Mouffe. As we have seen, Foucault's work on sexuality has been particularly influential in relation to anti-essentialism. His historical studies show how the naturalized identities of both "normal heterosexuality" and "abnormal perversions" have been constructed in institutions and discourses across society since the end of the eighteenth century. Foucault's work has been particularly influential in those areas of sociology in which "identity politics" within universities have been the key to setting the terms of study: gender studies, "queer theory," and, to a lesser extent, in the area of ethnicity and "race." In all these fields, there have been debates over the extent to which identity is "natural" or socially constructed. There are now many sociologists working on these topics who take Foucault's view that identities are socially constructed and an object of cultural politics rather than a given "fact of life" which society must somehow administer.

In more mainstream social theory, however, this conclusion has been resisted, particularly in relation to the individual. In the sociology of reflexivity, for example, the individual is seen as a sovereign agent, with capacities for interpretation and reasoning which make the agent – although not ahistorical, since the agent is seen as specific to modernity – somehow detached from the social practices in which he or she acts, reflecting on them from the position of an individual outside his or her social and cultural conditions. To borrow a striking metaphor used by Bhiku Parekh in another context, it is as if the individual put on his or her culture like a piece of clothing, and that in reflexivity, he or she was then able to take it off in order to reflect on its validity and implications (Parekh, 1995: 96).

In contrast, for post-structuralists, this sovereign individual is itself called into question; it is seen as having no essential attributes since it is a historically and culturally specific construction of discourse. It is, therefore, also a site of cultural politics. Any construction of what it is to be a subject is seen as privileging certain "ideal-type" characteristics and therefore as potentially exclusionary of those who do not typify its specific traits, and repressive of lived experiences and possibilities that do not conform to it. An obvious example here is the way in which women have long been seen as irrational in comparison with men. While it is possible simply to challenge this by "proving" that women are as rational as men – or, indeed, even more rational – post-structuralists would see this as unlikely to be effective if it did not also challenge the terms within which the assertion had come to be seen as true and valid. From a post-structuralist perspective, it would be necessary also to contest the constellation of forces which supported the "knowledge" that masculine reason is superior, the authorities which upheld it, however covertly, and the relations with other discourses and institutions which sustained it. This is not possible where rational subjectivity is seen as the essence of what it is to be a human individual, rather than a historically and culturally specific social construction.

(5) Given the multiplicity of perspectives from which social life is (and may validly) be seen, *there are no universal values and truths* to which all members of society subscribe. Associated particularly with the ideas of Jean-François Lyotard in *The Post-modern Condition*, some version of this view is increasingly adhered to even by those sociologists hostile to postmodernism. According to Lyotard, contemporary social life is marked by the loss of faith in the modern meta-narrative of the progress of reason toward a better society. The over-arching legitimation of modernity in the name of the Enlightenment values of scientific truth and social liberation is now seen as nothing more than a myth or story with pretensions to encompassing the totality of human experience.

Lyotard himself does not regret that meta-narratives are finished. On the contrary, he sees them as "terroristic" because of the way they re-describe everything in their own terms, often inappropriately. For Lyotard, in the postmodern condition all social life is made up of nothing but stories, with a historically and geographically specific, *local* validity, which are productive of the social positions, subjectivities, practices, and objects they relate. They embody in themselves the rules of pragmatic competence, "knowing how to speak," "knowing how to listen," and "know-how." His principal example of these local narratives, which he calls "language-games," is that of the Cashinahua of South America who always begin their stories with the phrase "Here is the story of — , as I've always heard it told;" in this way, the narration itself legitimates the authority of the story-teller (Lyotard, 1984: 20–1). Lyotard sees the end of meta-narratives in a positive light since it announces the possibility that the specificity of local narratives will be respected and imaginative invention from within them encouraged, rather than a standardized account being imposed on all. The pretensions of the Enlightenment project to universal moral values, underpinned by the universal truth claims of modern science, are themselves to be seen simply as narratives like any others; they no longer have the power to marginalize and de-legitimize others in the name of their supposed universality.

While Lyotard's analysis is endorsed by many, it is his optimistic reading of the situation that is generally found to be problematic. Sociologists and others find it difficult to accept a relativism of value which suggests that it is unacceptable to make moral judgments concerning any practices outside one's own "language-game," however cruel or repressive one might find them to be. In fact, the association of postmodernism with such relativism seems to be the main reason why no one, including Foucault, Derrida, Laclau and Mouffe and Lyotard (despite the title of his best-known book) is willing to adopt or accept the label. In the view of Best and Kellner (1997), it is associated above all with playful resignation to existing social forces, and it is this identity that is being resisted by those who want to retain a critical perspective while accepting much of the way in which postmodernism undermines the grounds on which radical critique has been founded.

Best and Kellner usefully identify two types of postmodernism. The first they call "ludic," or playful, advocating "anything goes" and inherently anti-political (Best and Kellner, 1997: 26–7). They see Lyotard's postmodernism as of this type, and also that of Jean Baudrillard. Baudrillard's work is perhaps the best exemplar since it seems to embrace relativism both of knowledge and of value. For Baudrillard, the development of consumer society and the media now mean that social reality itself has been undermined by "simulation" in which images and models have replaced people and things. We now live in the "hyper-real" in which reality has been replaced by technologically produced signs and media-produced spectacles; representations spawn more representations without ever referring back to what is "really" represented. Best and Kellner (1997: 101) give a good example of Baudrillard's thesis, that of Cindy Jackson, the "Barbie Doll Woman," who had over 30 surgical alterations in order to become the same shape as the doll, itself a representation of an impossible ideal rather than of a real woman.

Baudrillard's analyses of contemporary capitalism have been influential in new political sociology (Bauman, 1992; Lash and Urry, 1994). However, his thesis tends to be seen as exaggerated and therefore as exemplary of the "performative contradiction" of postmodernism: he claims to do what is impossible on his own account since he proposes an account of the real world while claiming that it no longer exists. In this respect, he actually goes much further than other post-structuralists. In his polemic *Forget Foucault*, Baudrillard argues that Foucault's account of power is limited, since "it is still turned toward a reality principle and a very strong truth principle" (Baudrillard, 1987: 12). In his view, Foucault fails to recognize that the production of sex he has so meticulously analyzed through the operations of power is no longer real, but hyper-real in such forms as pornographic videos, computer games and – eventually – virtual reality machines. As we have seen, however, as an empirical, investigative discipline, sociology depends – as indeed does Baudrillard – on producing accounts of the "real" world. Baudrillard is famous, for example, for pronouncing that the stock market crash of 1987 could only be a "virtual catastrophe," not a real event, since the economy today is purely fictional. However, as Kellner points out, given Baudrillard's claim that there is now no "real" world behind the simulations, it is contradictory for him to claim understanding of the economy as *really* "simulated" (Kellner, 1989: 213–14). While Baudrillard's insights into the commodification of culture are interesting and useful, his claims concerning the disappearance of reality are ultimately sociologically untenable.

Similarly, Baudrillard's version of postmodernism tends to be rejected as nihilist. According to Baudrillard, it is not worth taking a moral position, nor engaging in politics, because communication and human interaction has "imploded" into "the masses." In contemporary society, people are only concerned with what is

presented to them as a media spectacle; they do not express themselves, nor do they reflect. Indeed, since there is no longer any reality,
there is nothing on which to reflect (Baudrillard, 1983). This is
not, however, the view taken by most of those associated with postmodernism, nor by sociologists within the "postmodern turn." In
fact, Baudrillard's assertions are at odds with the way in which social
life is understood as increasingly politicized in the new political
sociology.

This brings us to the second type of postmodernism identified by
Best and Kellner: "oppositional postmodernism." It is this type
which has been most influential in sociology. Best and Kellner identify it with the influence of social movements which has led to the
questioning of Marxism and the reduction of all oppression to the
economic class struggle, to interest in the Foucauldian analytics of
power as operational in multiple sites and strategies, and in the normalization of identities in culture and everyday life. It is this form
of oppositional postmodernism which has contributed to the new
political sociology and the model of cultural politics with which we
shall be concerned in this book.

"Oppositional postmodernism" also raises problems of relativism,
but in a different way from "ludic" postmodernism. Oppositional
postmodernists see the "end of meta-narratives" in a relatively
positive light. Feminists, queer theorists, theorists of hybrid identities, and others all see opportunities for greater pluralism and
equality opened up by the displacement of the dominance of
Western reason. Like Lyotard, they suspect that the suppression of
complexity and the imposition of "objectivity" and "neutrality" in
modern knowledge was a repression of different stories and points
of view. However, while they endorse his view of knowledge, the
political commitments of "oppositional postmodernists" mean that
they cannot celebrate the fragmentation of social values as Lyotard
does.

The problem of value relativism arises in relation to the post-
structuralist thought on which oppositional postmodernism is built
in two main ways. First, it is seen as undermining the grounds for
moral values and political commitment. From a post-structuralist
perspective, there is no "objective" way of deciding between
conflicting points of view; it all depends on the perspective from
which such a conflict is approached. Secondly, post-structuralism is
deconstructive: it is above all concerned to break down what are

taken to be essential identities and necessary logical connections into contingent and accidental juxtapositions of elements. It shows the strategies of normalization and exclusion in what is taken for granted as natural and what is supposed to be universally "right." Stephen White (1991: 20) calls this deconstructive impetus the postmodern "responsibility to Otherness." The modern attempt at harmony, clarity, and order is seen as invariably producing devalued Otherness which is championed by postmodernists. As we have seen, this is evident in Foucault's anti-essentialism, Derrida's concern with what is repressed in stabilizing determinate meaning, and Lyotard's discussion of the multiplicity of narratives de-legitimated by the meta-narratives of modernity. According to its critics, however, this deconstructive ethic means that post-structuralism must always be suspicious of such concepts as "universal justice" and "political community" as potentially productive of excluded Otherness. Yet, without such concepts, effective resistance to the systematic injustices against the marginalized and oppressed detailed by post-structuralists would seem to be impossible (White, 1991: 115–16).

The first problem may be quite easily dealt with in a similar way to the problem of epistemological relativism we looked at earlier. Though there are no ultimate grounds for moral values and political commitments, we are, in fact involved in morality in our everyday lives, even if we do not always think of ourselves as making moral or ethical choices. We do not start discussing such issues from an "objective" standpoint, but we may still discuss what it is we do believe, why, what ideals are important, how far they may be compromised, and so on. Good reasons for holding certain beliefs can be given without necessarily basing them on some ultimate foundation such as "intrinsic human rights." The question that is raised by the "postmodern turn" is precisely who is the "we" who have enough in common to make such discussions possible?

This brings us to the second problem, which is a good deal more difficult. How can the postmodern "responsibility toward Otherness" be combined with standards of social justice applicable to all? If it is the case, as post-structuralists suggest, that supposedly inclusive principles of justice actually produce Otherness, the excluded and subordinated, must any attempt at a better society be abandoned as counter-productive? This is not an acceptable conclusion for oppositional postmodernists, and yet it is difficult to resist within the terms of the "postmodern turn." Perhaps, however, the important point is that this is a problem, not just for postmodern thought, but in practice. Claims for citizenship rights on the part of social movements and the decline of the old solidarities of class mean that new models of pluralist democracy must now be constructed which include the possibility of dialogue and negotiation across differences. The imposition of universal principles is suspect, but this does not mean an end to justice; it means, rather, finding new ways of realizing it. What is clear from a postmodern point of view is that new forms of democracy must be invented. They cannot be discovered by social scientists, nor elaborated in advance by political and moral theorists working on first principles of thought. As Foucault observed in an interview toward the end of his life:

> What is good, is something that comes through innovation. The good does not exist, like that, in an atemporal sky, with people who would be like the Astrologers of the Good, whose job is to determine what is the favourable nature of the stars. The good is defined by us, it is practiced, it is invented. And this is a collective work. (quoted in Weeks, 1993b: 190–1)

Arguably, the invention of new modes of democracy is already underway in the activities of social movements, the use and extension of international human rights, and attempts at global governance. For political sociologists, it is important to take a critical view of the democratization that is actually taking place in order to identify potentials for new forms of solidarity in which difference will genuinely be respected.

New political sociology

The following chapters each deal with a topic in the new political sociology from the point of view of the model of cultural politics developed in the "postmodern turn." In chapter 2, we discuss globalization, probably the most dramatic and widely acknowledged challenge to the old political sociology model of state-centric politics. Processes of globalization mean that the capacity of the nation-state to act independently in the articulation and pursuit of domestic and international policy objectives has diminished as its control over the traffic of goods, services, technology, media products, and information which crosses its borders has been reduced. Furthermore, the political authority of the state to determine the rules, regulations, and policies within a given territory has also been reduced by international political institutions and law which actively enforce limits on the state's jurisdiction over its citizens (Held, 1991).

In terms of the new political sociology, globalization clearly provides opportunities to reconsider the key issues of power and politics. The empirical changes brought about by globalization problematize the most basic concept of sociology, that of "society," by disaggregating the economic, social, and political processes previously seen as bound together within the borders of distinct national societies. This provides an opportunity to re-think social life in terms of multiple social structures and identities, and to think of power and politics as an aspect of social life rather than as separate institutions within a "society" governed by a single determining base, as in the case of Marxism, or a single inexorable logic, as in the case of the rationalization thesis of Weber. Globalization opens up issues which require a wider view of power and politics than that provided by the framework of old political sociology.

In chapter 3, we will review another challenge to this framework, the growing literature on social movements: feminism, campaigns for nuclear disarmament and against war, anti-racism, environmentalism, lesbian and gay liberation, and so on. Where social movements are concerned, the importance of cultural politics is very clear. They are at least as much concerned with personal identity as they are with policies and the law, and although they generally do make demands on the state, contesting the validity of its procedures and products, they are still more concerned with changing the rules and routines of everyday life. The state is often seen as biased, bureaucratic, and too blunt an instrument to bring about the detailed transformation in social relations which is their aim.

However, contrary to the claims of some theorists of social movements, the politics in which they are engaged should not be seen as *exclusive* to civil society. In chapter 4, we examine claims for citizenship rights made by social movements to the state. It is important to note that citizenship rights are as much a matter of cultural politics as the contestation of identity, lifestyle, media representations, and ethical consumerism in civil society. They involve questioning the model of the individual on which rights have been based in Western liberal democracies and how definitions of "the normal citizen" actually exclude groups such as women, ethnic minorities, gays and lesbians, and the poor from full citizenship rights. Social movements contest the very idea of universal rights, suggesting the possibility that rights should be different for different groups in society. At the same time, they also contest essentialist identities, questioning not only what it is to be a citizen, but also what it is to be a "woman," a "gay man," "black British," and so on. Definitions of identity and debates over the possibility of extending equal rights without compromising the freedom to redefine identities in the future are central to debates over citizenship in the new political sociology.

Finally, in chapter 5, we look at models of democracy which might be appropriate to the issues examined in the previous chapters. The two principal models of democracy in contemporary sociology – Habermasian deliberative democracy and post-structuralist radical democracy – give a central role to social movements. Both are concerned above all with the question of how democracy is possible in contemporary Western liberal democracies in which fragmentation and pluralism threaten to undermine social solidarity and where the state has been displaced as the center of political activity. We shall also look at David Held's model of cosmopolitan democratic governance as a way of dealing which the implications of globalization for democracy. It will be argued that the model of cultural politics outlined in this chapter and developed throughout the book may be used to understand how problems for democracy at the level of the nation-state which arise as a result of globalization may actually offer the potential for the realization of new forms of global democracy.

Notes

1 This definition of power is also adopted by Marxisant political sociologists (see Bottomore, 1993: 1).

2 They then go on to do just that. Although they argue for seeing politics as a class of actions rather than a set of institutions or organizations, in particular as the establishing of the rules of social organization, their primary focus is on government as a special set of this class, the setting of rules intended to be absolute. In practice, therefore, their main focus is again on the relation between state and society.

3 Although Weber did not actually theorize politics in this broad sense, restricting his analysis to politics at the level of the state, it is unsurprising that he saw power, and definitionally at least, politics, in a

similar way to post-structuralists since both have been influenced by Nietzsche. The influence of Nietzsche is evident in Weber's famous article "Science as a Vocation," although he does not explicitly acknowledge it. Weber's argument that morality, and ultimately truth, is a matter of personal responsibility comes close to Nietzsche's perspectivism, even if the article is stating the case for value-free scientific knowledge. Weber argues that science must be pursued in a disinterested way, but that the decision to become a scientist and to study a particular topic cannot be defended in terms of moral truth; it is a matter of choosing between irreconcilable values and there is ultimately no rational defence of the values one chooses. For Weber, as for Nietzsche, moral value is affirmed by the individual; it cannot be found in moral philosophies or theology, and it is no longer simply given in a disenchanted world (Weber, 1948b; Owen, 1994). It is but a short step from the claim that morality cannot ultimately be justified to the post-structuralist view that all existential choices are therefore a matter of politics. For post-structuralists, choices, whether made by a group or a series of individuals, involve issues of power in so far as they require the repression of alternatives with the consequence that these alternatives then become more difficult to realize socially. In a fragmented, pluralist world, there is politics wherever there is the repression – whether by force or persuasion – of the possible choices of others (Laclau, 1990: 31–6).

4 Although Weber's term is usually translated as "iron cage," Alan Scott has convincingly argued that "steel-hard housing," the casing which encloses machines, is actually a more accurate translation and a better metaphor for the constraints of modernity Weber wants to convey by it (Scott, 1997a).

5 Pluralism is categorized as Weberian here more on the basis of its intellectual orientation than its theoretical antecedents. It is better seen as founded by American political scientists, notably Robert Dahl and his school, than by Weber. Nevertheless, it may be taken as Weberian in relation to Marxism in so far as it insists on the autonomy of the political process, and sees power as dependent on the intentions and circumstances of social actors, rather than on socio-economic structures.

CHAPTER 2

Politics in a Small World: Globalization and the Displacement of the Sovereign Nation-state

Although globalization may be defined quite simply as increasing global interconnectedness, a number of complex and inter-linked processes are theorized under the heading "globalization," principally economic, technological, cultural, environmental, and political processes. Globalization involves flows of goods, capital, people, information, ideas, images, and risks across national borders, combined with the emergence of social networks and political institutions which constrain the nation-state. The most important point about globalization for sociologists is the way in which such flows problematize the founding sociological image of society as a bounded and coherent set of structures and practices governed by the sovereign nation-state.

In this chapter we will review theories of globalization in the light of the model of cultural politics discussed in chapter 1. This is a relatively obvious way to read much of the sociological literature on globalization since, although it does not always explicitly theorize politics in these terms, it invariably draws attention to processes structuring social life and identities which are not controlled through politics at the level of the nation-state. This does not necessarily mean that the state can now be ignored, that it has been rendered obsolete by processes of globalization. It is rather that the nation-state itself should be seen as one of the sites of cultural politics. Its political possibilities are currently being redefined and restructured in the light of global processes. While cultural politics is clearly significant outside the state – something the political sociology of globalization makes evident – as one of the most powerful players in global politics, it remains crucial in the new world (dis)order. The cultural politics through which this *internationalized* state is formed is, therefore, also very important.

Much of the debate in political sociology over globalization has actually turned on the periodization of the new world (dis)order. Is globalization simply another phase of capitalist expansion? Is it a development of modernity? Does it bring us into a new historical era altogether, that of "postmodernity"? In section 2.2 these debates, and the extent to which theorists working within relatively traditional frameworks have developed new sociological tools adequate to the empirical changes they identify, will be discussed.

In section 2.3 we look particularly at the issue of global culture and the way in which it may be seen as postmodern. It will be argued that it is radically heterogeneous and marked by the relativization of Western values. As it is understood in the sociological literature on global culture, which is itself part of the "postmodern turn," the problematization of liberal humanism, the flourishing of diaspora and hybrid identities, and the "glocalization" of consumer culture all signal the postmodern "end of meta-narratives."

Finally, in section 2.4, we turn to an article, "Disjuncture and Difference in the Global Cultural Economy" by Arjun Appadurai (1990) which offers an interesting way of theorizing globalization as a new, fluid, and dislocated condition. Although Appadurai's article is probably the single most widely cited piece of work on globalization, his ideas on "global scapes" have actually remained rather underdeveloped. Here we will consider how they might be used with our model of cultural politics to understand the structuring and restructuring of social life effected by processes of globalization. First, however, we must turn to an outline of what those processes might involve.

2.1 ASPECTS OF GLOBALIZATION

Currently at the center of sociological interest in globalization is its economic dimension. This includes the globalization of production and also of financial transactions. It is closely linked to advances in data-processing and information technology which allow instantaneous communication across vast distances, enabling the formation of a transnational financial system and facilitating the operations of multinational corporations (Thrift, 1988). Global production and mobility of capital are united in the operations of multinational corporations, usually taken to be at the vanguard of economic globalization, in which the company's production is not limited to the country in which it is based, but involves multiple sites of production in different countries based on direct foreign investment by the company itself. It is often argued that multinational corporations have consolidated and extended an already existing post-colonial division of labor, since they mainly operate from the developed world and take advantage of cheap labor and resources in the under-developed parts of the globe. A notorious example is the multi-national company Nike. With an annual sales turnover of 4 billion dollars in 1994, it employs 9,000 people in the US in design, marketing, and distribution, and subcontracts 100 percent of its goods production to 75,000 people in developing countries such as China, South Korea, Malaysia, Taiwan, and Thailand (Ashley, 1997: 109). Nike is notorious because human rights' campaigns have drawn attention to the poor pay and conditions of its workers and to the fact that it employs children who, if they lived in the West, would be legally under-age for work. Financial organizations, such as banks, and the infrastructures of a global financial system, including stock exchanges, tax havens, and so on, are also now more global in scale and orientation. In the 1990s, financial services accounted for over 50 percent of UK earnings, London being the leading center for transnational services in commerce and finance (Ashley, 1997: 123).

Economic globalization is widely understood to have led to the reduced control of nation-states over economic policy. It has involved a shift from the Keynesian post-war state in which governments, trade unions and heads of business compromised over economic policies designed to ensure high rates of employment and consumption, economic growth, and social security. Organized labor co-operated with capitalists in exchange for social security benefits and collective bargaining over wages; corporate capital ensured high levels of investment and the "scientific management" of workers for maximum productivity; the state undertook to curb business cycles through fiscal and monetary polices in order to ensure high levels of profitability for capital, and it invested in public works and welfare to reduce unemployment and to enable workers to spend on consumer goods, rather than saving for an uncertain future. Economic globalization means that the state is now in a much more difficult situation:

> called upon to regulate the activities of corporate capital in the national interest at the same time as it is forced, also in the national interest, to create a "good business climate" to act as an inducement to trans-national and global finance capital, and to deter (by means other than exchange controls) capital flight to greener and more profitable pastures. (Harvey, 1989: 170)

It must now attract multinational corporations, with all that implies in terms of discouraging militant trade unionism and creating tax incentives for global capital, rather than setting the terms within which a co-operative economic policy is pursued for the benefit of the nation as a whole.

It is important to be clear about precisely what is involved in economic globalization. Although the thesis is widely endorsed by politicians and the media, some sociologists have contested the very idea. Most notable is the recent work of Paul Hirst and Grahame Thompson. They see the thesis of economic globalization as an alibi both for the New Right, who then celebrate free-market liberalism, and also for the Left, for whom capitalism is at least straightforwardly rapacious under these circumstances and therefore easily understood (Hirst and Thompson, 1996: 176). They argue that the economy is *international* rather than global because nation-states are still the most powerful economic actors, both in terms of their domestic economies and in relation to agreements concerning the management of economic relations beyond national boundaries. They see the idea of globalization as suggesting the redundancy of national economic regulation, and since the nation-state has not been made powerless by international or transnational processes and transactions, there is no global economy (Hirst and Thompson, 1996: 10).

Hirst and Thompson's argument hinges on two main disputes with theorists of economic globalization concerning the operations of multinational corporations. First, they argue, multinational corporations do not dominate world trade and up to two-thirds of their assets are retained in their home countries; this means that they are subject to the control of national government policies. Secondly, they do not operate globally, but rather between partners within regions, notably Europe, the Americas and South and East Asia; again, there is considerable scope for national regulation of such trade. In particular, it is their view that there is little exchange of capital, labor, and goods between the First World and the Third; the Third World remains marginal both in terms of investment and trade apart from a few newly industrializing countries. Finally, they conclude that there is nothing new about the current internationalization of the economy and that it has existed in something like its present form since modern industrial technology began to be generalized from the 1860s, with some fluctuation due mainly to the two world wars in the intervening period.

Hirst and Thompson are right to suggest that theorists of globalization have tended to minimize the role of the nation-state. However, few actually maintain that it is redundant. The argument is much more likely to be that its role in managing the economy is now *problematic*, as we saw in the extract from Harvey (1989) above. It is not clear that Hirst and Thompson differ substantially from other theorists of globalization in this respect, though it is certainly true that they do give more emphasis to the continuing importance of the state than most.

Their rejection of globalization as a new phenomenon is also questionable. As Ash Amin (1997) points out, it is based on a largely quantitative analysis of trade and output, to the neglect of the *qualitative* shift in economic, social, and political trends which is supposed by other theorists of economic globalization. It may be that while the volume of trade is actually not so much greater now than it was in the nineteenth century, there are nevertheless new tendencies which suggest that a trend is growing. Trends do not necessarily continue, of course, but in so far as a global infrastructure for economic exchange is established, it may not be easy to reverse. In the words of David Held:

> there is a fundamental difference between, on the one hand, the development of particular trade routes, or select military and naval operations or even the global reach of nineteenth century empires, and, on the other hand, an international order involving the conjuncture of: dense networks of regional and global economic relations which stretch beyond the control of any single state . . . extensive webs of transnational relations and instantaneous electronic communications . . . a vast array of international regimes and organizations which

can limit the scope for action of the most powerful states, and the development of a global military order. . . . (quoted in Amin, 1997: 126)

There is considerable evidence that multinational corporations are taking a more global perspective than previously. While Hirst and Thompson are correct to point out that most of their activities are restricted to the developed world, the speeding up of the financial market means that multinationals now review their investments much more frequently than before and so are more likely to close down plants, acquire new assets, move swiftly into new markets and production, and so on, with all the consequences this has for the countries in which they operate. Furthermore, the interpenetration of capital is growing, albeit within the regions Hirst and Thompson specify, as a result of this activity (Thrift, 1988: 25).

It is important to note, as Hirst and Thompson argue, that the rise of a new world economic (dis)order does not give over-whelming power to multinationals. But, in a world in which multinationals account for up to one-third of world output, 80 percent of global investment, and two-thirds of world trade, their economic importance is hard to gainsay (Amin, 1997: 126). It is therefore equally important to understand that there have been changes so that there is now a greater transnational integration of capital than ever before and that economic management requires relations and institutions which extend beyond the structures of the nation-state.

All processes of globalization are, like economic globalization, linked to a greater or lesser extent to the development of new infor-mation technologies. In the case of cultural globalization this is very evident in the growth of mass communications which can reach around the world. Again, however, it is important to be clear about what is meant by cultural globalization. It is not that there is a growing tendency toward a single integrated global culture – an idea associated with the thesis of homogenization through Western-ization to which few subscribe today. The argument for cultural globalization is rather that there is increased cultural intercon-nectedness across the globe, principally as a result of the mass media, but also because of flows of people in migration, tourism, and the emergence of "third cultures" associated with the personnel of global economic and political institutions (Featherstone, 1990). Global cultural flows may contribute to our sense of the world as a single place, but even without such a global consciousness they affect how we live in our own locality in relation to others and to representations of others which come to us via the mass media. They may also produce new understandings of culture, nationality, the self in the world, what it is to be a foreigner, what it is to be a citizen, how people become politically engaged, and many other aspects of social life.

One of the most obvious forms of globalization, of which most people now have some awareness, is that of environmental degradation. According to David Goldblatt (1997), there are three forms of environmental globalization. The first is transboundary pollution, such as acid rain, which is obviously not bound by the territorial jurisdiction of the nation-state, although at the moment it is more likely to be regional than actually global. Secondly, there is environmental interdependence which means that causes set in motion in one place may have effects elsewhere, or they may be global in their impacts; the emission of greenhouse gases leading to global warming is an example. Thirdly, there may be degradation of the environmental commons, as in the case of pollution of the atmosphere and the sea, which potentially affects all living humans and future generations. Environmental problems are clearly linked to global politics since many can only be addressed at this level.

All these aspects of globalization – economic, cultural and environmental – have important implications for the sociological model of politics as centered on the nation-state. David Held makes a useful distinction between state autonomy and state sovereignty. The autonomy of the state involves its ability to act independently to articulate and pursue domestic and international policies (Held, 1995a: 100). Manifestly, the state has never been fully autonomous; as we saw in chapter 1, the extent to which the modern state has been subject to the imperatives of capitalist accumulation has been one of the most widely debated issues in Marxist political sociology. However, as we have seen in the case of economic globalization, the debate has taken on new life in that it is now argued that globalization systematically undermines state autonomy to the point where governments are reduced to managing processes over which they have no control, even in principle, since they are not contained within national borders. Economic globalization means that the monetary and fiscal policies of national governments are dominated by movements in the international financial markets to the point where many autarkic measures of national economic policy are now of doubtful value (Held, 1995a: 130–1; Amin, 1997: 128). In cultural terms, satellite communication systems bring new ideas, make censorship difficult, and threaten national broadcasting systems, charged with contributing to the social cohesiveness of nations, with redundancy. Finally, it is becoming increasingly evident that, since environmental damage does not respect national boundaries, it cannot be controlled by individual national governments.

At the same time, state sovereignty has also been undermined. The idea of sovereignty is integral to the development of the modern nation-state: it is the way in which the legitimacy of rule was conceived following the problematization of traditional authority in the religious and civil conflicts of early modernity (Held, 1995a: 38–9). State sovereignty has been ensured by the international state system which has grown up alongside it in a relationship of interdependence. Known as the Westphalian order, it supported the exclusive right of each nation-state to rule over its citizens and conduct its own internal and external affairs without intervention (McGrew, 1997: 3–4). Globalization has undermined this order in that new international and transnational institutions have been developed since the end of World War II, initially to deal with international conflicts but increasingly to address other issues of global import as well. These new political institutions pluralize sovereignty and displace the supreme sovereignty of the nation-state.

The most direct challenge to state sovereignty is international law. The Nuremberg Tribunal established the principle that where there are international rules protecting humanitarian values which conflict with state laws, so long as individuals are in a position to exercise "moral choice," they are legally and morally bound to transgress the state laws (Held, 1995a: 101). In international law the rights and duties of individuals as human beings now over-ride their rights and duties as the citizens of sovereign nation-states; for the first time in modern history a supranational legal authority compels citizens to ignore their own state. The European Convention for the Protection of Human Rights and Fundamental Freedoms of 1950 undermined state sovereignty still further by enabling citizens to undertake legal proceedings against their own governments (Held, 1995a: 102). The European Union is, however, exceptional among political institutions which go beyond the nation-state in having the authority to make laws which can be imposed on member states. It is, therefore, the only institution properly described as "supra-national." Others, like the United Nations, the World Bank, the IMF, the economic summit Group of 7, and so on, are better described as international since they are wholly dependent on the co-operation of nation-states for their operations. They have no means of collective enforcement of their policies other than this co-operation. However, intervention in the internal affairs of a sovereign state by international institutions has been legitimated in certain cases. It was seen as valid in the case of the UN interventions in Bosnia, for example, because of human rights violations. Another example is the practices of the IMF which may grant financial assistance to governments who ask for it under conditions which the government in question may have no part in negotiating (Held, 1995a: 109–110). At the same time, in almost every sphere of activity there are a growing number of transnational organizations, including social movements and social movement organizations like Greenpeace, but also large charitable operations like Oxfam and scientific and professional bodies like the International Association of Nutritional Sciences and the International Sociological Association (McGrew, 1995: 35).

The widespread network of international governmental organizations, combined with international non-governmental organizations (INGOs), provide the conditions for what is commonly known as global governance. Although there is clearly no world government – except in the case of the European Union there is no formal authority above the nation-state with the constitutional authority to make law backed by an administrative and enforcement apparatus – by co-operating with each other, and also with INGOs, states are actually engaging in global governance. As Rosenau describes it, global governance consists of "governance without government – of regulatory mechanisms in a sphere of activity which function effectively even though they are not endowed with formal authority" (quoted in McGrew, 1997: 15).

On these grounds it may be argued that in fact the nation-state has *not* been undermined by processes of globalization; it is rather that its role has changed in the new conditions, and in this way its power has actually been consolidated rather than weakened (Held, 1995a: 130; McGrew, 1997: 10–12). It is certainly the case that nation-states are the primary actors in global governance. Even in the case of the European Union, its powers were gained by the "willing surrender" of aspects of sovereignty by nation-states, and arguably this gave them greater scope for maneuver in the face of US dominance and the rise of Japan as an economic power (Held, 1995a: 112).

Nevertheless, as Held points out, sovereignty is now, to some extent at least, shared between national, international, and, in some cases, regional authorities; it is no longer the indivisible and illimitable power of individual nation-states (1995: 135). The very idea of a divided and plural sovereignty is, however, paradoxical from the point of view of the ideology informing the modern nation-state. We must, therefore, conclude that the very set of institutions named as "the state" should be understood in quite different terms from those of traditional political sociology. We will return to the question of the changing nation-state, and the formation of what could well be called the *internationalized* state, in the final chapter of the book, where we look at the possibility of global democratization.

2.2   GLOBALIZATION, MODERNITY, AND POSTMODERNITY

Globalization is closely linked to the question of the periodization of contemporary society. The "facts" of globalization are less disputed by political sociologists than the question of whether globalization indicates that we are now entering a qualitatively different era, that of postmodernity, or whether it represents a continuation of processes already set in motion in modernity.

Theorists of globalization as postmodernization tend to see it as a consequence of expansionary capitalism, set free from the restraints of the nation-state to develop new forms of exploitation across the world. In this view, postmodernity consists of a socio-economic base which is post-Fordist and an infrastructure of postmodern culture. These theorists identify themselves with Marxism, explicitly resisting the "postmodern turn." However, in so far as they attempt to theorize a new social formation in which postmodern culture plays a prominent role, the extent to which this is viable, or even consistent with their analyses, is doubtful. Ultimately, these theories are limited in their grasp of the new situation by their adherence to a sociological model developed under very different circumstances.

Theorists of globalization as modernization oppose themselves both to Marxism and to the view that we are now entering quite a different type of society. They maintain that there are many causes of globalization and that they are a continuation of the dynamic features of modernity. This multi-causal view is useful because it enables the recognition of the importance of cultural politics to the emerging social formations of globalization. However, the commitment to seeing globalization only within the terms of what is already known in modernity sets unnecessary restrictions on our understanding of how effective cultural politics might be in developing new forms of social life.

Globalization as a consequence of capitalism

The most traditional sociological approach to globalization is that of Marxists. Although, as we have seen, neo-Marxists have been very much concerned with the form and functions of the nation-state, the Marxist view of the essence of capitalism as a mode of commodity production based on the exploitative relationship between capital and labor does not require that it should be thought of as synonymous with a "society" organized as a territorially bounded nation. On the contrary, as a system which requires the maximum appropriation of surplus value, and which is characterized by class struggle, it is inherent in the logic of capitalism that it will seek out new sites of exploitation. Capitalism depends on the relentless search for low wages, cheap resources, and the creation of new markets for the goods it produces. The original premises of Marxist theory apparently need little alteration, then, to enable it to deal with the phenomena of globalization since on this understanding capitalism has inherent tendencies toward expansion beyond the societies in which it was initially developed.

The most highly developed application of Marxist theory in these terms is the world systems theory of Immanuel Wallerstein. According to Wallerstein, there is nothing new in the global scope and orientation of capitalism; it has, of course, expanded greatly in 400 years, to the point where it now forms a world economic system, but the logic of its expansion was there from its beginning in sixteenth-century Europe. Wallerstein sees capitalism as an integrating world system which has an internal dynamic of development; capitalism needs to expand its geographical boundaries in order to combat the regular slumps to which it is prone (Wallerstein, 1990). Although the world system is therefore driven by economic imperatives, Wallerstein's account is neo-Marxist in that he sees states as essential to the stability of global capitalism. The capitalist world system is historically unique in that it involves a global economy combined with a political system of sovereign nation-states; it is, therefore, quite unlike previous world economies which were regional rather than global, and centered on imperial states. The capitalist world system integrates what Wallerstein calls "political states" in a common international division of labor. The core developed states, such as those of the EU, Japan, and the USA, dominate on the basis of higher-level skills and greater capitalization, while peripheral areas with weak states, including the newly industrializing countries of the South, provide the conditions for capitalist expansion through their economic dependence on the core. In addition, there are semi-peripheral areas, including the "tiger economies" of South-East Asia, the oil-producing countries, and the former socialist countries of Eastern Europe, with moderately strong governmental structures and single-commodity or low-technology economies, which provide a buffer zone preventing polarization and outright conflict between core and periphery (Wallerstein, 1979; Waters, 1995: 22–6).

Wallerstein's world systems theory has been widely criticized for its practically exclusive emphasis on the economic aspects of globalization. Although politics actually features more centrally than class in his account, global integration seems to take place solely at the economic level: the relationships of trade and exploitation he sees as characterizing the world economy take place between relatively sovereign nation-states, each with its own relatively independent culture (Waters, 1995: 25). World systems theory therefore fails to address the changing form and role of the state in the context of the multiple and shifting sites of sovereignty which now characterize global governance (Held, 1995a: 26). Furthermore, as Roland Robertson points out, although Wallerstein has given up his original view that culture is epiphenomenal to economic processes, he tends to consider it only under the guise of "an ideological impediment" to the realization of socialism as a world system, or alternatively, as a resource for the "anti-systemic movements" he sees as opposed to the cultural premises of the core societies (Robertson, 1992: 65–8). These movements are, according to Wallerstein (1991), principally directed toward what he thinks of as political ends, at overthrowing or resisting state authorities. Culture for Wallerstein is either national, organized around and defined as such by the nation-state, or, alternatively, world culture, which would contribute to world socialism (Wallerstein, 1991). He is unable to take into account the multiple struggles within and about global culture which do not conform to this binary opposition, and, as we shall see in section 2.3, global culture is not readily seen as polarized in this way. He is also unable to give any consideration to the exponential increase in cultural products which other Marxisant theorists take to be the defining feature of contemporary globalization and which may indicate the development of a form of global capitalism quite different from that of any which has preceded it.

One of the most widely respected of these theorists is David Harvey. In *The Condition of Postmodernity* (1989) he links globalization with postmodernity and postmodernism, arguing that the new form of capitalism he calls "flexible postmodernity" can nevertheless be understood in classical Marxist terms: "Let us go back . . . to Marx's 'invariant elements and relations' of a capitalist mode of production and see to what degree they are omni-present beneath all the surface froth and evanescence, the fragmentations and disruptions, so characteristic of present political economy" (Harvey, 1989: 179). Globalization is not new to capitalism, according to Harvey, but flexible postmodernity involves the intensification of the time–space compression which characterizes it. Social life is speeded up to the point where space is reduced or collapses entirely, as in the case of the instantaneous transmission and reception of images around the world using satellite communications (Harvey, 1989: 241). According to Harvey, since 1970 there has been an intensification of time–space compression as a response to a crisis in the Fordist regime of capitalist accumulation; new forms of information technology and communications are now used to bring about a more flexible form of capitalism. By 1970 market saturation and falling profits exposed the disadvantages of a system based on Fordist techniques of mass production and Keynesian corporatism involving agreement between the state, capitalists, and trade unionists to guarantee high levels of employment, investment, and consumption. Capitalists successfully dismantled Fordism by introducing new manufacturing and information technology enabling small-batch, "just-in-time" production aimed at specialized "market niches;" by gaining greater control over workers with the division of the labor market into skilled, adaptable, and therefore well-paid and secure core employees, and peripheral workers who are less skilled and frequently insecurely employed; and by deregulating the global financial market so that capital flow is now to a large extent outside the control of nation-states (though they may be called upon to intervene in new ways, in unstable financial markets, if currency is in danger, for example).

We are currently in a period of transition, then, to a flexible postmodernity characterized by post-Fordist techniques and relations of production. Most importantly, for Harvey, finance capital has been empowered at the expense of the state and organized labor. The nation-state has lost a good deal of the control over economic policy and labor relations it enjoyed in Keynesian corporatism. It has been forced to become "entrepreneurial," disciplining workers and curbing the power of trade unions in order to attract capital investment (Harvey, 1989: 168). Flexible postmodernity is a new, more virulent form of capitalism in which the state and organized labor are at the mercy of finance capital.

According to Harvey, flexible postmodernity produces a postmodern culture. Following Jameson's (1984) influential argument that postmodernism is the "cultural logic of late capitalism," he sees cultural production as increasingly integrated into commodity production resulting in a new aesthetic sensibility. The relentless search for new markets, the rapid turnover of goods, and the constant manipulation of taste and opinion in advertising produces the postmodern celebration of ephemerality, of surface images rather than depth of meaning, of montage and juxtaposition of styles rather than authenticity, and of heterogeneity, pluralism, discontinuity and chaos rather than meta-narratives of reason and progress (Harvey, 1989: ch. 3; see pp. 71–88 on postmodern culture). For Harvey, postmodernism is epiphenomenal, a by-product of a new stage of the capitalist mode of production dependent on the accel-

erated consumption of signs and services, rather than on manufactured goods. Nothing more than "froth and evanescence," it does
not require the development of new theoretical tools appropriate to
the object since it can be understood entirely from within the terms
of Marxist political economy.

In fact, as Krishan Kumar (1995) points out, it is possible to read
Harvey's work against his own conclusions. Rather than seeing postmodernism as simply a change of style, a surface gloss on capitalism
as the driving force of contemporary social life, it is possible to conclude that if postmodernity is capitalism with a new face, then the
novelty of the situation warrants more than simply a return to business as usual. Without denying the importance of the economic
dimension of postmodernity, it is important not to reduce the cultural and political dimensions to an economistic determinism of
capital accumulation and ceaselessly extending commodification
(Kumar, 1995: 192–5). Despite his sensitivity to cultural forms, from
the position Harvey takes within a political economy developed to
deal with a very different kind of social life, one in which signs were
less obviously effective in identity formation and contestation and
in the structuring of social practices, he ignores the contemporary
significance of culture in this respect. In reducing cultural forms to
economic determinism, Harvey is unable to theorize the productive
role of representations and images in the mass media and consumer
culture, and so cannot engage with the potentially transformational
strategies of cultural politics.

For Harvey, real politics is essentially class politics. Although on
occasion he commends social movements for "changing the structure of feeling" and articulating the rights of the marginalized to
speak in their own voices ("women, gays, blacks, ecologists, regional
autonomists:" Harvey, 1989: 48), at the same time he suggests that
such movements tend toward "place-bound" resistance which only
serves the fragmentation upon which flexible accumulation feeds
(1989: 303–5). As Meaghan Morris (1992) notes, he gestures toward
acknowledging the equal importance of "differences" and "otherness" and the necessity of incorporating them into a more inclusive
historical materialism, but he continually re-writes "differences"
as "the same;" ultimately, all these groups are simply further victims
of capitalist exploitation. For Harvey, it is only class politics that
can be genuinely emancipatory (Harvey, 1989: 355, 1993; Morris,
1992).

In *Economies of Signs and Space* (1994), Scott Lash and John Urry expound a similar argument to Harvey, using a Marxist framework to explain globalization. Like Harvey, they also see the terms "post-modernity" and "postmodernism" as usefully summing up new features of contemporary life, while grounding them in the continuity of dynamic capitalism as the driving force of history. However, Lash and Urry do integrate these new features into their account of what they call alternatively "disorganized capitalism" and "postmodernity" to a greater extent than Harvey. In fact, it may be argued that a postmodern account of postmodernity almost breaks through the modern Marxist paradigm to which they are anxious to remain committed.

Lash and Urry see themselves as giving more emphasis than those who think in terms of post-Fordism and flexible specialization to *consumption* as a leading practice in contemporary capitalism. For them, it is consumption and service industries rather than finance capital and post-Fordist production that demonstrate the progressive features of disorganized capitalism and which are therefore at its core (Lash and Urry, 1994: 17, 60). This is an important difference in emphasis because it leads them to place culture and symbolic value at the center of their analysis. In their view, the economy is now based primarily on the circulation of signs: the cognitive signs that are informational goods and the aetheticized signs of what they call postmodern goods such as media products, leisure services, and designer products (1994: 4). It is in this respect that they link post-modern aestheticism and postmodernity. Postmodernism is central to postmodernity because, alongside the changing *objects* of capitalism, it also involves the emergence of a new, more highly reflexive *subjectivity*. This is, in turn, both cognitive and aesthetic. In cognitive terms, it involves the monitoring and formation of the self in the reflection on information given by experts. In aesthetic terms, it involves the interpretation and formation of the self through the consumption of goods, ideas, and images. Lash and Urry see reflexivity of both kinds as central to the reproduction and modification of the socio-economic processes of postmodernity; it is both the result and the condition of a continual "de-tradition-alization" which constantly revolutionizes patterns of production and consumption.

For Lash and Urry, postmodernity is intrinsically global. Organized capitalism was centered on the nation-state: like Harvey, they see the previous capitalist system as one in which class interests were incorporated into a Keynesian national agenda set through negotiated compromises and state regulation (Lash and Urry, 1987). Disorganized capitalism cannot, however, be analyzed as a society, a set of structures bounded by the nation-state (Lash and Urry, 1994: 320–2). Flows of capital, technologies, information, images, and people do not recognize territorial boundaries and collapse the globe as they circulate across greater distances at greater velocity. Expanded and speeded-up flows across borders are increasingly outside the control of national governments, or, indeed, of any individual organization or group. Nothing is given or fixed in disorganized capitalism, according to Lash and Urry, and the reflexivity resulting from ever-increasing knowledge and information serves only to disorganize it still further (1994: 10–11).

Lash and Urry begin and end *Economies of Signs and Space* by invoking the name of Marx, to resurrect the "dinosaur," as they put it. However, it is arguable that the theory they present breaks significantly with the economism of orthodox Marxism in seeing the circulation of goods, capital, and labor in symbolic terms and therefore as at least as much a matter of culture as of economics. On one hand, they seem to argue for a weak version of economic determinism, seeing postmodern culture, reflexivity, and other features of postmodernity as caused by global economic flows, as "effects of [the] highly informationalized socio-economic core" (1994: 13). However, as Kumar notes, at the same time they also see the postmodernized economy as inseparably intertwined with culture, rather than as occupying a separate sphere from which it could be said to be causing cultural effects (Kumar, 1995: 118). They argue that what it is important to grasp in order to understand contemporary capitalism is precisely "the extent to which culture has penetrated the economy itself, that is, the extent to which symbolic processes, including an important aesthetic component, have permeated both consumption and production" (Lash and Urry, 1994: 60–1). This second thesis is also a good deal more consistent with the idea of reflexivity as productive of the flows in which it is embedded; flows of goods, information, people are modifiable just to the extent that they are, as Lash and Urry argue, meaningful for those engaged in them because they are imbued with symbolic value. The reflexivity of the economy is both cause and effect of the way in which it is, in Lash and Urry's terms, informationalized and aes-

theticized. In fact, Lash and Urry's theory of capitalism is barely recognizable in terms of Marxism's privileging of the economic sphere
as determinant of social relations and cultural forms. Their analysis
thus gestures toward a more thoroughly postmodern, and more comprehensive, theory of globalization as postmodern than either
Harvey or Wallerstein can provide from within the terms of orthodox Marxism.

Lash and Urry give little consideration to politics in either the
narrow or the wider sense. They see the nation-state as increasingly
internationalized in that many attempts to govern globalized
capitalism can only be made at the level of the international
political order. However, they do not discuss politics at this level in
any detail. Nor do they explicitly address the issues of cultural
politics we are concerned with in this book. Nevertheless, their
analysis of reflexive postmodern capitalism does allow for an understanding of cultural politics as it is concerned with the formation and
contestation of identities and social practices. In their account, the
individual is forced to make choices concerning his or her consumption habits, lifestyle, work patterns, family relations, and so on,
and in so far as such decisions are linked to global social movements,
ethical consumerism, and so on, they are political, with implications
for social structures which go beyond the individual him or herself.
Lash and Urry's analysis of postmodernity might be seen as pessimistic in that disorganized capitalism is characterized in terms of
the demise of organized labor and the power of the nation-state to
regulate capitalism in the interests of citizens. However, their theory
of postmodernization actually points toward the way in which the
social is necessarily actively constituted through the manipulation of
meaning, and therefore to the possibility of a globalization which
would not necessarily be dominated by the imperatives of capitalist
expansion.

Globalization as modernization

This understanding of cultural politics is much more highly
developed in the sociology of reflexivity, the main alternative to
Marxism as a way of theorizing globalization from a starting
point within the terms of traditional sociology. These sociologists,
notably Anthony Giddens and Ulrich Beck, advocate a multi-causal

explanation of globalization in which it is seen as a consequence of modernity, rather than the mono-causal account of Marxists in which capitalism is presented as its driving force (McGrew, 1992: 69).

Giddens (1990) sees globalization as the outcome of the dynamism of modernity which involves what he calls the disembedding of social relations in time–space distanciation and the reflexive appropriation of knowledge. He contrasts modernity with previous epochs in which time and space were always linked to place, to the immediate location of co-present social actors. In modernity, time and space are "emptied;" abstracted from particular social rhythms of life, they are represented by clocks and maps which allow them to be used independently of any particular social location. Time–space distanciation makes possible the development of disembedding mechanisms which "lift out" social activity from localized contexts and reorganize it across time and space. There are two types of disembedding mechanisms, according to Giddens: symbolic tokens, of which the only one he discusses is money, used as a universal token of exchange; and expert systems in which technical knowledge is used to organize material and social environments: that of engineers, architects, doctors, psychologists, and so on. Expert systems contribute to the reflexivity of modernity, to the continual monitoring of what is known, and to the decisions that have to be made concerning how to proceed in everyday life. In modernity, there can be no reliance on tradition, since every aspect of life is potentially subject to reason and can only be justified in the light of this consideration. The reflexive monitoring intrinsic to human activity is thus radicalized in modernity: social practices are continually constitutively altered by the understanding social actors bring to bear on them in their daily routines (Giddens, 1990).

According to Giddens, the dynamism of modernity leads inexorably (if unpredictably, since there are always unintended consequences in social life) toward the globalization of its institutions: capitalism, industrialism, and the administrative surveillance and control of the means of violence which are concentrated in the nation-state. In Giddens's view it is the importance of the rise of the nation-state, and now of the nation-state system of global governance, which is neglected in Marxist accounts. He agrees with Wallerstein that capitalism is inherently expansionist, but he argues that the concentration of power in the nation-state enabled the mobilization of social, economic, and military resources far beyond those available to pre-modern systems and that this, combined with capitalism and industrial production, is what has made the expansion of the West irresistible (Giddens, 1990: 62–3). Giddens sees the nation-state as retaining its importance in globalized modernity in so far as there is no area of the earth's surface which is not under the legitimate control of a state and in so far as states continue to have a successful monopoly over the means of violence within their territories. However, the modern state has always been involved in a dialectic in which it trades control over practices within its territories for more global influence by joining with other states. Working through international agencies, a state may gain control over military operations, for example, which do not depend solely on the control it exercises within its borders; at the same time, it loses a degree of independence of action through that co-operation. In late modernity, given increased time–space distanciation in all areas of activity and the resulting flows across territorial borders, there is a tendency toward a greater degree of co-operation and a consequent diminishing of autonomy for the nation-state.

As Giddens sees it, then, we are still within modernity, albeit a radicalized modernity which has many of the features others attribute to postmodernity. He sees radicalized modernity as characterized by a disenchantment with teleological models of history involving the progress of some intrinsic human capacity or activity, such as reason or labor, and also by the dissolution of foundationalism in which the absolute and fundamental grounds for truth or morality are sought in reasoned reflection. In this respect, his work is an example of the "postmodern turn" away from "meta-narratives." For Giddens, however, anti-foundationalism and "the end of meta-narratives" are a result of modernity's reflection on itself, a process of clearing away traditional forms of thought which is obscured by the term "postmodern" (Giddens, 1990: 51; see pp. 38–9).

Despite his commitment to a modern framework, Giddens has developed one of the most detailed accounts of cultural politics in relation to globalization. He compares the "emancipatory politics" of modernity, including Marxism, liberalism, and conservatism, with the "life politics" of the contemporary period of late modernity in which both the political end and the means are the transformation of the self. He gives rather a sketchy account of emancipatory politics as concerned with liberation from exploitation, inequality, and oppression and as seeking justice and participation through democratic participation (conservatism is seen as a reaction to these ideals in radicalism and liberalism). It works with the conventional modern notion of power as the capability of an individual or group to exert its will over others that we have encountered as the dominant definition in political sociology (Giddens, 1991: 210–14). By contrast, "life politics" is a politics of individual lifestyle. It involves the individual in continually making choices in a reflexively ordered environment where tradition no longer provides the parameters of everyday life. It is closely connected to globalization, according to Giddens, "where globalizing influences intrude deeply into the reflexive project of the self, and conversely where processes of self-realization influence global strategies" (1991: 214). The connection is evident, for example, in the case of the extensive public awareness of the impact of lifestyle decisions on the environment, but it is also there whenever global processes impact on individuals' projects for self-actualization and vice versa.

Giddens does not see the nation-state as irrelevant in life politics. The state remains crucial to democratization, emancipatory rights are still important and issues of life politics are likely to become increasingly significant in the public and juridical arenas of states. However, life politics are currently more prominent outside the state, often carried by social movements, as exemplified in the feminist slogan "The personal is political." They may, therefore, according to Giddens, lead to new forms of political organization appropriate to their concerns (Giddens, 1991: 226–8). As we shall see in the final chapter, it is indeed the case that global social movements offer important possibilities for democratization both of the nation-state and beyond it.

Ulrich Beck's theory of cultural politics is strikingly similar to that of Giddens in many respects, despite their different starting points (Beck, 1992: 7–8). Beck is best known for drawing sociologists' attention to the way in which contemporary social life is characterized by an unprecedented degree and number of fabricated risks, many of which are global in scope, such as environmental pollution or nuclear war, and which are likely to become more so as the overproduction, which is currently a feature of advanced industrial societies, intensifies across the world. Risk society is necessarily global, in Beck's view, because it produces dangers which are not clearly limited in space and time. Furthermore, responses to risk may also be global: modernization is the driving force of globalization, but risk accelerates it in so far as modernity is reflexive. Beck argues, from rather an optimistic point of view, that we are now on the threshold of a radicalized modernity in which "global dangers set up global mutualities" such that self-conscious, collective reflection on risk displaces the modern privileging of progress and wealth production in order to avoid global destruction (Beck, 1992, 1996: 29).

In Beck's view, the realization of the potential for reflexive modernity depends on what he calls "sub-politics." For Beck, it is very clear that new forms of politics are developing which do not directly address the nation-state. Modernity has resulted in a gap between the state as the supposed political center which actually has no influence over the most important decisions concerning risk, and the decisions taken outside this arena, in different institutional contexts where contingent decisions must be made in the light of the knowledge of different possibilities with different implications for different groups (Beck, 1992: 222). A new political culture which by-passes the institutions of formal government has been produced by the successes of modernity in which civil rights of free speech and an independent judiciary are guaranteed. Citizens now have something of a public voice in media debates, in citizens' campaigns, in decisions concerning ethical consumption, in petitioning the courts on matters of public concern and in private lifestyle choices, all of which must be taken seriously by governments, multinational corporations, and other citizens. As Beck sees it, in reflexive modernity, there is a moralization of economic and social life in which the supposed objectivity and necessity of technical requirements and the outcomes of government policies are continually called into question and opened up to new opportunities for democracy. Beck's principal example here is the politics of the environmental movement which has been largely effective outside political parties and the bureaucratic procedures of the state.

Beck, like Giddens, is committed to the view that we live in reflexive modernity rather than postmodernity. However, some of his formulations concerning the status of reflexive knowledge are actually made in terms of a version of discourse theory very similar to that argued for by post-structuralists. In this respect, he is more explicitly within the terms of the "postmodern turn" than Giddens.

He argues that while scientific knowledge should not simply be seen as "truth," such that risks must be taken to be "real" if they are verified by scientific procedures, nor should it be seen as socially constructed, *tout court*. Social constructionism is inadequate, first, because it is unable to take into account the way in which particular cultural constructs enter into the constitution of nature itself in "hybrids" of technology and nature, in the contemporary malleability of the human body, for example, or the reproductive techniques such as *in vitro* fertilization, surrogate motherhood and the like which make "biological motherhood" so complex. And, secondly, because it fails to account for the reality of certain social constructions, the way in which some constructions rather than others come to (re)produce "reality-as-it-is." In Beck's view, we should understand knowledge as effective if it is carried in "discourse coalitions," by actors and institutions which put constructions into practice, in decisions and material production which actually constitute reality (Beck, 1996: 10). Beck's view clearly understands "discourse" as embedded in social practices here; they are not simply linguistic.

Furthermore, Beck's analysis of "sub-politics" goes beyond Giddens's theory of reflexive modernity in offering the theoretical possibility of a complete transformation of social forms, even if they remain, according to Beck, within modernity. For Beck, it is always possible that decisions made in sub-politics may alter the institutional contexts in which they are made; such decisions precisely concern the realization of one course of action, and thus the constitution of one possible institutional form, among various possibilities. One of the examples he gives is that of the use of information technology in industrial organizations; there are many ways in which everyday working life could be transformed by the use of this technology, such that the relations within and between the economic institutions of radicalized modernity might be quite different from those that have gone before (Beck, 1992: 215–23).

Similarly, Beck argues that the state is currently being remade behind the façade of the modern nation-state. While, historically, nation-states have been formed and sustained by and for war, the situation is very different where populations are faced with global risks. This is particularly evident with the end of the Cold War and growing concern with environmental dangers. The state itself must now adapt to the new situation of the risk society and the sub-

politics of social movements, citizens' initiatives, professional associations, and so on. In the most favorable case, this would lead to
the establishment of the "round-table" state in which different
groups discussed national and international policies (Beck, 1998:
152). The modern military state would be completely transformed
by changes within its bureaucratic institutions.

Giddens also allows for the complete transformation of modernity by advocating a "utopian realism," including, for example, the
global redistribution of wealth, demilitarization, the humanization
of technology, and increased democratic participation, all of which
he sees as possible future outcomes of current social change
(Giddens, 1990: 163–73). Furthermore, he theorizes the process of
social change in so far as his concept of reflexivity allows him, as we
have seen, to identify new forms of politics. However, his focus on
the particular institutions and dynamics he attributes to modernity
means his theory is committed to a framework in which the far-
reaching transformations taking place within social practices and
institutions may be overlooked as they develop.

The question of the transformation of the nation-state is a good
example. Giddens has actually given more consideration to the
changing role of the nation-state than most theorists of globalization. However, when he refers to "the modern state" there is a tendency to flatten out and reify a complex, pluralist set of practices.
This makes it difficult to trace in detail the way in which the state
is produced from a plurality of institutional practices and discourses
in which power is exercised. From the point of view of Giddens's
rather abstract theorization of the modern state, as involving the concentration of the means of violence and surveillance, its practical and
discursive construction and continual reconstruction are difficult to
understand. This is particularly problematic because it risks obscur-
ing the precise means by which the state is currently being contested
and reconstructed in innovative ways with potentially far-reaching
effects in an era in which globalization is accelerating. Without
the close attention to the details of the discursive construction of
"the internationalized state" of global governance implied by Beck's
model of sub-politics and "discourse coalitions," for example, the
analytic possibility that it might develop in ways that go beyond
modernity is difficult to discern. In so far as Giddens sees life politics as taking place within the framework of modern institutions,
his theory of globalization puts conceptual limits on our under-

standing of the changes it may bring about in a way that Beck's model of sub-politics does not.

2.3   GLOBAL CULTURE: GLOBALIZATION AS POSTMODERNIZATION

Although very few theorists of globalization actually identify their work explicitly as post-structuralist or postmodern, as we have seen, globalization has been linked with postmodernity and theorized in terms which are recognizably within the "postmodern turn" in sociology. Similarly, global culture is often seen as postmodern: fast-changing, fragmented, pluralist, hybrid, and syncretic. That global culture should be seen as postmodern is, in some respects at least, unsurprising. Global culture is inevitably fragmented and pluralist since it is not *world* culture: no theorists of globalization are of the view that there is a single global repertoire of beliefs and styles (Smith, 1990). The question of global culture arises because the scope and pace of communication networks around the world suggest that there is a flow of meanings as well as of people and goods. The term "global culture" is used to refer to the *globalization of culture*, rather than to the constitution of a single, integrated culture, a version of national culture writ large.

However, seeing global culture as postmodern goes further than recognizing that it is heterogeneous, fragmented, and fluid. It also means thinking about the way in which Western cultural values have now become just one way of looking at the world among many, sometimes conflicting, perspectives. In postmodern terms, it has become one narrative among others rather than the defining "meta-narrative" it saw itself as in modernity. In this respect, seeing global culture as postmodern offers the opportunity of a greater openness and "responsibility toward Otherness" as cultural differences are seen as valid rather than suppressed or destroyed.

Globalization and the relativization and pluralization of the West

Western culture has been relativized by globalization. The values once seen as unproblematically universal, valid for everyone, at all times and in all places, are now in retreat. It is acknowledged that they were developed in particular ways, by particular groups of people, with particular historical and social experiences. At the same time, Western culture has become more evidently pluralized. It is, in fact, plausible to argue that there has never been a homogeneous "West," that such an idea could only have been constructed through encounters with Others seen as radically different. However, it is undoubtedly the case that there is now, largely as a result of migration, a significant presence in the cities of the West of many people who do not see themselves, and are not seen by others, as Western. Nevertheless, given that most come from countries previously colonized by Europeans, their history must also be seen as that of the West. New identities, such as "Asian-American," "British black," and for that matter "British white," mean that Western culture itself is now pluralized to an unprecedented extent.

This is a very complex topic. Western culture in modernity has always had a dual aspect. On one hand, it was seen as universal, embodying values which everyone should hold, representing the best in human nature and endeavor and encoding the highest possible ideals. This liberal humanist view of culture was famously defined in the nineteenth century by Matthew Arnold as "the best that has been thought and known" and was held to be the path to enlightenment and self-realization (Jordan and Weedon, 1995: 25–6). On the other hand, however, it has also always been taken to be particular to a nation, to be a single, integrated organic way of life, including the traditional thoughts and habits of the people in whatever artefacts and rituals they were produced (Guibernau, 1996: 55–6). Although this conception of culture is more closely associated with conservatism than liberalism, and includes "folk culture" as well as "high culture," in practice national culture and liberal humanist culture have been conflated, particularly since the nineteenth century. In modern nations there has been a concerted effort to identify humanist culture with national culture, particularly through compulsory systems of mass education (Jordan and Weedon, 1995: 67–71). Arnold, for example, was actively involved in developing the study of English literature "for the English" as a way of uniting classes, allaying unrest and promoting social cohesion (Jordan and Weedon, 1995: 38–40)

Modern culture is still more complex because the construction of both humanist culture and national culture involves relations which actually go beyond the nation. Following the enormously influential work of Benedict Anderson (1983), it has become commonplace to see nations as "imagined communities": "imagined" because members of nations never meet most other members; "communities" because the nation is always conceived in terms of deeply felt comradeship. For Anderson, nationalism is itself a cultural product, produced in practices of identification with fellow-nationals. The imagined community of the nation was developed following the replacement of the sacred languages of the Middle Ages – such as Latin, Arabic, and Chinese, each of which united a vast territory – with regional, vernacular languages which were then standardized and spread through the printed word in novels and newspapers. In eighteenth-century Latin America and North America, the development of print enabled millions of individuals to represent their fellow-readers to themselves as compatriots; this was particularly marked in the case of newspapers in which the reading is imagined as more or less simultaneous (Anderson, 1983). Belonging to a nation is, then, an ongoing process of construction and identification rather than an objective fact or a timeless loyalty to the land and people (though it may well be imagined in such terms).

Although, as Anderson is keen to point out, nationalism depends at least as much on love as on hate – people see themselves as willing to die for their country, not so much to kill for it – the "imagining of communities" is very much facilitated at times of crisis when there is the threat of an external Other against whom unity must be ensured. This is expressed in the (in)famous saying of Mrs Thatcher on the eve of the Falklands War: "We are one nation tonight" (Featherstone, 1995: 111–12). Most modern nations were formed through relations of conflict and competition with other nations and peoples, especially since the nineteenth century as the form of the nation-state has been generalized across the world (Balakrishnan, 1996). Unlike the "great global communities" they superseded (Anderson, 1983: 21), nations are necessarily limited by other nations and national culture is seen as coterminous with the territory of the nation-state. National cultures are dependent for their identity, then, not just on the homogeneity with which they are endowed by those who "imagine the community," but also on their opposition to the nation's "Others," those who cannot be included within it.

A subtle example of the construction of a national culture formed in opposition to its Others – although, unusually in this case, the Others inhabited the same territory without being included in the nation – is Toni Morrison's analysis of white American culture as dependent on the subordination of black Americans in slavery. Early cultural commentators in the United States, like Ralph Emerson, were quite self-conscious about the need to develop an explicitly American national culture. According to Morrison, in order to do so, the writers engaged in this project did not look only to Europe to establish a difference, they also used the "very theatrical difference underfoot," that of race (Morrison, 1992: 39). As Morrison sees it, the characteristics of American literature – individualism, innocence, a virile, powerful heroism, and social engagement (all of which, she notes, are also associated with masculinity in these works) – were developed in relation to an "Africanist" presence. Blackness and enslavement enabled the construction of a polarity for white writers in which "not-free" and "not-me" were combined in the literary imagination (Morrison, 1992: 38). Even though black characters are rarely prominent in this literature and slavery is not always explicitly at issue, the "Africanist" representation of blackness is so dominant that: "It provides a way of contemplating chaos and civilization, desire and fear, and a mechanism for testing the problems and blessings of freedom" (1992: 7). It is through their imaginative "playing in the dark," as Morrison calls it, that white writers created the tradition of the American novel in which whiteness is equated with authoritativeness, ethical sensitivity, compassion, even in some cases genuine humanity (1992: 76), as narrated through a creative opposition between self and Other and in comparison to subordinate blackness.

We see, then, from this last point, how national culture, although avowedly particularistic in its specificity as national, shares on occasion the universal pretensions of liberal humanism. If white American males are the only genuine human subjects, then only what they have produced is genuinely "the best" of human culture. There is a tension between particularism ("we are the best because our nation is best") and universalism ("we are the best because we are truly human") in national culture. There is a similar tension in liberal humanism.

This is nowhere more apparent than in the arguments of liberal political philosophers. Liberalism presents itself as a reasoned reflection on the human condition in which each individual is to be equally respected as capable of exercising his or her human capacities. In practice, however, liberals have held on some occasions that some individuals have not developed their capacities so that the rights to which they are entitled as humans may legitimately be withdrawn or over-ridden. This has been very much the case where liberals have been actively engaged in projects of colonialism.

The liberalism of John Locke, who had financial interests in the development of the New World, is a good example of the way in which the ostensibly universal principles of liberalism are actually exclusionary of those who do not exhibit the requisite cultural credentials. For Locke, although Native Americans undoubtedly had the human capacity for reason which would enable them to develop the land of North America, it was evident that they did not have the industry, enterprise, and self-discipline to enable them to do so since they had not enclosed it and did not use it to its full advantage. The English colonizers had both a right and a duty, therefore, to take this land and, indeed, ultimately this would be in the best economic interests of the Native American tribes themselves. Locke did not apply the same understanding to land which lay undeveloped in Europe since he saw it as forming part of the territory of political societies whose independence and integrity had to be respected. What was decisive in the case of the Native Americans was that they did not have structures of political authority resembling those of Europe, nor did they exhibit cultural homogeneity in terms of language, nor the development of arts and sciences as Locke understood them (Parekh, 1995).

A similar gesture to that of Locke's in relation to early colonialism is repeated throughout the history of liberal thought: the individual to whom universal human rights are attributed turns out to be highly specific, exhibiting just those characteristics valued by the writer and his milieu and excluding those for whom they are irrelevant or inappropriate. Liberal universalism, ostensibly inclusive of all human capacities and endeavors, is actually particularistic and exclusionary: the attributes and achievements of liberalism's Others, including women as well as those of different cultures, is often not counted as genuinely human at all (Pateman, 1989).

The globalization of culture is postmodern because it fragments and pluralizes the very engagement of the dominant Western definitions of culture as universal and as national. Decolonization and the rise of economic and political centers outside Europe and North America mean the decline of the power of the West to define its culture in universal terms and to legislate over others as inferior. At the same time, post-colonialism has meant a massive movement of people from the global periphery to the metropolitan centers, in search of relief from economic and political problems, to participate in the good life now shown in the media across the world, and also to contribute to family economies in their countries of birth. In Stuart Hall's words, " 'The Rest' is in 'the West' " (Hall, 1992a: 306). Even if the West continues to dominate in economic and technical terms, the ostensibly universal culture of the West has been relativized – localized historically and geographically – in the way in which the cultures of colonized societies have long been relativized by the West. Furthermore, Western national cultures have been pluralized by the co-existence of quite different cultural orientations "under the roof" of the nation-state. It has become evident that the nation-state is no longer, and in fact never was, the container for a single, unified, and integrated national culture.

There is no better example of the relativization and pluralization of the West in global culture than the case of the writer Salman Rushdie. His book, *The Satanic Verses*, was taken to be blasphemous by certain Muslims, both in Britain and around the world, and so outraged them that they supported the death sentence passed on him by the Ayatollah Khomeini of Iran. He was in hiding for his own protection for nine years until 1998. Rushdie defends his work on cultural grounds, arguing that his writing represents the experience of minority ethnic groups in the West – a defence which is not quite made in universalist liberal terms since he claims to be representing a particular group, but nevertheless in cultural terms of literary merit. This defence, however, has no validity for his opponents who are concerned with the sacredness of the Qur'ān which they see as defiled by certain passages in *The Satanic Verses* and which they were determined to protect from the corruption of secular Western beliefs. As members of a minority in Britain, they felt strongly that they had to defend a traditional way of life which is threatened on all sides (Hall, 1992a: 311).

Most of us probably find it difficult to decide which side to support in this affair, even if ultimately we do feel bound to take a position. The dilemma clearly illustrates Lyotard's thesis that we live in a historical moment marked by a loss of faith in the modern meta-narrative of the progress of reason toward a better society (Lyotard, 1984). In postmodern culture there are conflicts between different world-views with no over-arching set of absolute principles that allows us definitively to validate one rather than the other. In fact, simply in order to be able to understand the issues on both sides we have to move from one to the other; there is no common set of terms within which the values of both can be compared. In so far as liberal humanism continues to have any purchase, it is as a local narrative, productive of the West as it relates itself and not the bearer of universal values. The experience of flexibility in trying to understand the conflicting perspectives of Rushdie's liberal defenders and devout Muslims attempting to safeguard a threatened way of life, the willingness to try different frames and models in order to make sense of images and practices, is an important feature of postmodern, global culture (Featherstone, 1995: 82).

It is important to note, however, that the experience of relativization is itself specific; it is predominantly the experience of Western intellectuals. As Zygmunt Bauman (1987) argues, intellectuals, including sociologists, are no longer in a position to legislate for society. They no longer hold the position as legislators that Enlightenment thinkers prescribed for them, as those who should establish rational social organization, using the resources of the state to mould society according to universal precepts of reason. This is largely, he argues, because, although the state has made extensive use of "professional experts," it has relied much more on the strategies of surveillance and normalization analyzed by Foucault and, more recently, on the seductions of consumerism and the market to maintain social order. According to Bauman, it is as a result of the loss of their political role that intellectuals have lost faith in the "Western values" to which they remained committed as long as the socio-political system seemed hospitable to their vision. However, since the Enlightenment project has lost the legislative purchase it once had, intellectuals have become postmodernists, acknowledging and even celebrating the pluralization and relativization of modern meta-narratives (Bauman, 1987).

Bauman wants to retain a role for critical sociology which does not depend on discredited meta-narratives. He argues that sociologists should give up any attempt to legislate along the lines of "obligatory truth and universally binding norms," but that this is only an insuperable problem seen from the point of view of the modern conviction that political decisions can only be made where there is absolute certainty (Bauman, 1992: 85–6). Contemporary sociologists are liberated from such restraints to produce reflective and critical accounts of social and political reality which contribute to the self-understanding of the community and provide guidance in the face of the multiple, contingent choices with which it is faced (1992: 86–7). Postmodern sociology is *dialogical*, Bauman argues, following Richard Rorty's definition of philosophy: its goal is "not to achieve the truth about ourselves but to keep the conversation going by constantly calling current agreement into question and sending the conversation off in new directions" (Rorty, quoted in Bauman, 1992: 83).

While Bauman's recommendations for sociology are commendable, it is important to be clear about precisely what is involved in "interpretation." At other points of his work, Bauman calls for sociologists to remain detached from the postmodern condition in order to make analyses of its "objective" conditions and potentials as a system. To do sociology from within postmodernism, he argues, would be to produce highly specific, contextualized accounts and thereby to embrace relativism (1992: 65). Presumably, then, Bauman thinks of his account of the development of postmodern intellectuals as more than simply an interpretation, as an "objective" account of the development of the "postmodern condition."

From the postmodern point of view, this is highly suspect. In so far as sociologists suppose themselves to be producing an "objective" account, a "view from nowhere" rather than acknowledging and monitoring their own partial perspective, they again risk erasing the production of Otherness in which they are engaged. Let us return to the case of Salman Rushdie as an example. Although, as we have noted, from the point of view of "the West," or at least of Western intellectuals, recognition of the validity of the claims of "the Rest" is now compelling, from the point of view of the "Muslim fundamentalists" the point is precisely the opposite: the West retains its power to define "the Rest" as deviant. Many points could be made in support of this view: Rushdie's life was protected by all the force of the British state; that same state refused to extend the blasphemy laws to give Islam the protection enjoyed by Christianity; the Western intervention in Iraq during the Gulf War would not have been as ferocious if it had been a non-Islamic society that was being attacked, and so on. From this point of view it may be argued that, focusing on processes of globalization as postmodernizing from a Western perspective, sociologists risk producing the marginalization and repression of the accounts of non-Western "Others." Western values are seen as relativized and pluralized so that Western intellectuals are seen as tolerant in a way that is apparently not available to those "dogmatic" fundamentalists for whom religious truth is absolute.

In order to be genuinely productive of "responsibility toward Otherness," sociologists must acknowledge the partial, perspectival nature of the accounts they produce. "Interpretation" is always multiple. It is always possible to see the same events, history, or way of life from many different points of view. It does indeed suggest the possibility of dialogue, since, where it is a matter of interpretation, there is always room for uncertainty and change. Bauman's suggestions for sociology as interpretation are interesting because they offer the potential for a positive development from the relativization and pluralization of the West: dialogue across differences rather than their repression. However, given that it is precisely in the name of "objective" knowledge that differences have been repressed in the past, in order to realize that potential it is important that sociologists' interpretations should also be seen as such.

Diaspora culture

Studies of diaspora culture contribute to the potential "responsibility toward Otherness" suggested by seeing global culture as postmodern since they explicitly and self-consciously adopt the point of view of "the Rest" in "the West." In this respect, theorists such as Stuart Hall and Paul Gilroy are also more overtly concerned with culture as politics than other theorists of global culture. They see the emergence of diaspora cultures as involving resistance to the claimed superiority and exclusivity of supposedly integrated national cultures. The title of Gilroy's first book proclaims, *There Ain't No Black in the Union Jack* (Gilroy, 1992). Black Britishness therefore problematizes the "naturalness" of the unified national culture. Of course, it is possible to argue that the hybridity associated with diaspora culture was actually always there in modernity, but that it was repressed in the Western idealization of national culture as homogeneous. Britain, for example, includes England, Scotland, and Wales; it is not a single nation at all.

What is clear, at any rate, is that hybridity has come to prominence as a topic in sociology coincidentally with the mass migrations from the global peripheries to the overdeveloped metropolitan centers of the world, a culmination of the long processes of colonization and decolonization. Diaspora studies focus on transnational cultures and the construction of new hybrid identities as an aspect of globalization. In this context "diaspora" refers to the dispersion of a people across the world, as in the Jewish diaspora from which the word comes. In the way it is used by theorists of postcolonialism, however, the desire to return to a sacred homeland is not a feature of diaspora culture as it is in the Jewish experience. On the contrary, it denotes the experience of hybridity as a result of a dispersion which cuts across the boundaries of national cultures (Hall, 1990: 235).

According to Hall (1990), there has been a shift in the cultural politics of ethnic minorities, at least in Britain and the United States. From the 1960s onwards, black artists and intellectuals have been involved in what Hall calls a "politics of the relations of representation:" the way in which black culture has been marginalized by the white community is contested and black people demand the right to represent their history and experiences in their own terms. The immensely popular TV series *Roots*, for example, was produced in 1977 as a way of representing black history from the point of view of those who had been subject to slavery. More recently, Hall argues, there has been a shift to a "politics of representation" in which what is at stake is the contestation of the way in which black people are represented, whether by black or white, and in particular an emphasis on the diversity of experiences and identities which compose the category "black." "Black" itself is seen as a constructed, political identity within which there are multiple, sometimes conflicting, perspectives, divided in terms of gender, ethnicity, religion, generation, sexuality, and so on. One of the first popular examples of such a politics is the film by Stephen Frears and Hanif Kureishi, *My Beautiful Laundrette*, which tells the story of a young South-East Asian man in love with a white skinhead who had previously been a "Paki-basher." As Hall sees it, it is continually transgressive in its representation of the complexity of identities and relationships within the black community which unsettle stereotypes and simple accounts of what it is to grow up black in British society (Hall, 1991a, 1992b).

Hall uses ideas drawn from post-structuralism to theorize this new cultural politics which, in fact, he sees as itself informed by post-structuralism (Hall, 1992b: 254). He draws on Derrida's idea of *différance* as a useful tool with which to analyze the continual production of cultural identity through the binary oppositions of "self" and "other," which is never complete: "difference" is at the same time the "deferral" of an ultimate, fixed meaning such that no cultural identity is ever finally complete and singular in meaning (Hall, 1990: 229). For Hall, as for post-structuralists and for others engaged in a "politics of representation," it is only in representations that identity is, partially and incompletely, constituted. There is no "authentic," already existing identity which can be "discovered" behind representations. To illustrate this point, he recalls growing up in Jamaica and the way in which no one there, however black or brown, ever thought of themselves as having any connection with Africa. It was only with the construction of an Afro-Caribbean identity in civil rights struggles, Rastafarianism, and reggae that "Jamaicans discovered themselves to be 'black' – just as, in the same moment, they discovered themselves to be the sons and daughters of 'slavery'" (Hall, 1990: 321).

For Hall, Afro-Caribbeans are people of a diaspora, a transnational people without a home for which they might long. The Afro-Caribbean identity is a hybrid one, constructed from a great diversity of experiences, cultures, and histories: different islands have different relations to the metropolitan centers of Europe; different groups have different experiences of being brought to the Caribbean from Africa and also from Asia; and there are many different religious affiliations which pre-existed, and have been transformed, in Caribbean spiritual life.

Paul Gilroy analyzes the hybridity of black identity in this sense in a highly original study of what he calls the "black Atlantic." Gilroy differentiates his analysis of the black Atlantic from Hall's idea of "new ethnicities," arguing that what is missed in the latter is the recognition of continuing racialized subordination (Gilroy, 1993a: 32). However, like Hall, he is concerned above all to develop an understanding of culture which does not reduce it to a form of "authentic" ethnicity. He therefore opposes the ethnic absolutism both of white nationalism and of black Afro-centrism.

The discourse of white cultural purity is a form of "new racism" which has achieved the status of common sense for many. "New racism" denies that there is a biological hierarchy of races, arguing that everyone is equal. It is further argued, however, that there are absolute cultural differences between ethnic groups which make them incompatible. Effectively, in "new racism" culture is relativized and pluralized, but it is also made absolute in the sense that strict and unchanging divisions between the different cultures is supposed. In the most extreme cases it leads to calls for the repatriation of ethnic minorities who can neither assimilate to the majority, nor share their social institutions, because they are intrinsically culturally different (Barker, 1981). Black Afro-centrism similarly constructs an ethnic absolutism, tracing the roots of black cultural identity to Africa and sometimes arguing for black superiority on the grounds that civilization originated there. As Gilroy sees it, it is wholly inadequate to theorize black culture as if the intervening history of slavery and diaspora were irrelevant to its formation. What is needed, rather, is an understanding of the transnational and intercultural exchanges between the intellectuals, artists, and musicians who have produced the culture of the black Atlantic (Gilroy, 1993: 188–96).

Gilroy's most striking examples come from popular music, although he is also concerned with literature and social and political theory. He describes the borrowing, cross-referencing, and influences which pass between blacks in Africa, the US, the Caribbean, and Britain in such cases as Funki Dred's "Keep on Moving" which was "produced in England by the children of Caribbean settlers and then mixed in a (Jamaican) dub format in the United States by Teddy Riley, an African-American" and included samples from American and Jamaican records (Gilroy, 1993a: 16). He also includes examples of African musicians influenced by black musicians from elsewhere, such as the influence of James Brown on the Nigerian musician Fela Kuti, to illustrate the two-way traffic between African and diaspora culture and to problematize the binary opposition between "authenticity, purity and origin" and "hybridity, creolization and rootlessness" (Gilroy, 1993a: 199).

Music is also the most important example for Gilroy because it involves performance. Gilroy sees black Atlantic culture as directly political since it embodies a counter-cultural critique of modernity. This involves two dimensions. The first Gilroy calls a "politics of fulfilment" which is expressed as the normative content of black cultural forms – though not necessarily literally – as the demand that modernity should live up to its own principles of non-racialized justice and the rational organization of socio-economic forms. The second he calls a "politics of transfiguration" in which utopia is realized in the actual expression of the music, a community "of needs and solidarity" is created through the performance itself. Both dimensions are realized in performance, but the politics of transfiguration is only really possible where there is music and dancing as well as singing, because its "magical" claims cannot be represented solely in words (Gilroy, 1993a: 37–8).

The diaspora culture of the black Atlantic is, then, explicitly political, according to Gilroy, as well as aesthetic and ethical. For him, it expresses a far more radical and total critique of capitalism than any currently articulated by anti-capitalist movements focused on the struggle between capital and labor (Gilroy, 1993b: 44). Gilroy's work also goes beyond discourse theory and post-structuralism in theorizing non-verbal expression as a political possibility. For Gilroy, like post-structuralists, politics is a matter of contesting meaning, but he sees meaning in less cognitive terms, less a matter of representations or even meaningful practices and more a matter of lived memory and emotion. For Gilroy, black Atlantic as the counter-culture of modernity springs from, and preserves, the memory of slavery from which is generated a total critique of contemporary social and political existence and at the same time a utopian ideal which can be realized through artistic expression in the present (Gilroy, 1993a: 38–9).

Gilroy's careful tracing of black Atlantic political culture situates it, then, very much within modernity; he is explicitly concerned to show how mutation, hybridity, and intermixture produce *modern* cultural forms which have been marginalized in Western thought and practice. In fact, as Stuart Hall points out, it is not just transnational cultures which are hybrid, national cultures are too. We have already seen this in the case of Britain, which is actually multinational, but all the societies of Western Europe which seem homogeneous are made up of different languages, traditions, religions, and so on, integrated into a more or less uneasy alliance under the auspices of the nation-state (Hall, 1992a: 297). This has become a good deal more evident in recent years with the growth of regional independence movements like that of the Bretons and the

Basques. Nor is the hybridity of national cultures solely "internal;" it has also been produced by transnational processes of globalization throughout modernity. One of the most striking examples of the cultural hybridity of national cultures, also striking for the way it represents the repression of that hybridity, is that of the noodles Marco Polo brought from China which have become such an important element of "authentic" Italian cooking as pasta (Friedman, 1995: 74).

However, in so far as there have been extensive migrations in the post-war period, as well as the massive acceleration of processes of globalization with the development of new technologies of mass communication, it may reasonably be supposed that hybridization will become an ever more prominent feature of social life. In this respect, and as a way of marking the difference from the supposed homogeneity of national cultures, hybridism may be said to be post-modern (Pieterse, 1995).

Postmodernization as "glocalization"

Finally, there is still another way in which global culture may be said to be postmodern; this is in the more straightforward sense in which it involves Westernization, sometimes called "Coca-Colonization." In so far as the media and consumer culture of the West is post-modern, involving the commodification of every aspect of life with consumption as the main form of self-expression and the disruption of traditional beliefs and values with the continual innovation in the production and marketing of goods, then the export of this culture to the rest of the world with the expansion of mass communications may be said to be productive of a postmodern global culture (Waters, 1995: 140).

This brings us to one of the central issues in globalization studies: the relationship between the local and the global. The nation-state is by-passed by cultural processes to the extent that it is unable to control images and ideas which pass across its borders, directly by satellite TV, radio, and the Internet, and more indirectly by multi-nationals who bring new products, advertising, and the commer-cialization of traditional ways of life. Under these conditions, the "global" might be seen as representing the threat of homogenization, while the "local" stands in for particularity and place-bound, traditional, or "authentic," differences in ways of life. While the terms "global" and "local" do have these resonances to some extent, in contemporary studies of cultural globalization they are somewhat out of date. It is actually a previous generation of theorists of the mass media who tended to see the worldwide spread of mass communications as a form of Western political, economic, and cultural dominance, of "Western cultural imperialism," or "Americanization" (Lull, 1995: ch. 5). The very term "postmodern" is a denial of the homogenizing effects of global culture, and even when theorists of globalization do not actually use the term, they tend to see global culture in this way. (This includes, as we have seen, those like Harvey and Lash and Urry who are critical of the expansion of the consumer capitalism they see as producing it.)

The globalization of culture tends not to be seen as homogenizing because the global is not seen as absolutely opposed to the local. It is rather that both are intimately linked such that they are both produced by the same dynamic, sometimes known by the Japanese marketing term *glocalization*. As Roland Robertson (1995) argues, there is a tendency to see globalization as involving large-scale macro-sociological issues and processes, but this neglects the way in which globalization is spatialized. Globalization always takes place in some locality, while at the same time locality is itself produced in discourses of globalization as a particular place. According to Robertson, we should not see globalization simply as linking already existing localities together, such that the integrity of each place is invaded and subjected to the homogenizing effects of world markets, products, images, and ideas. He prefers the term "glocalization," which in its original definition means "a global outlook tailored to local conditions" – or, in the more prosaic language of marketing in which it was first developed, the way in which goods, services, and advertising are created for differentiated local markets. It better sums up the inter-relations of the global and the local in which heterogeneity is continuously produced and reproduced in processes of globalization, while at the same time there is a homogeneity in the terms in which the differentiation of localities is discussed (Robertson, 1995).

Cases for which the term "glocalization" is appropriate abound in studies of global culture. First, there are numerous examples of the post-Fordist techniques of production, distribution, and marketing by means of which goods produced by multinationals and sold on worldwide markets are tailored to the choices of particular groups of consumers. This is most famously the case in the production and distribution of Coca-Cola, which is modified slightly to suit the tastes of those it is aimed at in different parts of the world. Coca-Cola is a particularly interesting example, because, in its most recent advertising campaign in Britain, it seems to have represented itself in terms of an explicitly postmodern sensibility, re-inventing locality for quite a different locality, half-way across the world. Instead of celebrating its status as a world brand, with the world singing in harmony, the recent British advertisement for Coke used pictures of children playing cricket in the streets of Pakistan to the songs of a well-loved Pakistani singer, Nusrat Fateh Ali Khan, who is also popular among world music fans in Britain. In this case the production of locality is used to denote globality for a particular group of consumers in quite a different locality, a particularly complex and self-referential example of "glocalization."

Secondly, global culture is understood as heterogeneous because the way in which media consumers make their own culturally specific interpretations of images and products is now very well documented in globalization studies. The most commonly cited example is that of Katz and Liebe's (1984) study of different cultural interpretations of the glossy soap opera, Dallas, which would seem to represent the epitome of the American dream. Interpretations ranged from misreadings of the text to a refusal of its terms. A group of Arab viewers found it unacceptable that one of the characters, Sue Ellen, having left her husband, should go to her lover's house, so they "read" into the program that she returned to her father's house; while a Moroccan Jew felt he had learned from the program to be grateful for being Jewish, because the family relationships were so confused in the series that the babies "are almost all bastards" (Fiske, 1987: 71–2). The products of global media and consumer culture may, then, be taken up in quite unforeseen ways according to locality. Another example, explored in detail in the work of Jonathan Friedman, is that of *les sapeurs* of the People's Republic of the Congo, who display the designer clothes they acquire at great expense in France and Italy in a ritual *danse des griffes* in which the labels are sown on outside the clothes to be shown to maximum effect. This should not simply be seen as a matter of fashion. According to Friedman, *les sapeurs* gain enormous local prestige in this way because the clothes are taken as the immediate expression of the degree of life-force possessed by the man wearing them, to the point where they represent a serious threat to the status stratification of Congolese society. In this case, consumption of Western goods may have quite an unexpected effect on the structuration of a particular, non-Western society (Friedman, 1990: 314–19).

Thirdly, "glocalization" involves the production of locality from within the locality itself as a way of taking advantage of the global market. This is particularly notable where cultural sites are re-invented for tourists. Friedman's work again provides a good example, that of the Ainu, an ethnic minority who are economically and politically marginalized in Japan. In the 1970s, a cultural movement began among the Ainu in which the language and traditions are taught to those who have lost them and to children, while at the same time villages were rebuilt in which handcrafted goods are produced for tourists who come to watch them being made, learn about Ainu mythology, ritual, and history, taste Ainu food and even stay in Ainu homes. Tourist production and display is a central element of the reconstruction of Ainu ethnic identity. Interestingly, according to Friedman, the commercialization of Ainu culture is not felt to be at odds with its authenticity: in the words of one man interviewed: "We make carvings because we cannot stop. It is in our blood. If we can make a profit, well we do not think there is anything wrong with that" (Friedman, 1990: 321).

Finally, locality is produced in global culture in so far as it is perceived as Westernization and is refused in various ways. This is the case, for example, where there is strong identification with cultures of origin among ethnic minorities in the West, or the construction of strong "counter-ethnicities" as in the identification of second-generation Afro-Caribbean youth with an African heritage through Rastafarianism (Hall, 1992a: 308). It is also the case in the revival of religious orthodoxy, or fundamentalism. In some cases, like that of Muslim fundamentalism, this involves a refusal of Westernization. It may, however, equally be a reaction against the confusions, conflicts, temptations and disappointments of media and consumer culture. According to Akbar Ahmed, Christians in the US, Hindus in India and Buddhists in Thailand all exhibit the religious fanaticism and intolerance associated with fundamentalism as an attempt to deal with the uncertainties produced by postmodernism (Akbar, 1992). Both "counter-ethnicities" and religious fundamentalism, while undoubtedly local in some respects, are often also global, not only because they are produced in global processes but also because those involved are members of "imagined communities" constructed via communications systems which are not under the control of the nation-state. This is the case, for example, in the Muslim funda-mentalist opposition to Salman Rushdie which extends across the world. In contrast, at the same time there has been a resurgence of nationalism across Europe. This may also be linked to globalization in so far as it involves the assertion of the homogeneity of national culture in the face of multi-culturalism within the nation and in some of the images and ideas relayed by the global media (Hall, 1991b). It would seem that the very heterogeneity of global culture is contradictory.

2.4   CULTURAL POLITICS AND DISJUNCTURES IN GLOBAL "SCAPES"

The uneven nature of global culture is well captured in Arjun Appadurai's highly regarded article, "Disjuncture and Difference in the Global Cultural Economy" (1990). He constructs a theoretical framework to enable the analysis of the uncertainties and fragmen-tations in global culture, describing disjunctures which cannot be understood using older models of the world as organized in terms of center and periphery. Economic, political and cultural realities are no longer as closely linked as they were when societies were more readily seen as organized around nation-states, and we need a dif-ferent model to deal with the complexity of the global cultural economy (Appadurai, 1990). In fact, although Appadurai's sugges-tions are promising, their potential has been relatively little devel-oped. Once we have looked at his article in some detail, we will try to see how his ideas might be extended using the model of cultural politics developed in chapter 1.

"Disjuncture and difference in the global cultural economy"

Appadurai's understanding of global cultural economy stresses its heterogeneity. It is to be seen as "a complex, overlapping, disjunctive order" (1990: 296). To this end, he proposes a theory of what he calls "scapes," suggesting five dimensions of global cultural flow: ethnoscapes, technoscapes, finanscapes, mediascapes, and ideoscapes. In each case the suffix "scape" is used to indicate, in Appadurai's words:

> that these are not objectively given relations which look the same from every angle of vision, but rather that they are deeply perspectival constructs, inflected very much by the historical, linguistic and political situatedness of different sorts of actors: nation-states, multinationals, diasporic communities, as well as sub-national groupings and movements ... These landscapes thus, are the building blocks of what, extending Benedict Anderson, I would like to call "imagined worlds," that is, the multiple worlds which are constituted by the historically situated imaginations of persons and groups spread around the globe. (Appaduria, 1990: 296–7)

By *ethnoscape* Appadurai means "the landscape of persons who constitute the shifting world in which we live" (1990: 297), tourists, immigrants, refugees, exiles, and so on, who travel ever greater distances. They form fluid, transnational, imagined communities which have an increasingly dislocatory effect on the politics of and between nation-states. By *technoscape* he means the development of both mechanical and information technology which make multinationals possible. They render obsolete any notion of political economy which fails to take into account the complex transnational relationships within and between these huge corporations. *Finanscapes* are Appadurai's term for the flow of global capital through currency markets, national stock exchanges, and commodity speculations which affect national economies in ways that cannot be controlled by any individual nation-state. There are, he argues, deep disjunctures between ethnocapes, technoscapes, and finanscapes which make the outcomes of movement in any one of them unpredictable since they are all inter-related and each has its own constraints and incentives.

Building on these disjunctures, Appadurai argues, are mediascapes and ideoscapes. *Mediascapes* concern both the distribution of the electronic capabilities to produce and disseminate information – increasingly available to public and private interests across the world – and also the image-centered, narrative-based strips of reality from which imagined worlds are fashioned. They provide repertoires of pictures and stories from which ethnoscapes, in particular, are constructed.

Ideoscapes are similarly based on images and narratives, but they have to do with the ideologies of states and counter-movements. As Appadurai sees it, they are all loosely based on the meta-narrative of the Enlightenment. Terms like "freedom," "rights," "sovereignty," and "democracy" are frequently invoked, but they are organized differently according to the ways in which different nation-states have used them to justify particular regimes. Although ideoscapes originated in Europe and America, then, their diaspora across the world has indigenized them in different ways in different localities. Ideoscapes are, in themselves, disjunctive in so far as the same words are understood differently by different audiences; Appadurai asks us to consider how "democracy" is used in China, Poland, and the United States. They are also disjunctive with regard to mediascapes which present very different images and stories, with ethnoscapes in so far as they are not accepted, or are disseminated beyond their original constituencies, by diasporas, and with technoscapes and finanscapes in so far as these movements may outstrip, or lag behind, changes in ideoscapes.

As a result of transnational flows and de-territorialization, Appadurai argues that there is now a radical disjuncture between states and nations, which attempt to "cannibalize each other" (1990: 304). While groups claiming nationhood try to capture states, states attempt to monopolize nations. As Appadurai sees it, this is due to the contradictory position in which states are now placed. On one hand, they have to keep their borders open to transnational flows in order to attract investment, skills, and ideas which will promote economic growth. On the other hand, they try to control images and ideas which challenge their vision of the nation and what is good for it. States feel themselves to be under siege, while national minorities who identify with transnational communities find themselves repressed by the states which have jurisdiction over the territory in which they live and increase their efforts to achieve self-determination as a people. Paradoxically, the very processes of globalization which are weakening the nation-state are promoting the desire for national autonomy among those who feel that they do not have it.

Appadurai apparently sees himself as a Marxist (although it is only in a footnote to the article that he states this affinity: 1990:

308). However, Appadurai's "scapes" are very much like discourses. They are social practices which are produced, re-produced, contested, and transformed only in so far as they are meaningful for specific, situated, social actors. The idea of "scapes" replaces older sociological ideas such as "structures" or "institutions" in such a way as to make possible the analysis of dislocated and non-totalizing social practices which are neither simply objective, nor subjective (in the sense of individually created). In this respect, it must be seen as closer to post-structuralist understandings of discourse than to any versions of Marxism. For Appadurai, as for discourse theorists, social life is cultural "all the way down."

It is true that, as we have seen, Appadurai claims that mediascapes and ideoscapes are *built on* ethnoscapes, technoscapes, and finanscapes. This does suggest that he subscribes to the Marxist metaphor of the "economic base" on which the "ideological and political infrastructure" depends. However, it is difficult to understand his theory of scapes using this metaphor because he does not distinguish between the different types he has identified as more or less material, nor as more or less determining. For orthodox Marxists, the economic base is material, whereas the ideological and political infrastructures are nothing more than ideas. They therefore produce little or no effect in the world in comparison with economic forces. David Harvey's view, discussed earlier in this chapter, that postmodern culture is no more than "froth and evanescence," a mere by-product of the post-Fordist mode of production, is exemplary of such a position. For neo-Marxists, following Althusser, ideology is not seen as mere ideas; it is always embedded in social practices. Appadurai's idea of scapes as "imagined worlds" is quite close to Althusser's theory of ideology in this respect. However, what makes Althusser a Marxist is his view that "in the last instance" the economic base is determining of the other "levels" of society, of ideology and politics (see pp. 7–9). According to Appadurai's theory, however, the disjunctures of global cultural flows mean that it is no longer possible to establish any logic of socio-economic development. Nor does he discuss why we might see any one of the scapes he discusses as having greater efficacity than any other. On the contrary, the way in which social formations are constructed according to Appadurai's theory of global scapes seems to be better described as like a kaleidoscope than like a building which needs stable foundations. In a kaleidoscope there are recognizable patterns, and similar shapes and colors are used to make each one, but none takes precedence over any other and none is supporting the others.

Appadurai's theory of global scapes as a matter of disjunctural cultural flows, rather than of socio-economic structures conforming to scientific laws of history, make global processes inherently unpredictable. Nevertheless, it may be seen as contributing to a discussion of how the uneven and risky development of globalization might be regulated, whether by states or less formally. What is of value in this contribution is that it takes seriously the perspectival nature of social reality, the way in which it is seen in different ways from different points of view. Appadurai's theory of scapes offers a map of kinds, but it is one in which everything but the barest outlines remains to be filled in according to the specificities of the different perspectives which are brought to bear on its construction. It offers a map in which the precise shape of the land is uncertain, to be established by the cultural politics in which actors are currently engaged.

Global "scapes" and cultural politics

Here I will do no more than suggest a number of ways in which cultural politics is actually being conducted within the limits of global scapes. Global scapes may very readily be understood in terms of the model of cultural politics developed in chapter 1. The construction of a particular scape involves the contestation of identities and possibilities for action which figure in it and the horizons – or limits – of the scape. As processes of globalization are contested, it is possible to see how different scapes are formed where certain issues are in question. Furthermore, it is clear that definitions of interests and possibilities structure the flows of resources and differences of power which result from the resolution of contestation. The institutionalized social practices in which global scapes are embedded involve establishing particular perspectives on how they might be formed.

In recent times, the extent to which global processes can be regulated and how this might be carried out is highly contested in relation to a number of issues. At the moment, these issues are extremely unsettled and the outcome is quite open, though it is clear that in each case there are a number of emergent scapes. Clearly, the institutionalization of a particular scape is not simply a matter of ideas as such; some scapes are already well established in existing social practices, while others have little bearing beyond being ideals. However, the future shape of global scapes depends on the ongoing contestation of the terms of both existing and ideal scapes: how the issues are framed and what is made possible or impossible; who is empowered as an actor and who is disempowered; the social practices and institutions which are established and those which are destroyed or become obsolete. Global scapes both provide the terms within which cultural politics is conducted and are also the outcome of the agreement which results from the contestation of those terms. At the moment, contestation is very much to the fore.

The following paragraphs suggest some of the main ways in which the global scapes identified by Appadurai might be understood in relation to the cultural politics of globalization which are currently at issue.

ETHNOSCAPES In terms of cultural politics, ethnoscapes are among the most contested of the global scapes identified by Appadurai. The most dramatic examples are those he discusses in which groups claim the status of a nation on the basis of their ethnic identity and demand self-determination. There has been an explosion of this nationalist seeking of states throughout the former Soviet bloc following the downfall of communism.

Within Western liberal democracies the cultural politics of ethnoscapes tend to be concerned with the distribution of resources with respect to citizenship rights. There are attempts to establish to what extent existing rights depend on ethnic identification and how far this is legitimate. There is widespread criticism of existing citizenship rights as too restricted with regard to ethnic communities. In this case, ethnoscapes are seen quite differently: the nation and the state are not seen as isomorphic as in the previous case, and the question is raised of how far the state *should* be constructed within the limits of a given ethnoscape. Multi-cultural citizenship rights are a way of constructing the state as a reference point for a number of different ethnoscapes, rather than as indissoluble from the one in which it was initially constructed.

At this point, especially where the question arises of those who do not have citizenship rights in the country in which they live, the

ethnoscape may be cut across by the ideoscape of "human rights."
Increasingly, ethnoscapes are regulated by international law on
human rights, mobilized by organizations working on behalf of
ethnic groups to by-pass nation-states. Ethnoscapes are transnational, and regulation is increasingly internationally agreed and
enforced.

Finally, as we have seen above in the section on diaspora and
hybrid cultures, there is the politics which contests all given
ethnoscapes and attempts to construct new, more pluralist and
hybrid ethnic identities. The actors engaged in this politics should
not be mistaken as calling for a limitless ethnoscape – an impossible
view without a horizon. It is rather that they want to see limits as
relatively arbitrary historically, negotiable, and fluid. They are
arguing for de-naturalized horizons, a way of seeing ethnic identities
as always already political. However deeply ethnic identity might be
felt, its contours and horizons are nevertheless different when viewed
for different purposes and from different positions. How far this is
compatible with establishing citizenship rights to ethnic difference is
open to question. We shall look in more detail at the cultural politics of citizenship rights in chapter 4.

TECHNOSCAPES Technology seems invariably to take on some of
the features of the natural world for us, as though it develops
along the inevitable, because rational, lines of scientific progress.
However, in the case of contemporary technoscapes, there is currently a good deal of contestation concerning the possibilities of
new information technology. Appadurai draws our attention only to
how mechanical and information technology makes multinational
exploitation possible. However, there is also a counter-claim:
information technology could contribute to greater democratization.
Those who argue that such developments as the Internet and digital
TV are empowering see them as providing information directly to
users without it being processed by the media, states, or hierarchical organizations. Furthermore, by using such technology, people can
communicate directly with each other. It may therefore empower
individual citizens who are free to engage in critical discourse with
fewer restrictions of information or of time and space than was
previously possible. Individual members and local groups of such
organizations as Friends of the Earth already use information

technology to communicate, convey information, and prepare political strategies across the world (Washbourne, 1999). It may even be possible for citizens to participate more directly in government since personal computers linked to the Internet make referendums much more easy and cheaper to carry out than has previously been the case.

On the other hand, questions must be raised about the limits of this technoscape of empowerment. It risks excluding those who are too poor or who lack the education to participate in the electronic revolution, both in advanced and Third World countries. Furthermore, technoscapes are also heavily contested in the less idealistic terms of flows of economic resources. The term "information superhighway" was first coined by the US government under Clinton's presidency. It refers to a telecommunications infrastructure which can carry information and enable communication. However, while the idea has been enthusiastically adopted by many governments, in practice the development of telecommunications has been marketled with limited state regulation. The technoscape of the "information superhighway" looks rather different from this point of view, a matter of giving consumers what they want rather than empowering citizens. If it is dominated by media corporations, it might come to resemble already existing media systems, with standardized "infotainment" broadcast and interaction restricted to channel selection (Wheeler, 1997). The question of who is to be empowered by technoscapes – transnational corporations, citizens, consumers, or even states, in the unlikely event that they might take charge of providing telecommunications infrastructures – is highly contested in cultural politics.

FINANSCAPES The most important point about finanscapes is that the current global free-market in capital is not simply technologically determined – it is not because it is now technologically possible that it has happened – nor is it simply a matter of expansionary capitalism. It is actually the outcome of a neo-liberal political project. Deregulation introduced by nation-states in the 1980s and encouraged by international financial institutions like the World Bank and the IMF eliminated restrictions on cross-border financial flows and introduced new instruments of transnational financial exchange, so permitting the explosion of the financial market (Ashley, 1997: 122;

Scott, 1997b). Until the late 1990s, however, finanscapes had come to be seen as inevitably dominated by global flows of capital; nation-state economies could only work within the limits imposed by this reality.

More recently, fears of a collapse in global capitalism with the "crisis of Asian capitalism," the disintegration of Russia and the possible failure of the Brazilian economy have radically changed finanscapes. Russia has effectively opted out of the global economy, refusing to repay its debts, there is talk of reviving Keynesianism in Europe, and Malaysia has introduced exchange controls, something economists claimed it was no longer possible for individual nation-states to do. The current instability of the global economy means that the future development of finanscapes is highly contested, with all the opportunities for more equitable flows of resources and the dangers of deepening divisions between "haves" and "have-nots" implied by this cultural politics.

Finanscapes may be constructed as more or less inclusive. The least inclusive option is new forms of protectionism. If the US and the countries of the European Union close their borders to withdraw from the global economy, it will undoubtedly lead to depression in weaker economies. Furthermore, minimizing trade with countries of the Third World will do nothing to contribute to their development. A more inclusive option would involve the international regulation of global capital flows. It would be a new form of the Bretton Woods agreement which provided the horizon of a stable international finanscape after World War II. This involved fixed exchange rates, a fixed gold standard, and funds, collected by the IMF, to be distributed to nation-states to enable them to ensure high levels of employment and to avoid currency devaluation and welfare cuts. The Bretton Woods agreement was under-written by the US which provided most of the funds for the IMF. However, it was also dissolved by the US, which unilaterally introduced floating exchange rates in the 1970s and used its power in the IMF to impose economic liberalization on the Third World, the ex-Soviet bloc, and China (Cox, 1997: 54). Any new agreement would have to be more democratically instituted to prevent a similar outcome in the future.

MEDIASCAPES The main question concerning mediascapes is similar to that concerning technoscapes: to what extent is it possible to construct them in such a way that they are empowering rather than disempowering? It is undoubtedly the case that media regulation by states is increasingly difficult with the development of technologies such as satellite broadcasting and fibre-optic cable services which enable the reception of material transmitted anywhere in the world. It is not impossible, however. Famously, French governments since the 1980s have restricted the free-market wherever possible, in film for example, while investing substantially in French national culture to prevent it being over-whelmed by the perceived Americanization of the mass media (see Street, 1997a).

The most important question in the cultural politics of media-scapes is whether regulation is desirable. Those in favor of deregu-lation see the free market as the way to ensure free speech. Although the motives of media moguls who advocate this option are suspect, there is no doubt that the global media do offer a way of avoiding state censorship. Furthermore, this may have progressive outcomes. It does seem to be the case, for example, that TV images received from the West played a part in bringing down the totalitarian regimes of the Eastern bloc.

For those who are opposed to a deregulated mediascape, on the other hand, it is clear that, far from enabling free speech, it will actu-ally be dominated by transnational media corporations. The televi-sion coverage of the Gulf War, for example, was dominated by CNN and broadcast around the world. It was clearly structured in favor of the US, presenting the Iraqis as "Muslim fundamentalists" and Saddam Hussein as "Hitler" (Wheeler, 1997). However, the effects of the media are notoriously difficult to ascertain because they are dependent on how images and stories are interpreted. In terms of Appadurai's model, we might say that mediascapes are cut across by ethnoscapes and ideoscapes. It is likely, for example, that such cov-erage would be interpreted by those sympathetic to the Arab cause as confirming their anti-Americanism.

From still another point of view, while the mediascape is domi-nated by pro-Western media corporations, it may also be empower-ing. John Thompson (1995) argues that the media open up new modes of publicness, in which images and stories are presented which cannot be completely controlled by ruling groups, whether corpora-tions or states. They therefore offer the possibility of gaining a hearing for marginalized views. For example, Thompson notes the

way in which the video of Rodney King being beaten by the Los
Angeles police was shown all over the world and provoked riots in
Los Angeles and elsewhere when the police officers were acquitted
(Thompson, 1995). Douglas Kellner (1995) argues that alternative
media, such as film and video production, community radio, and
computer bulletin boards are especially appropriate to what he
calls radical "media activism." He sums up the cultural politics of
mediascapes:

> These technologies can be used as instruments of domination or lib-
> eration, of manipulation or social enlightenment, and it is up to the
> cultural producers and activist intellectuals of the present and future
> to determine which way the new technologies will be used and devel-
> oped and whose interests they will serve. (Kellner, 1995: 337)

IDEOSCAPES As Appadurai has noted, the ideoscape with the widest
horizon is undoubtedly that of "democracy." At the end of the twentieth century, there is practically no political regime in the world
which does not try to legitimate itself as democratic. However, the
term itself is highly contested. The ideoscapes within which "democracy" is a key term are very different across the world. In former
communist countries, for example, it has been closely linked to economic liberalization, while in Western liberal democracies social
movements play an important role in contesting the legitimacy of
"really existing" democracies.

The contestation of democratic ideoscapes involves many questions. What kind of democracy really counts as such? To what extent
are the formal institutions of representative democracy sufficient?
What is the role of rights in democracy and how can they be safeguarded? Who is to be included as a genuinely participating citizen,
and are certain groups excluded by the way in which representative
democracy actually works?

Above all, it raises the question of global democracy. If it is the
case that nation-states no longer enjoy the degree of autonomy
they once had, while sovereignty is now shared between states
and international political institutions, democracy at this level looks
increasingly inadequate. It is undoubtedly still important, given
the continuing power of states to shape global scapes. However, in
so far as much regulation is effective only at the international

level, if citizens are to participate in global governance, they must be able to ensure that their voices are effective there too. As we will see in chapter 4, this is increasingly an issue in the European Union, where political rights lag significantly behind the opening up of borders to transnational economic flows and legal regulation (pp. 208–11).

Cultural politics is inherently democratizing. Even where the horizons and contours of global scapes attain a degree of temporary fixity, as in the case of neo-liberal finanscapes in the 1980s, they are continually "de-naturalized" by the disjunctures produced by the processes of globalization itself. The instability which results continually raises questions about how social life should be organized and how individuals should live. It continually opens up the possibilities of shaping global scapes in new and more inclusive ways. Of course, there is always also the very real possibility of instituting more *exclusionary* global scapes. Nevertheless, the fact that the outcome is open, that it is a matter of realizing a definition of what is possible in the world, is potentially empowering for progressive political movements. It is in this context that an ideoscape of democracy in which democratic rights and sites of negotiation are instituted is important. Democracy should ensure that cultural politics is not limited, that participation in redefining global scapes is encouraged, and that the power of states and international political institutions is used to keep possibilities open. In chapter 5, we shall consider the potential for global democratization in more detail.

CHAPTER 3

The Politicization of the Social: Social Movements and Cultural Politics

Social movements play a very important role in new political sociology. First, they have been directly influential in its development within the university. That social movements have such a central place in the understanding of new forms of politics in the field is largely due to the way in which they have been placed on the research agenda by those sympathetic to, or actively involved in, those politics. In particular, in the 1970s, it was those who identified with social movements who worked to make dimensions of inequality and exclusion other than class significant. Similarly, debates in the 1980s over whether identity is best seen as a fixed "essential" property of the person or a social construction were closely related to the "identity politics" of social movements. Secondly, the understanding that members of social movements bring to bear on social life has been important. Where society is widely seen by social actors in terms of struggle and conflict – again, not necessarily assimilable to class struggle – sociological explanations which treat the reproduction of the social order as practically inevitable are likely to be discredited, even to be seen as complicit with the status quo. This has been the fate of Marxism, now seen as over-deterministic and insufficiently sensitive to the possibilities of radical change at the micro-sociological level. Thirdly, as a topic of study, social movements problematize older models of sociological explanation in so far as they see politics as organized solely around the nation-state. Social movements see themselves, and they are analyzed in the new political sociology, as involved in struggles over the definition of meanings and the construction of new identities and lifestyles as well as in more conventional politics. They therefore bring the consideration of cultural politics to the center of sociological concerns with social change.

The topic of cultural politics, although it is not named as such, is central to the development of both the major traditions of social movement research. Those who work in Resource Mobilization Theory (RMT), which was initially developed to analyze individual choices and social movement organizations, have become increasingly concerned with the construction of collective identities and the contestation of social events and problems. We shall look at this work in section 3.2, examining the development of the RMT tradition and the way in which it has taken a "postmodern turn" toward cultural politics. Those who work in New Social Movement Theory (NSMT), which began with an understanding of the centrality of cultural politics to social movements, have elaborated on that understanding and dropped the vestiges of determinism which kept it tied to old sociological models. We shall look at this work in section 3.3. RMT and NSMT began from quite different premises, the former in liberal individualism, the latter in Marxism. Nevertheless, they have converged in their focus on cultural politics to the point where it is now possible to synthesize the two traditions around a common core of research interests. In section 3.4 we shall look at an attempt at such a synthesis, discussing it in the light of our concern with cultural politics. In section 3.5, we examine a very important, but underdeveloped aspect of social movement research, social movements in relation to globalization. Remarkably little work has been done in this area, but it is nevertheless possible to suggest ways in which social movements are shaped by the need to act transnationally and internationally, and the way in which globalization is in turn shaped by social movements.

First, however, it is necessary to consider how social movements became a significant area of research in sociology, in the guise of "*new* social movements." "New" here is indicative of the way in which social movements seemed to erupt on to the social scene at the end of the 1960s, especially the student movement which was so active in universities, organizing demonstrations, sit-ins, and so on. Such forms of politics seemed to represent quite a startling new direction. The term "new" is now seen as somewhat inappropriate, but the debates which ensued concerning precisely *how* social movements might be new has been important for the development of subsequent research in political sociology.

3.1   SOCIAL MOVEMENTS: WHAT'S NEW?

The term "new social movement" is used to describe movements which have come to prominence since the 1960s. They include the student movement of that time, the civil rights movement, the women's movement, the environmental movement, the peace movement, and, more recently, anti-racist movements, movements for the rights of indigenous peoples, the "anti-political" movements of Eastern Europe, and so on. They have been seen as "new" in two main respects, both of which have been subject to extensive debate. First, they are characterized by a set of features which distinguishes them as quite different from previous social movements. Secondly, their novelty is due to their appearance in the context of a new social formation: they are taken to be new because they are exemplary of new social and political relations.

New movements?

Those features of new social movements said to make them novel in terms of their orientation, organization, and style may be listed in a kind of ideal-type construction. On this view, new social movements are distinguished from others because they are:

1   Non-instrumental, expressive of universalist concerns and often protesting in the name of morality rather than the direct interests of particular social groups.
2   Oriented more toward civil society than the state:
    (a)   suspicious of centralized bureaucratic structures and oriented toward changing public views rather than elite institutions;
    (b)   more concerned with aspects of culture, lifestyle, and participation in the symbolic politics of protest than in claiming socio-economic rights.
3   Organized in informal, "loose," and flexible ways, at least in some aspects, avoiding hierarchy, bureaucracy, and even, sometimes, qualifications for membership.

4 Highly dependent on the mass media through which appeals are made, protests staged, and images made effective in capturing public imagination and feeling (Scott, 1990: ch. 1; Crook et al., 1992: 148).

These particular features of new social movements are picked out by theorists on the basis of a more or less explicit comparison between the new and the "old" social movement: the labor movement. This is characterized as directing its attention toward the corporatist state with the aim of economic redistribution and the extension of citizenship rights, as organized in bureaucratic trade unions and parties which defend members' interests, and as showing very little concern with wider issues or more inclusive political participation.

Perhaps unsurprisingly, this sharp and rather simplistic contrast between old and new is not sustainable once it is looked into more closely. While it is certainly true that sociology took the class struggle of industrial society to be central to modernity (even defining of it in the case of Marxists), there has, in fact, long been a multiplicity of social movements. As Craig Calhoun (1995) has shown, in the early nineteenth century there were many movements, including the feminist movement, nationalist and religious movements, and even aspects of the class movement itself, such as the utopian communitarianism of Robert Owen, which were less like the conventionally defined labor movement than they were like new social movements. Very much concerned with lifestyle and identity politics, they were often organized in non-hierarchical ways in order to prefigure the social order they aimed to bring about, and they used unconventional means, such as direct action, rather than working through the "normal" political institutions of the state (Calhoun, 1995).

On the other hand, however, it is also the case that recent social movements share some of the features attributed to this "old" movement. This is most notable when their organization is considered in more detail. Some aspects of the organization of new social movements do clearly distinguish them from formal political organizations, to the extent that the term "network" is often a better description than "organization:" they are often locally based or centered on small groups rather than nationally oriented, organized around specific issues rather than offering general solutions, experience vacillations of high and low activity rather than enjoying a relatively stable membership, and are run by fluid hierarchies and loose authority structures (Scott, 1990: 30). However, the organizational forms of social movements are best seen as a continuum, and at the other end of it they may be as bureaucratic and hierarchical as any other organization. This is the case where political parties have been formed to take the movement into the arena of formal politics, as in the case of the green parties associated with the environmental movement (though there has been much discussion in these parties about how to avoid bureaucratization and hierarchies). It is also the case wherever centralized movement organizations are developed which rely on the subscriptions of members without involving them in decision-making or action. Greenpeace, for example, is a well-known example of this type of environmental organization; its members are not themselves involved in the well-planned, dangerous, and often illegal direct action it undertakes. In contrast, Friends of the Earth is run more on the basis of the participation of members who are actively involved in their own localities.

It is also unreasonable to see a complete contrast between old and new social movements in terms of their orientations toward the state or civil society. It is certainly important to note that a large proportion of social movement activity is addressed to changing practices and identities in civil society. This is clear in the case of the women's movement, for example, which has been extremely influential in opening up virtually all aspects of the relations between the sexes to public debate and in creating the necessity for individuals to make lifestyle choices in terms of their personal relationships and employment practices; in recent so-called "political correctness" disputes, which largely concern the contestation of language; in questions raised by the environmental movement concerning ethical consumerism; and in struggles over ethnic identity, often articulated around music, dress, and in relation to the construction of historical narratives. Legislation is too blunt an instrument to deal with most of the issues raised by social movements, and changes in the law and social policy are often less the direct objective of their activities and more a consequence of changes in civil society which they have brought about. However, it is also the case that all social movements which organize to improve their constituents' social conditions have aimed to extend citizenship rights. This is not a unique feature of the workers' movement; it was the case for the civil rights movement, for example, and it has long been a feature of at least some aspects of feminist activities. Furthermore, it is evident that social policy and the law are important agents of social change, so that it is unlikely that any movement concerned with social transformation would ignore the state altogether. Again, it is perhaps not so much that new social movements have introduced new forms of politics since the 1960s, but rather that those forms which did not easily fit the modern sociological paradigm have been overlooked so that they are now taken to represent a radical departure from the norm. New social movements might more reasonably be seen as marking a change of emphasis, both of orientation and in terms of organization and activities, rather than a completely new form of politics.

New social context?

This brings us to the second sense in which new social movements are seen as new: the way in which they are situated in a new social context. The most limited views of this new context see it in terms of changes in the class structure of advanced capitalist societies. The most extensive link social movements to the transformation of society, beyond industrial modernity to post-industrialism and postmodernity.

Claus Offe is among the most prominent proponents of the first view, arguing that it is the relative prosperity of social democracy, high levels of education, and the growth of service-sector employment which have provided the conditions for the emergence of the new social movements. It is the new educated middle classes, according to Offe, especially those employed by the state, and "decommodified groups" such as students, housewives, and welfare recipients, who are receptive to the universalist concerns of new social movements. According to Offe, these groups are most likely to be aware of the irrationalities of the contemporary capitalist system, or to experience its disadvantages most directly. He argues that since there are clear structural determinants of participation in social movements, this form of politics is a "politics of class," but since, unlike previous class movements, it does not make demands for its own specific advantage, it is not politics "*on behalf of a class*" (Offe, 1987: 77).

Offe's analysis is certainly empirically borne out to the extent that the highly educated are proportionally over-represented in social movements, though this is less than conclusive since they are over-represented in conventional political organizations too. However, it is unsatisfactory for two main theoretical reasons. First, like all attempts to analyze social movements in terms of class, it begs the question it set out to answer: what is it about the heterogeneous collection of groups and individuals Offe describes as a "new class" which makes it appropriate to designate it as such? In recent years, the classification of social strata in terms of occupational structure has become increasingly problematic for sociologists with the growth of a service sector in which there is an enormous range of occupations, many of which do not share the middle-class conditions associated with white-collar jobs, the increase in women workers who often do not fit class categories designed with traditional male roles in mind, and the large section of the population which is now economically inactive (see Pakulski and Waters, 1996). Classification along class lines is increasingly arbitrary, so that Offe's designation of a "new class," while it cuts through all the problems with which stratificationists are currently concerned as his main class division is in terms of education, seems equally arbitrary. The diverse groups he classifies as "the new middle class" do not share similar backgrounds, conditions of employment or opportunities in the way we would expect from the use of the term "class;" Offe's use of the term trades on analytic associations established by sociologists of stratification which are not supported by his theory. Secondly, by eliminating the link between class locations, the interests of those who fill class locations, and their membership in movements, Offe gives us no reason to suppose that it is the class structure itself which determines that membership, rather than some other aspect of participants' lives. On the contrary, since members have reasons for becoming involved in movements, without which they would presumably take no action, it seems more reasonable to see those reasons as the causes of their participation, rather than structural determinants which are, in fact, hard to specify given the diversity of experiences among the groups he classifies as forming the "new middle class." In fact, the movements with which he is most concerned, the environmental movement and the peace movement, contain within themselves such a range of different possibilities, in terms of ideological commitment, degrees of participation, types of organizational structure, and so on, that it seems unlikely that a single orientation would be adequate to describe participation in general. Explanations of new social movements which analyze them in terms of class unnecessarily complicate the question of how it is that they have become so significant in recent years by refusing to consider the terms in which participants themselves see their activities.

Another popular socio-economic explanation of new social movements which links them to developments in advanced capitalist societies is that of Jürgen Habermas. He sees the extension of commodification, resulting from the growth of a consumer economy and of the bureaucratic post-war welfare state, into what was previously considered private life as contributing to the emergence of new social movements. For Habermas, they have emerged mainly to defend what he calls the "lifeworld" – the values of the community and family – against the commodification and bureaucratic administration which increasingly threaten it from the economic and political systems in modern societies. This understanding of social movements remains constant throughout his work. On the other hand, however, Habermas also delineates a progressive potential of social movements which he sees in different ways at different points in the development of his theoretical work. In *Legitimation Crisis* (1988) he argues that, especially where they involve the members of the new class identified by Offe, they may demand that the system itself is made rationally accountable. The extension of the state and the market undermines traditional motivations and values, according to Habermas – for example, deference to status hierarchies is undermined by increasing meritocracy – which are necessary for the reproduction of the system. The resolution of this tension depends on the increase in communicative rationality demanded by progressive social movements to replace non-rational, traditional acceptance of the system by adherence to a fairer, more participatory, and more rationally ordered society.

As Scott (1990) points out, many of the features of new social movements do realize the more progressive aspects of Habermas's analysis rather than defending the lifeworld: they often seek to extend citizenship rights to excluded groups and to involve a rationalized state in minimizing social inequalities in civil society; and they also often attempt to extend the state's accountability to rational decision-making, as in the case of the anti-nuclear and peace movements. On the other hand, however, there are cases where movements are defensive against those features of modernity which Habermas sees as necessary and progressive. The enormously influential German green movement, for example, rejects the notion of progress as linked to industrial development in a way that would be difficult for Habermas to accept, and it also rejects the universalist morality which is essential to Habermas's ideas on rational accountability, seeking the reconstruction of community in quasi-religious and mythological experience. As Scott argues, because his idea of industrial society is linked to Marxisant ideas of historical development evolving as a result of systemic contradictions and crises, he is inclined to neglect those aspects of industrial societies which do not conform to this view of the direction of history (Scott, 1990: 70–80).

In his later work, Habermas distances himself from the totalizing functionalism of *Legitimation Crisis*; the lifeworld is no longer seen as necessary to the reproduction of society as a whole, but as an arena which, with its own rationalizing dynamic of de-traditionalization, is quite opposed to the systemic logic of the economy and state. In this later work, innovative social movements are again seen as defensive in their attempt to return formally institutionalized activities such as "work" and "politics" to the community (Outhwaite, 1994: 106–7). However, they are also seen as playing a potentially progressive role as they could influence the formal political process through rational criticism and democratic deliberation in the public sphere. Habermas's later understanding of social movements is more concerned with the normative potential they offer for democratic renewal than with the sociological understanding of why they have emerged and how they operate. We will look at this in more detail in chapter 5 (see pp. 226–34).

An alternative to socio-economic explanations of new social movements like those of Offe and Habermas are socio-cultural accounts based on generational factors. According to Pakulski's reading of the research, the social profile of ecological movement activists in the US, Western Europe, and Australia is very close to the social profile of the under-forty age group in the population as a whole. Although this age group is also more highly represented in Offe's "new middle class" than older people, such that the two groups significantly overlap, he claims that the empirical evidence is more supportive of the generational analysis (Pakulski, 1995: 65). More importantly, however, as Pakulski points out, a socio-cultural explanation, like the influential theory of Ronald Inglehart (1990), based on the shared experiences and values of generations, does not have the difficulty of class explanations which have to *suppose* a common orientation (Pakulski, 1995: 69). Inglehart's view is that the post-World War II generation developed "post-materialist values" in which more emphasis is placed on quality of life than on economic goals. He sees this as a result of the fact that they enjoyed an unprecedented degree of economic security. The claims underlying Inglehart's theory are, first, that people value most highly those things which are relatively scarce; and, secondly, that a person's basic values reflect the subjective conditions which prevailed during their pre-adult years. These claims he sees as borne out in the results of extensive survey research carried out across the world: there are strong correlations between age, post-materialist values, and membership of social movements. According to Inglehart, there has been a shift toward a new style of left-wing politics which is more concerned with creating less formal, more intimate relationships with others, the growth of personal self-esteem, and intellectual and aesthetic satisfaction, than with the issues of economic growth and distribution characteristic of the politics of the old left, dominant in a society marked by scarcity and economic insecurity. Although he acknowledges that there were forerunners of the new social movements which were less concerned with deprivation than with quality of life, he argues that participation in these movements was very low. The novelty of the new social movements is the mass scale of their support (Inglehart, 1990).

Because Inglehart's theory is based on shared beliefs and ideals, he is able to explain the similar orientation of the members of social movements – at least in so far as data on values collected by the survey method may be said to be reliable – without having to *presuppose* that similarity of outlook as a consequence of structural change, as class explanations do. However, as a general theory of the conditions of new social movements, Inglehart's socio-cultural explanation suffers from a similar problem to class-based explanations: it does not take the members of social movements seriously in their own terms. The theory that a generation shares a general set of values, however well supported empirically, is quite unable to account for why people join one social movement rather than another, nor why they differ in their degrees of participation, nor why they are active in different types of organization. While Inglehart's explanation seems to go some way toward providing an account of the exponential increase in social movement activity in recent years, it is only a partial account – it cannot explain why it is that particular social movements come to the fore at particular moments of history. Similarly, it is partial in that it ignores the impact of social movements themselves on changing patterns of belief and attitudes. Inglehart sees values as much more profoundly held than ideological beliefs, as an aspect of personality structure produced through socialization and rooted in feelings rather than as susceptible to rational persuasion, and therefore as practically impossible to change. Since, for Inglehart, social movements are governed by ideologies *based on* deep-rooted values, they must be seen as having relatively little effect on social values and beliefs. While Inglehart's attention to the emotional resonances of politics provides insights into a much neglected dimension of political life, there is no room in his theory for an understanding of the impact of social movements on deeply felt aspects of the self. It is, however, counter-intuitive to suggest that, for example, the women's movement and the gay liberation movement, explicitly concerned as they are with aspects of gendered and sexual identities, have had no influence on emotional relations to ourselves and others.

Finally, there are much bolder theses of the changing social context in which new social movements have come to the fore which concern the transcendence of industrial society altogether. The idea that it is because of changes in society that social movements have now come to the fore is generally held by those designated as New Social Movement Theorists, especially Alain Touraine and Alberto Melucci whose work we shall be looking at in detail later in the chapter. Touraine first developed the idea of post-industrialism as a way of understanding the new context of social movements. Whereas industrial society was organized around manufacturing production, in the post-industrial society it is knowledge and information that are the key resources. For Touraine, this leads to new forms of conflict which are more cultural than economic. Class conflict is displaced by conflict over the control of knowledge, particularly between those well-educated sectors of society who are nevertheless marginalized and those who use it to manage the new society. Writing shortly after *les évenements* of 1968 in Paris, Touraine was particularly thinking of the student movement (Touraine, 1971). More recently, Melucci has added two further points to Touraine's thesis. First, post-industrial society is globalized, an interdependent world system in which no one and nothing is external to its limits. Secondly, it is increasingly individualized: the principal actors in society are no longer groups defined by their class consciousness, religious affiliations, or ethnicity, but rather individuals who must try to give meaning to their lives through social action (Melucci, 1989: 184).

Social movements have also been closely linked to postmodernity. Crook et al. (1992), for example, see their rise since the late 1960s as related to the decline in importance of class conflicts. In their view, the post-World War II corporatist agreements between working-class organizations, management, and the state have been undermined, partly by processes of globalization, as the modern links between markets, culture, and politics organized around the nation-state are unravelled, and partly because class is no longer the main focus of political mobilization. They see evidence of what they call "class decomposition" in the fragmentation and de-polarization of the major political parties in liberal democracies and the declining identification of voters with those parties as the representatives of class interests. The contemporary fragmentation of politics they attribute to the disillusionment of the electorate with established bureaucratic structures, and also to a weakening of the milieux – the communities and, above all, the occupations – on which class constituencies were based. Social movements are increasingly important in postmodernity because they are at least as much concerned with moral and cultural issues as with issues of self-interest, and they orient themselves toward the mobilization of public opinion at least as much as toward the state. They are particularly suited to the new form of society because culture takes pre-eminence as the medium through which identity, ways of life, and social structures are stabilized, in so far as this is possible at all in postmodernity (Crook et al., 1992; see also pp. 241–3).

Social movements and new political sociology

There is still a third way of seeing the novelty of social movements. They may be seen as novel for sociology in so far as it is now oriented toward seeing their activities as significant. This is the conclusion of Craig Calhoun (1995). He asks why it is that traditional sociology ignored social movements other than the labor movement, so that social movements were discovered as "new" in the 1960s, when, in fact, religious movements, nationalism, the women's movement and others continued throughout the nineteenth century and into the twentieth? As Calhoun sees it, this is due to the rationalist, instrumentalist bias of sociology itself. Once the labor movement was institutionalized in the late nineteenth century with the extension of the vote, it came to be seen as *the* social movement of industrialization and progressive social change. Other movements, at least as much concerned with transformations of the self, lifestyle choices and aesthetic criteria for judging personal and social arrangements, were ignored as irrelevant to rational, material progress (Calhoun, 1995).

Calhoun's conclusions can clearly be understood in relation to the "postmodern turn" in sociology. It is in so far as sociology adopted the modern "meta-narrative" of rational progress toward human emancipation that it neglected social movements other than the labor movement, seen as the dynamic force of change for equality and freedom in a future socialist society. Modern sociology neglected the small, local narratives of other social movements. The "postmodern turn," on the other hand, allows for a more pluralist understanding of social life as made up of different, limited narratives, seen as appropriate only for circumscribed groups and individuals. It is therefore much better placed to analyze not only contemporary society but also, following Calhoun's argument, the features of modern society which were obscured by the sociological adherence to the modern meta-narrative. According to this understanding, it is not that society has become postmodern, it is rather that a postmodern understanding is actually more appropriate to modernity than modern sociology.

However, as Calhoun himself acknowledges, it is also the case that the labor movement *actually* marginalized other social movements from the mid-nineteenth century. As Charles Tilly (1984) has shown, the labor movement and the modern state developed together. The extension of the franchise and the relative willingness of state elites to respond to working men's concerns meant that the very form of the state itself was shaped by the labor movement. This process culminated in the corporatist welfare state, in the period following World War II, in which negotiations between capitalists, workers, and government were formalized (Tilly, 1984). As sociological theory was established at the same time as these developments, sociologists were also led to focus on the state as the site of modern politics and the labor movement as the dominant political force. This resulted in the narrow understanding of politics in traditional political sociology that we looked at in chapter 1. It also meant that social movements which did not conform to the model of the labor movement, with its organized political parties and instrumental demands for improved social conditions, were not seen as political. Before the eruption of "new" social movements in the 1960s, social movements which were not part of the organized labor movement were seen as irrational and analyzed in terms of unmotivated outbursts caused by strains in the social system. At the same time, the way in which politics developed around the labor movement and the state actually marginalized alternative movements. For example, although it is true that the women's movement never completely disappeared, following the extension of the vote to women in the early twentieth century it was absorbed into mainstream politics. Women's groups worked either within the state, advising on liberal policy and lobbying ministers, or in the working-class movement, campaigning for better social conditions for poor wives and mothers (Pugh, 1992). The more lifestyle-oriented politics of the earlier links between feminism and socialism were marginalized to the point of extinction (see Taylor, 1983).

From this point of view, the eruption of social movements in the 1960s did represent something new, not only for sociological theory, but also, relatively speaking, in relation to the politics which had hitherto dominated – the organized politics of the labor movement. Although there is no sharp contrast between "old" and "new" social movements in terms of organizational forms and orientation toward politics in civil society and/or the state, nevertheless, social movements in the 1960s and 1970s did exhibit features which required a revision of the traditional sociological model of politics as centered on the state. It is in this respect that the social movements of the

1960s were "new." Similarly, the social context in which they arose is also "new" in so far as there has been a decline in identifications made in terms of class, a withdrawal of support from political parties organized to represent "class interests" and the politicization of identities such as gender, sexuality, ethnicity, and nationality, which were previously marginalized in mainstream politics. Again, it is not necessary to conclude that there has been a sharp historical break, or even that we are now in a transition to a completely new form of society, in order to conclude that these changes nevertheless amount to a "new" social context which requires the re-thinking of the traditional assumptions of political sociology, rooted as it is in understandings of society as stratified principally along divisions of class.

Social movements have, then, required and contributed to the re-thinking of political sociology as a result both of actual changes in politics and also because they have drawn attention to forms of politics previously neglected by the traditional focus on politics at the level of the nation-state. As we shall see, this re-thinking is evident in the development of social movement research, even in the case of RMT where it began from very rationalist, instrumental premises. Furthermore, it is closely related to the "postmodern turn" in political sociology we considered in chapter 1. Above all, this body of work has contributed to an understanding of social movements as engaged in cultural politics: they are engaged in contesting identities and redefining the terms within which social life is structured.

3.2   RESOURCE MOBILIZATION THEORY AND BEYOND

Resource Mobilization Theory (RMT) is based on the liberal view that social phenomena are the result of individual decisions and actions. It was explicitly developed on the premises of rational choice theory, that individual participation in social movements is rational, in order to oppose previous explanations in American sociology in which it was seen as psychologically motivated, as a more or less irrational response to social conditions. In theories deriving from the work of Le Bon and popularized in functionalist accounts like that of Smelser, collective action was seen as related to outbursts of uncontrolled behavior as a result of social dysfunctioning. This work was driven by concern to prevent the rise of fascist and authoritarian movements, but by the 1970s sociologists were much more likely to be sympathetic to the claims of new social movements, if not actively involved in them, and could not subscribe to such a view (Offe, 1987: 81; Scott, 1990: 40–6). The other popular theory against which RMT was developed was that of relative deprivation: it was held that protest is the result of expectations expanding more rapidly than real opportunities, so that groups who experience themselves as marginalized and lacking in influence – students, civil rights protestors, women – will turn to collective action to redress their grievances. Resource Mobilization Theorists have a very simple and convincing rebuttal of any theory of social movements in which they are seen as the result of social grievances: since there are always grievances in a society, their mere existence cannot explain participation in collective action (Zald and McCarthy, 1987: 16–18). For Resource Mobilization Theorists, what needs to be explained is why individuals are purposefully involved in collective action as a result of rational consideration of their own interests: social action is not caused by structural conditions.

In recent years, the premises of RMT in rational choice theory – itself rooted in classical neo-economics – have been subject to extensive criticism, there has been an awakening of interest in less rational aspects of individual motivation, and theorists sympathetic to the tradition have attempted to develop a more sociologically satisfying account of participation in social movements. This had led to an interest among Resource Mobilization Theorists in subjectivity and culture. They have incorporated ideas from the interactionist sociology of Erving Goffman into the approach as a way of enriching its conception of individual decisions. However, Resource Mobilization Theorists resist the implications of the "postmodern turn" they have taken, simultaneously maintaining the realist epistemology and rationalist premises on which the tradition was founded. This has resulted in inconsistencies in the approach which can only be addressed by recognizing those implications.

It is not only its methodological individualism which makes RMT a liberal approach, but also the way in which it implicitly takes the state as the arena of politics proper. For Resource Mobilization Theorists, although social movements may initially have a problematic relation to government in so far as their members do not see themselves as properly represented in dominant political parties and institutions, success for a social movement involves achieving routine access to the political process. This premise is also problematized, however, by the incorporation of concerns with subjectivity and culture into the theory. If participation in a social movement depends on how individuals understand themselves and their situation, there seems to be no good reason for ignoring the contestation of perspectives and the transformation of identities in civil society as if this were not itself an aspect of politics. The extension of RMT to include such issues, however, again points beyond the liberal paradigm, and is therefore somewhat difficult for its adherents to accept.

Resource Mobilization Theory: the premises

The contribution to rational choice theory which has been most influential in RMT is *The Logic of Collective Action* (1968) by Mancur Olson. As Scott points out, the theory of social behavior outlined in this book is established on the basis of two premises drawn from neo-classical economics: First, that social choices are to be explained with reference to individual preferences; and, secondly, that individuals act rationally to maximize their interests and minimize their costs (Scott, 1990: 10). Olson is interested by the idea that there is no necessary connection between collective interests and collective action. On the contrary:

> If the members of a large group rationally seek to maximize their personal welfare, they will *not* act to advance their common or group objectives unless there is coercion to force them to do so, or unless some separate incentive, distinct from the achievement of the common or group interest, is offered to the members of the group individually on the condition that they help bear the costs or burdens of the group objectives. (Olson, 1968: 2)

This is the famous "free-rider" problem of rational choice theorists. It is in the very nature of a public good that no individual in a particular group can feasibly be prevented from benefiting from it if it is enjoyed by others in that group. Because the participation of a single individual makes so little difference to the achievement of a public good, it is more rational to gain it without participating in collective action, unless the group can somehow reward or punish particular individuals in direct proportion to their degree of participation. This is very difficult to do, impossible even, for a social movement intent on changing the very rules and structures by which a category of persons is systematically disadvantaged in relation to others.

Olson was not himself aiming to provide an explanation of the formation of social movements. On the contrary, he was interested in showing why it is that people *do not* take part in collective action, despite their individual interests in collective goals. The existence of social grievances is not a sufficient condition for the rise of a social movement. However, for Resource Mobilization Theorists impressed by rational choice theory but interested in studying actually existing social movements, given that people *are* participating in collective action, the question becomes rather different: how are resources mobilized in such a way as to make that participation rational for self-interested individuals?

This is the question addressed by Anthony Oberschall, who extended Olson's theory to explain the historical emergence of oppositional social movements. Oberschall defines resources widely enough to include material resources, such as jobs, money, and the right to goods and services, and non-material, including authority, commitment, friendship, skills, and so on. By mobilization, he means the processes by which groups manage resources for the pursuit of their goals (Oberschall, 1973: 28). Like Olson, Oberschall supposes that individuals faced with their own resource management decisions participate in collective action to the extent that they rationally choose to pursue their interests in this way. However, he is able to show that such participation is more common than one would suppose on Olson's theory by taking into account aspects of the social situations in which individuals find themselves, something Olson largely ignored. In the case of movement leaders he argues that, although the costs of their participation are very high, as indeed may be the risks where they are involved in activities which are opposed to vested interests, so too are the potential benefits in terms of social status and power within the movement, and a successful career as a result of the leadership role if it succeeds. This is particularly the case where "normal" opportunities in the wider society are closed to members of a particular social group, in which case the benefits to leaders as individuals should they succeed will be very high, and the costs relatively low. Oberschall also considers the social context of the rank-and-file members of social movements, arguing that they do not exist as isolated individuals as Olson assumes; in fact, they often live in communities in which everyone stands to gain from collective action so that each individual is under social pressure to participate in a movement working toward common goals. This is particularly likely to be successful because the costs of that kind of participation are low. In fact, Olson himself thought that social sanctions and rewards are among the kinds of incentives that can mobilize a group, but he believed they only work among small, friendship-based groups (Olson, 1968: 60–1). Oberschall extends that idea to give a more sociological account of individual preferences as shaped by social conditions. He remains clearly committed to Olson's methodological individualism, however, arguing that consideration of action as based on anything other than rationally chosen self-interest is mere speculation (Oberschall, 1973: 118).

RMT was further developed by the sociologists Mayer Zald and John McCarthy, who were the first to coin the term as such and who developed many of the ideas on which the empirical research program it stimulated has been based. Zald and McCarthy focused particularly on social movement organizations, arguing that it was, above all, the fostering of such organizations which was responsible for the exponential growth of social movements in the 1960s. Again, they largely accepted the premises of rational choice theory and Olson's ideas on the fundamental incompatibility of individual self-interest and collective action. For them, any satisfactory explanation of social movements would have to be consistent with those premises.

According to Zald and McCarthy, the professionalization of social movement organizations responsible for the increase in social movement activity involves the development of career opportunities for the individuals they employ. Often experts in social policy, the law, or a "social problem," they move "in and out of government agencies, private agencies, community organizations, foundations and universities," committed above all to programs and policies rather than to a particular organization or to their profession (Zald and McCarthy, 1987: 397). These opportunities were linked in the 1960s and 1970s to a growth in funding for "worthy causes" provided by charitable foundations, corporations, churches, and also the state.

Zald and McCarthy define resources more narrowly than Oberschall and Olson – setting the terms within which the research agenda of RMT was to develop – as involving legitimacy, money, the labor of supporters, and facilities. In practice, however, the resource with which they are most concerned is money. This is the second important factor Zald and McCarthy see as contributing to an increase in social movement activity: the general increase in wealth of developed societies. The increased wealth of the new middle classes, who are able and inclined to provide such resources, is significant, according to Zald and McCarthy, as it helps to form "the social movement sector," consisting of the total activity and membership of all social movements in a society. Social movement organizations compete with each other to convert what Zald and McCarthy call "adherents," those who are sympathetic to the aims of their movement, into "constituents," those who provide its resources, from within much the same social group. Especially important in this respect are "conscience adherents," likely to have considerable resources and to be receptive to the claims of more than one movement. Zald and McCarthy further distinguish what thy call "potential beneficiaries," those who stand to gain from the movement's activities, who may fall into none of the previous categories. For example, a woman without disposable income who happened to be opposed to rights for women might nevertheless benefit from increased opportunities won by the women's movement.

As Zald and McCarthy see it, their version of RMT, emphasizing as it does the importance of social movement organizations, provides a full response to Olson's claims concerning the lack of rationality of collective action. The free-rider problem does not arise where the participation of most individuals is virtually cost-free, requiring nothing more than an annual subscription and/or occasional donation, while there are considerable benefits in terms of employment and career opportunities for those who do take an active role in the collective action of social movements. According to Zald and McCarthy (1987: 27), their theory turns Olson's thesis on its head:

Though it may be individually irrational for any individual to join a social movement organization that already fights on behalf of his [sic] preferences, the existence of a social movement made up of well-heeled adherents calls out to the entrepreneur of the cause to attempt to form a viable organization.

In fact, far from being the outcome of individual action to redress social wrongs, Zald and McCarthy suggest that social movement organizations may even create grievances which are not felt as such by members of the population concerned.

The influential work of Zald and McCarthy and their various collaborators (see Zald and McCarthy, 1987, 1988) went some way toward situating social movement organizations in relation to the wider political process in so far as they suggested that, since the sources of funding they identified as contributing to those organizations were established elite institutions, it is likely that there would be difficulty in mobilizing resources in support of radical causes seen as seriously challenging to the existing order. It was the work of Charles Tilly, however, particularly in *From Mobilization to Revolution* (1978), which provided the tools for the investigation of political opportunity structures.

The most important aspect of Tilly's work is the way in which he deals explicitly with what is often implicit in other studies based on RMT: the importance of the state. Tilly argued that, as the most powerful political actor in modern industrial societies, the state selectively represses or facilitates social movements and/or their activities according to the perceived interests of state elites. That the state represses certain movements and organizations is evident: terrorist organizations are to be repressed by definition, for example; those who take direct action in opposition to government policies or state power are not usually tolerated; and even those organizations which act within the limits of the law may find themselves outside it if a change in policy is seen as desirable and practicable (as in the case of trade unions in Britain in the 1980s, for example). By the same token, some social movements are tolerated, even encouraged, to the point where they become part of the *polis*; that is, where they gain routine access to the government. Tilly suggests that the American state creates three main destinations for a social movement: its dissolution (as a result of repression); the merging of organized activists into an existing political party (absorbing it into the polity – this is how the labor movement became established in the corporatism of post-World War II Western Europe, for example); or the constitution of an enduring pressure group working on the government and political parties (the most frequent outcome for social movements in the United States). There is a fourth destination, common in countries in which there are single-constituency and single-issue parties – where the electoral system is based on proportional representation, for example: the creation of a new, possibly temporary, political party (as in the case of the German greens) (Tilly, 1984: 312–13).

According to Tilly, in comparison with social movements before the nineteenth century, those with which we are familiar today are organized and oriented toward effecting change through the nation-state to an unprecedented degree. In fact, he calls such movements "national movements" to distinguish them from the less organized, more defensive, and more local movements which were particularly prominent during the aggressive expansion of states in the seventeenth century. The rise of national movements is due to the growth of electoral politics and the consequent widening of access – at least in principle – to the political process, according to Tilly: where movements see themselves as having routine access to government agencies they are likely to take their grievances there; where they do not, they will resort to other means. It is also due to the learning of what he calls "repertoires of collective action." A repertoire of collective action includes all the ways in which a group uses its resources to bring about a common end. In twentieth-century North America, for example, these include striking, petitioning, and organizing pressure groups, but rarely rioting, machine-breaking, or rebellion – common actions in previous times. It is Tilly's contention that movements learn from each other: the success of a particular tactic on the part of one movement is likely to lead to its adoption by another.

Tilly's work fits within the RMT tradition in so far as he is above all concerned with how resources are mobilized by social movements to deal with collective grievances. However, it differs from that of Zald and McCarthy in at least two important respects. First, he rejects the premises of the rational choice theory in so far as he adopts the more radical, Marxist view that interests cannot be reduced to the preferences expressed by an individual at any particular moment. It is possible to be mistaken about one's "real interests" and, in fact, part of the task of agencies working on behalf of the status quo is to obscure such interests where their articulation could be threatening to it (Tilly, 1978). Secondly, the theory of political opportunity structures and repertoires of collective action gives quite a different emphasis to the development of social movements than does Zald and McCarthy's focus on formal organization. It directs attention to the development of resistance in grassroots settings as an important aspect of that development, rather than toward professional organizations as the necessary condition of social movement mobilization.

This difference in emphasis does not necessarily make the two approaches incompatible. It may be rather that, in different instances, different aspects of the development of social movements are prominent (McAdam et al., 1996: 4). Such a view is developed in Sidney Tarrow's influential work on "cycles of protest" (or, as now calls them, "cycles of contention"). He argues that social movements do not arise individually, but rather as part of a general wave of social unrest, generally precipitated by some unpredictable event and facilitated by changes in political opportunity structures. At the beginning of the cycle, mobilization takes place directly among existing social networks. As it develops, collective action increases and is diffused across a wider range of social groups. Social movement organizations are formed at the peak of the cycle of protest and compete with one another for constituents within the social movement sector. At this stage, they tend to be demanding of members' time and energy and have little to offer in return except enthusiasm, a feeling of solidarity, and the joy of rebellion. They therefore contribute to the escalation of direct action which characterizes this stage of the cycle of protest. The student movement of the 1960s was led, for example, to employ increasingly radical tactics to challenge the authorities, eventually leading to violent clashes with the police. This escalation actually contributes to the beginning of the decline of the cycle, as participants reject increasing violence or simply become exhausted and as the state either exercises effective repression or, in rare cases, capitulates to the demands of the protestors. The decline often, however, results in the consolidation of social movement organizations, which adopt a more measured and long-term approach, and which act to mobilize resources on this basis. Moreover, it does not necessarily mean defeat of the protestors' aims. Often the effects of the peak of the protest are not felt immediately, but become apparent later in the agendas of political parties, policy decisions, and changes in attitudes and values among the general population. The cycle of protest initiated by the student movement of the 1960s may be seen as an example. Initiated among groups of friends and colleagues, reaching its peak with demonstrations and clashes between police and students and young workers, it resulted in the formation of the "new" social movements which became prominent in the 1970s, and which continue to have far-reaching, though diffuse, effects in the 1990s (Tarrow, 1989, 1998: ch. 9).

Tarrow's analysis of cycles of protest is well supported empirically. It also complements Zald and McCarthy's analyses of the importance of social movement organizations and Tilly's work on political opportunity structures. However, both Tarrow's and Tilly's emphasis on grassroots mobilization has one main weakness from the point of view of RMT. It returns sociologists working in this tradition to its starting point: why is it that rational individuals participate in collective action? If, as Tarrow argues, social movement organizations are only effective once a cycle of protest is underway, how does it begin? He tentatively suggests that people revolt when new grievances are heaped on the old, or when new political opportunities develop (Tarrow, 1989: 51). However, his model of cycles of protest presupposes that individuals have motivations apart from their rational self-interest for initiating collective action since, as we have seen, from a rational choice perspective this is not sufficient to make participation worthwhile. The question of individual motivation and participation in social movements with which the RMT tradition began is also the question which has led to its transformation into quite a different perspective from that premised on rational choice theory.

The "cultural turn" in Resource Mobilization Theory

From the very beginning of the development of RMT, there have been criticisms of its excessively rationalist and instrumentalist approach to social movements. The most frequent and extensive criticisms concern the model of the social actor on which it is premised. It is argued that to see individuals acting solely out of rational self-interest ignores how actors are always socially situated. Individuals are not detached and solitary, with merely instrumental relationships to others, but always already members of groups and communities, with feelings, beliefs, ideas, and values about shared, collective identities. As we have seen, Oberschall criticized Olson's view of the individual as essentially isolated very early in the development of RMT, but it is nevertheless Olson's individualistic assumptions which have been dominant in RMT research.

A further criticism related to the assumptions of rational choice theory is the neglect of actors' perceptions; it is assumed that an individual somehow immediately knows what is in his or her most rational self-interest. In fact, even if self-interest is always the dominant motivation in any individual decision – an assumption which is either tautological, assuming that whatever the individual does is necessarily in his or her rational interest, or else doubtful in the extreme – this depends on a calculation of costs and benefits which are themselves socially constructed. It is rational to pursue certain ends only if those ends are of value, and value itself is socially constructed; it is not something decided on by an individual in isolation (Scott, 1990: 117–28; Morris and Mueller, 1992).

In response to such criticisms of the atomistic, over-rationalist model of the individual on which the approach has been premised, those working within the RMT tradition have attempted to develop a better account of subjectivity and culture. The most influential work in this respect is that of David Snow, in association with various colleagues. They draw on Goffman's ideas of framing to analyze how actors negotiate meanings and commit themselves to social movements. This work is intended to supplement RMT, to provide it with the tools to understand how individuals make the choices so difficult to account for from a rational choice perspective and also, to a lesser extent, to understand the "meaning-work" carried out by social movements. However, the attempt to combine a social constructionist approach with the methodological individualism of rational choice theory is actually more problematic than Resource Mobilization Theorists suppose. They stop short of accepting the full implications of the understanding of culture they have adopted, which actually brings the development of the approach within the "postmodern turn" of new political sociology.

According to Snow and his associates, it is through "frames" that social actors define grievances, forge collective identities, and create, interpret, and transform opportunities in order to bring about social movements. A "frame" works because "it simplifies 'the world out there' by selectively punctuating and encoding objects, situations, events, experiences, and sequences of actions in one's present or past environment" (Snow and Benford, 1992: 137). Frames enable the interpretation of what would otherwise be a mass of complex data, fleeting impressions, and confusing ideas. It is "collective action frames," in particular, which work to mobilize the members of social movements: they "punctuate" or emphasize the intolerability of some aspect of a group's social condition, defining it as requiring corrective action; they make what Snow and Benford call "diagnostic attributions" – attributing blame to individuals, groups or social structures – and "prognostic attributions" – suggesting how the problem could be ameliorated; and they "encode" an array of events, observations, and experiences into meaningful "packages" for the targets of mobilization (1992: 137–8).

Influenced by Goffman, Snow and his associates consider mobilization to take place in face-to-face interaction, in what they call "micromobilization." Building on earlier work concerning different processes of recruitment into different social movements, on how movements "solicit, coax, and secure participants," they locate mobilization in the face-to-face interactions of everyday life (Snow et al., 1980: 799, 1986: 464–5). Social movements recruit and secure adherents by linking individual interpretations with those of the movement in an ongoing process which Snow et al. (1986) call "frame alignment." There are four strategies of frame alignment, as they see it, which depend on how far individuals are from the orientation of the movement: "frame bridging" in which "ideologically congruent but structurally unconnected frames" are linked; "frame amplification" in which there is the "clarification and invigoration" of an already existing interpretation; "frame extension" in which the objectives of the movement are portrayed as continuous with the values and interests of potential adherents; and "frame transformation" in which a movement puts forward a radically new set of ideas and must therefore totally reframe old understandings of issues and problems (Snow et al., 1986).

In more recent years, while still focusing on micromobilization in so far as they see framing and reframing as interactive, Snow and his associates have turned their attention to the wider context in which social movements mobilize resources, to look at the "master frames" through which a variety of movements are created and constrained (Snow and Benford, 1988, 1992). This enables them to take a more historical view, and they argue that, using this concept, they can explain the well-documented "cycles of protest" which characterize the activities of new social movements. Like collective action frames, master frames are modes of punctuation, attribution, and encoding, but they are more universal and less context-specific. They are powerful if they make claims which resonate with central ideas and meanings already existing in the population, and as such they contribute to the escalation and intensity of collective action which characterizes the upswing of a cycle of protest. In fact, Snow and Benford argue that without the construction of an innovative frame there will be no mass mobilization. Similarly, the deterioration of the master frame due to changes in the prevailing cultural climate, or its displacement by a more potent master frame, has a significant effect on the decline of a cycle of protest.

Tarrow sees the American civil rights movement of the 1960s as a good example of Snow and Benford's theory of framing, arguing that its dominant theme of "rights" was resonant with widely shared values, both among black middle-class members of the movement and the white liberal "conscience constituents" who supported it. However, this easy relationship between the movement and American cultural understandings also contributed to the decline of the cycle of protest initiated by the civil rights movement: the rights frame was appropriated by disparate groups across society, including even those who saw affirmative action as an infringement of their rights, while more radical black groups, rejecting the symbols of white liberalism, failed to find resonance in an oppositional subculture and became increasingly isolated and ineffectual. As Tarrow sees it, success depends on "maintaining a delicate balance between the resonance of the movement's message with existing political culture and its promise of new departures" (Tarrow, 1992: 197).

Resource Mobilization Theorists have attempted to integrate the framing approach with the more familiar concepts in the tradition: "political opportunities" and "mobilizing structures." In their introduction to an important collection of articles intended to do just that, McAdam, McCarthy and Zald argue that in order to fully understand social movements it is necessary to analyze the dynamic relations between political opportunities, mobilizing structures, and framing processes, to examine how they condition and constrain each other to shape movements' aims and activities (McAdam et al., 1996). To further this analysis, they propose the study of social movements through time, over the course of their development. The initial emergence of movements, they argue, is due principally to social changes which make the political order more vulnerable to change. However, the political opportunities created in this way are only opportunities in so far as they are defined as such by a group of actors already sufficiently organized to take advantage of whatever openings the political system might offer. In the case of the revolutions in Eastern Europe in 1989, for example, the relaxation of state control in the wake of Gorbachev's reforms provided the conditions for mobilization, but it only became a real possibility because already existing dissident groups had defined regimes as illegitimate and were ready to act against the authorities. It is the dynamic interaction between political opportunities, mobilizing structures, and framing processes which produces the emergence of a social movement.

McAdam et al. (1996) further suggest that the form of mobilization, as well as its timing, is affected by perceptions of political opportunities. To take the example of the Eastern European revolutions again, Elena Zdravomyslova argues that in 1988, following relaxation of state control, the Democratic Union was formed in Leningrad/St Petersburg; it exploited the more tolerant policy on public gatherings by staging disruptive demonstrations. In contrast, following a law granting popular elections passed in the same year, the Leningrad People's Front was formed to mount an electoral campaign (McAdam, 1996: 10). The divergent form of these movements was the result of perceived political opportunities available during their mobilization, according to McAdam and his associates. Further, they argue that, as a movement develops, it may create its own political opportunities, again illustrating the dynamic interaction between different aspects of a movement's activities across time. A good example of mobilization *creating* political opportunities is that of the civil rights movement; as a result of electoral access to Southern political structures, and a consequent rise in the number of elected black officials, the political opportunities available to the movement as such, as well as to its beneficiaries, were significantly altered (McAdam, 1996: 36).

In fact, McAdam et al. (1996) suggest that a movement is increasingly the author of its own fate: organizations claiming to represent the movement consciously shape shared understandings of it in contestation with other collective actors claiming to represent it, with the state, and also with counter-movements. However, the degree of control over definitions and opportunities that McAdam and his associates suppose in this respect is somewhat exagerrated. As Tarrow notes, social movement leaders do not have complete control over how the collective frames of action they propose will be received, nor over how far their supporters will be prepared to follow their lead. In his words, "framing is less like a completed symphony than like improvisational jazz: composers provide the initial 'head' for a jam session, but the improvisations depend on a group of players over whom they have little control" (Tarrow, 1992: 191).

McAdam et al.'s mistaken view of the possibilities of controlling framing processes is actually indicative of a wider problem concerning the "cultural turn" of RMT. The understanding of actors' motivations for collective action as socially constructed cannot simply be grafted on to the RMT approach, as if its premises in rational choice theory were irrelevant. The turn to culture in RMT does not explicitly draw on post-structuralism (although Zald, 1996: 264 has acknowledged its influence within sociology), but in some respects it does imply a radical constructionism which brings it within the terms of the "postmodern turn." This is an unexpected and unwelcome consequence for Resource Mobilization Theorists. It can no longer be assumed that participation in social movements is rational, the realist epistemology on which analyses of political opportunity structures is based becomes untenable, and RMT's understanding of politics as centered on the state becomes problematic. These conclusions are avoided because Resource Mobilization Theorists tend to see culture simply as a resource, to be manipulated by an actor who is somehow outside it, using it rationally as the best means to reach a given end. However, this is unsatisfactory, even within the RMT tradition, since it means that the question the "cultural turn" was supposed to address – how it is that social actors become involved in collective action – remains unanswered.

McAdam et al. (1996: 6), for example, see framing as "the conscious strategic efforts by groups of people to fashion shared understandings of the world and of themselves that legitimate and motivate collective actions." On this model, framing takes place after the (rational?) decision to undertake collective action on the part of the social movement's organizers. For Snow and Benford, however, whose view of framing McAdam and colleagues specifically commend for its clarity, frames provide the initial motivation for individual involvement in collective action. According to Snow and Benford, as we have seen, they do so in so far as they resonate with the ideas, experiences, and values of potential adherents; that is, with already existing frames within which social actors locate themselves. It is on the basis of these existing frames, and their "fit" with "collective action frames," that social actors identify themselves as members of the group for which the movement exists, or as sympathizers with its cause who are prepared to commit their support, and possibly money, time, and energy to achieve its ends. In this case, collective action in the form of the contestation of actors' identities and the framing of cultural understandings is *prior* to the individual calculation of the costs and benefits of collective action.

If McAdam et al.'s view is followed, the question remains unanswered of how it is that the instigators of the social movement come to decide to participate in collective action, if not on the basis of cultural framing. On Snow and Benford's account, there is no need to conclude that the process of mobilization is fundamentally different for leaders and followers: micromobilization may take place in networks and friendship groups, from which social movements grow in momentum. However, if framing processes are seen as fundamental to mobilization, as indeed McAdam et al. themselves suggest in their proposed synthesis of approaches within RMT, this suggests conclusions which are more radically constructionist than theorists within the approach have acknowledged.

First, the implication of framing as fundamental to movement mobilization is that individuals may never act in ways which Resource Mobilization Theorists would find rational. If individual decisions to join social movements are made on the basis of the internal validity of the frames within which they are situated as social actors, the link between actual political opportunities and collective action is severed. As Gamson (1992: 69–70) puts it, "A successful theory of framing must be based on an epistemology that recognises facts as social constructions and evidence as taking on its meaning from the master frames in which it is embedded." This is not to say, as Gamson points out, that *the success of a movement* cannot be assessed on the basis of the actual political opportunities available to it, regardless of how those involved in it see them, but *the action of those involved* cannot be assessed as rational aside from the terms in which they themselves construct it as such. In fact, Gamson argues that adherents are more likely to act if they make an over-optimistic assessment of the chances of a movement's success; ironically, from a rational choice perspective, they are more likely to act irrationally, without a realistic assessment of the opportunities available to them.

Secondly, the framing approach suggests that, rather than objectively and scientifically studying social movements as social phenomena "out there" in the world, Resource Mobilization Theorists are actually much more implicated in that world than has hitherto been supposed on this approach. The assumptions on which RMT is based are themselves cultural constructions. According to the RMT account, in order to participate in collective action one must see oneself as having an interest which can only be realized in common with others, as capable of acting with them to bring about change, and as gaining from that activity. In other words, one must frame one's identity as a rational calculator of the costs and benefits of collective action. In so far as it is the case that social actors *do* frame their identities in this way, then, it is not that Resource Mobilization Theorists provide a detached *explanation* of social movements; it is rather that both share the same master frame. The implications of this are clear: if, as Gamson has clearly pointed out, the framing approach is based on an epistemology in which "facts" are internal to a particular frame, there is no possible independent verification of the way in which RMT frames social action. Resource Mobilization Theorists cannot step outside the cultural frame in which they are situated anymore than any other social member. As we have previously noted, such relativist conclusions need not be an insuperable obstacle to doing sociology (pp. 33–4). RMT, however, is based on a realist epistemology in which the objects of study are, or have been, real resources and political structures which exist independently of their meaningful construction by social actors. The implications of adopting a framing theory of social action which is incompatible with this realist epistemology have not yet been fully considered.

Finally, the cultural framing approach also has important implications for the RMT view of politics which have not yet been taken into account. If social action is based on definitions and meanings made from within cultural frames, then there is no reason to see the contestation of definitions and meanings as simply a preliminary to collective action, a mobilizing strategy to enable a social movement to realize the real goals of influencing political structures and effecting socio-economic change. On the contrary, the theory of framing suggests that what is at stake in much collective action is the contestation and transformation of the meanings actors attribute to events, experiences, and perceptions, and the attempt to construct and reconstruct one's view of oneself and others. This is the understanding of cultural politics of the "postmodern turn" in political sociology.

Traditionally, RMT has focused on social movements as political actors concerned above all with achieving change to the socioeconomic structure through the nation-state. It is true that, as Scott has pointed out, the way in which RMT sees social movements on a continuum with conventional political organizations such as parties and pressure groups does effectively account for much social movement activity (Scott, 1990: 115). It is important not to neglect the relationship between social movements and the state, nor to ignore the fact that integration into the political process in the way Tilly describes may facilitate the realization of a movement's aims, rather than representing its co-option and neutralization (as, for example, Touraine would see it). However, this is very different from the understanding of politics which is the consequence of RMT's "cultural turn." On this understanding, the ongoing contestation of social identities and structures and the broader social change effected as a result must also be seen as political. At this point, the RMT tradition joins "new social movement" theory, to which such an understanding of the cultural politics of social movements has always been central.

3.3 NEW SOCIAL MOVEMENT THEORY: CONFLICT AND CULTURE

In contrast to the liberal premises of RMT, New Social Movement Theory has its roots in Marxism, which it rejects but from which it nevertheless gains certain of its presuppositions. It is based on the centrality of conflict to society and, rather than beginning from the starting point of isolated individuals, it takes the collective nature of that conflict as given. In particular, due to the influence of Alain Touraine, the activity of social movements is seen as involving conflict between dominators and dominated which is inherent in all societies and which provides the motor of social change. Theorists of new social movements in this tradition emphasize, therefore, the revolutionary dimension of social movement activity, even if revolution is not seen in Marxist terms. The aim of a true social movement is not to influence the political process, as in the RMT tradition, but to break the limits of the current system and to lead the transformation of society. New Social Movement Theorists are often criticized, as we shall see, for their utopian ideals, particularly since they are inconsistent with other aspects of their work. However, it is their understanding of cultural contestation as a vital element of social conflict which makes the contribution of this tradition so important.

Alain Touraine: social movements and the sociology of action

According to Alain Touraine, social movements are the central topic in sociology. Since the ordering of social relations is the product of social action, and social movements are the collective agents of social action, social movements are not exceptional and dramatic events, as they are for Resource Mobilization Theorists: "they lie permanently at the heart of social life" (Touraine, 1981: 29).

Touraine explicitly develops his view of social movements in opposition to the structural determinism of Marxism and functionalism, dominant in European and American sociology respectively in the 1950s and 1960s. According to Touraine, functionalism's neglect of social action means that it suffers from an uncritical acceptance of social institutions and values as they happen to have solidified at any particular moment; functionalists fail to see how the apparent unity of a social system is nothing more than the imposition of a dominant movement over the dominated (Touraine, 1981: 34–5). Similarly, Marxism is flawed in so far as it shares the determinism of structural-functionalism. Although conflict is central to Marxism, it is attributed to underlying structural conditions; a contingent social formation is explained in terms of evolutionary laws of history which again fail to acknowledge the role of social action in the production of society. While Marxism imputes interests and motives to class actors which they themselves might not recognize but which Marxists see as produced by socio-economic structures from which they cannot escape, Touraine (1991: 57–9) argues that the terms in which social movements present themselves as actors must be taken seriously if social action is to be properly understood.

Nevertheless, despite Touraine's opposition to Marxism, much of his sociology of action has clearly been influenced by the central idea of Marxist theory: all history is the history of class struggle. According to Touraine, every society is formed by two opposing social movements, which he goes so far as to call class movements. He does not see these classes, however, as struggling over ownership and control of the means of production of a society, as Marxists do, but rather over the control of what he calls "historicity." By "historicity," Touraine means something like "reflexivity" as we have looked at it already in the work of Giddens, Beck, Lash and Urry (see pp. 62–71). It involves the processes by which society is produced as a result of conscious reflection and action on social action and its conditions.

In every society, according to Touraine, there is one key conflict between opposed social movements: the conflict between the dominant class which has appropriated historicity, changing it into order through organization, and the dominated who attempt to re-appropriate it, to break down the status quo, reveal the conflict it conceals, and introduce innovatory ways of thinking, working, and living. Touraine agrees with Marxists that in industrial society the key conflict was between capitalists and proletariat, though he thinks it is a mistake to think of it solely in economic terms since, although it was a struggle over the distribution and control of material resources, this was as a means to the control of historicity rather than as an end in itself. However, we are now living through the transition to a "post-industrial" or "programmed" society: there has been a shift from manufacturing toward knowledge-based industries in which education, training, information, design, and so on are central to production. In such a society control over information and knowledge are the immediate stakes of social conflict and technocrats are the dominant class to the extent that the interests of the society as a whole are identified with the technological development and management of organizations they achieve. The opposing class is not made up solely of workers, but of all those subject to technocratic control; for example, consumers or simply "the general public." According to Touraine, class struggle in post-industrial society is no longer in the name of political or workers' rights, it is not related to economic class struggle, but for people's right to choose and control their own lives.

In Touraine's view, since social movements now struggle directly over the social conditions of self-determination, contemporary society works on itself directly through culture to a greater extent than ever before. In his concern with social transformation through cultural politics Touraine is an important forerunner of the new political sociology and an important influence on the "postmodern turn." His definition of social action makes clear his view of the importance of cultural contest: "Action is the behavior of an actor guided by cultural orientations and set within social relations defined by an unequal connection with the social control of those orientations" (Touraine, 1981: 61). He sees control over historicity as involving control over "the great cultural orientations" by means of which a society's relationships are normatively organized (1981: 26). The conflict between social movements which produces social transformation is principally a conflict over interpretations shared by both sides of the conflict; if actors do not share the same values in the broadest sense – what Touraine calls the "stakes" of the struggle – a conflict cannot be said to be social (1981: 32–3). In Touraine's view, culture not only provides the motivations for collective action in the normative orientation to such issues as "progress against tradition" and "universalism against particularism," it is also the principal object of class struggles.

Touraine does not use the term "cultural politics." He actually restricts the term "political" to activities directed at representative institutions organized at the level of the state. However, he is sympathetic to what he calls Foucault's "denunciation of power" as inherent in all social relations. He sees it as contributing to critical social thought by revealing how apparently rationally organized social relations have actually been established through conflicts and clashes between dominators and dominated. Moreover, although Touraine criticizes Foucault for failing to consider the source of power in society, arguing that it originates in the apparatuses of the ruling class – in post-industrial society, from centers of technocratic domination – like Foucault, he sees power as operating in every social sphere rather than as possessed or produced by the modern state (Touraine, 1981: 21).

For Touraine, social relations are relations of power in so far as they are fixed in certain patterns by class domination. Struggle for the control of historicity takes place in conflicts across the social field, wherever domination tries to impose itself. Touraine's theory of social movements therefore minimizes the importance of the state in the transformation of society. In his view, genuine social movements struggle in the social realm, not through the state. He considers engaging with the political system to be co-option into the status quo and antithetical to the radical changes social movements may achieve.

Touraine's theory of social movements has undoubtedly made an important contribution to the development of the new political sociology. As Giddens has noted in the context of his influential argument against the dominant structuralist-functionalist orientation of sociology, the neglect of social movements in sociology up to the 1970s was quite unjustified in a century in which revolutions and struggles over radical social change have been so prominent (Giddens, 1984: 203–4). Furthermore, although Touraine has no theory of cultural politics as such, he has been highly influential in the "postmodern turn." The importance Touraine gives to struggles over interpretations of norms and values in civil society allows us to see much social movement activity as political in the widest sense, not just in relation to the political process narrowly defined.

However, there are also problems with Touraine's approach which limit the development of an understanding of cultural politics based on his work. First, he over-emphasizes ideology in social movement conflicts. This is well illustrated by his study of the anti-nuclear movement in France in the 1970s. Touraine's interest in anti-nuclear protest lay in his hope that it might be the central social movement of post-industrial society, replacing the workers' movement of industrial society. In order to establish whether or not this was the case, he used his unconventional method of "social intervention." The first aim of this method is to study collective action as directly as possibly, by looking at the self-analysis of a militant group in confrontation with its opponents. Secondly, the researcher actively intervenes to help collective struggle take shape as a force for social transformation by challenging the assumptions with which activists work and raising their action to a "higher level of struggle." It is this aim which has earned Touraine's method the epithet "sociological Leninism" (Cohen, cited in Pickvance, 1995: 127). Finally, the researcher also tries to get the group to develop an alternative, progressive model of modernity. In the case of the nuclear protestors Touraine found so promising, he hoped that they would develop an anti-technocratic vision of society as a whole for which they could fight. In fact, however, he found that they were unable to fulfill the criteria he specified as those of the central movement of post-industrial society. Motivated above all by fear rather than by a vision of the future, they were unable to identify a concrete enemy – attributing problems to "the system" – and were eventually tempted by the utopian ideal of a retreat into community and withdrew from engagement in the struggle to bring about social transformation (Touraine, 1983).

As several commentators have pointed out, Touraine's methodology, particularly the way in which he attempts as a researcher to bring the movement to the realization of its potential, seems to suggest that the most important aspect of bringing about social transformation is to have the right ideas. This is manifestly not the case; since action takes place in practice and so is subject to constraints and is implicated in modifications and consequences which cannot be foreseen in advance, even the best plans may be thwarted. In Touraine's work with social movements, furthermore, it is not ideas of strategy which are at issue, but rather the "true" definition of the social actors involved in the struggle and the cultural orientations at stake (Pickvance, 1995: 127).

His approach may usefully be compared with the quite different understanding of cultural politics developed from discourse theory and discussed in chapter 1. While this model of cultural politics involves the contestation of ideas (although only as a type of symbol among others), they are ideas which are actually effective in structuring social life and identities. It is not that social movements must establish the "true" identities of their opponents, nor the "realities" of the situation in which they are engaged. It is rather that they necessarily engage in strategic and persuasive exchanges in which they try to bring others into their project for change, redefining the terms within which the battle lines have been drawn, changing people's views of their real interests, and convincing them to see the world and themselves in a different way. Social change is not achieved by revealing the truth, as Touraine seems to suppose, but rather by challenging received understandings and introducing new frameworks within which change becomes possible and desirable.

Secondly, from the point of view of this model of cultural politics, Touraine retains some of the problems of the Marxism he rejects, notably – and ironically – its determinism. The problem lies in Touraine's view that there is a single appropriate social movement for every type of society which will bring about the transition to another type of society. As Scott (1996b) points out, this is at odds with his definition of social action as having no a priori direction or foreseeable outcome. The emphasis Touraine gives to actors' interpretations of social action as its cause, rather than underlying structures which work themselves out in a "logic" of development "behind people's backs," as in evolutionism, is testimony to the idea that social action takes place in an open system, potentially transformable in any direction. On the other hand, his diagnosis of the transition from industrial to post-industrial society depends on a theory of society as moving from one relatively closed system to another. Furthermore, he supposes that what is most important in this transition is changes in techniques of production which produce changes in societies as totalities. It is clear from his discussion of anti-nuclear protestors that, rather than analyzing social action in its own terms, as he recommends, his theoretical commitment to the movement for post-industrial society means that what he actually does is to compare the aims of any social movement to the "higher level" anti-technocratic aims he ascribes to it. Apart from problems of inconsistency in his own theory in this respect, Touraine is therefore bound to ignore the diversity of actual social movements and their significance for less total social transformation (Scott, 1996b).

Alberto Melucci: developments in "new social movement" theory

Alberto Melucci, Touraine's one-time student, has taken up many of the insights of Touraine's approach, while at the same time avoiding its inconsistent and untenable determinism and its idealist excesses. In order to avoid the determinism of structural approaches such as that implied in Touraine's theory, he incorporates some ideas from the RMT tradition concerning mobilization and political opportunity structures. In some respects, then, Melucci is concerned to work out a synthesis of RMT and NSMT, but his emphasis on culture and the importance he gives to struggles in civil society make his work very much closer to the latter tradition than to the former. Furthermore, the way in which he has developed Touraine's ideas brings Melucci explicitly within the terms of the "postmodern turn." Although he does not use the term "cultural politics," his view of social movements as engaged in the contestation of collective identity in the practices of everyday life is very clearly akin to the understanding of cultural politics identified with the new political sociology and developed in this book.

For Melucci, Touraine's theory that there is a single progressive social movement in every societal type is a clear case of the typically mistaken view of seeing social movements as *personages* – unified actors playing out a role on the stage of history. In his view, this idea comes from the workers' movement which was relatively unified in terms of its aims, the spaces in which it operated, and its membership among male manual workers. Contemporary social movements, however, are inherently plural: they consist of different levels of action – from political conflicts, narrowly defined, to defensive reactions and challenges to the codes of everyday life – and also of different groups of actors with different reasons for their involvement in collective action. Melucci gives the example of mobilization against a proposed nuclear power station in a rural area, arguing that for the peasants of the community it may represent a threat to traditional ways of life, while for a group of young people who have returned to it from the city, it may symbolize something quite different, for example, a threat to their right to live autonomously (Melucci, 1989: 203–4).

In Melucci's view, the most important point about collective action is that a more or less stable, composite, collective identity – a "we" – must be constructed out of very different ends, means, and forms of solidarity and organization. It must be understood as an ongoing *process* through which actors communicate and negotiate the meanings which produce the social movement as such. It is, of course, also Touraine's view that social movements are the product of social action, as we have seen; however, he reintroduces structural determinism when he interprets collective action in terms of its capacity for leading the transformation from one type of society to another. In such a case it seems that the actors do not necessarily recognize the "highest meaning" of their action until it is brought to their attention by the researcher. For Melucci, on the other hand, social actors must know the meaning of their action, even if they do not know it completely, since collective action is nothing but the multiple meanings they give to it (Melucci, 1995b).

Melucci's emphasis on the construction of meaningful collective action is also a response to Resource Mobilization Theorists. In his view, RMT is useful for the way in which it stresses the external relationships of social movements to the field of systematic opportunities and constraints within which action takes place. Its focus on *how* social movements are formed and maintained is a good corrective to Touraine's emphasis, and also that of Offe and Habermas, on *why* they have become so important in contemporary society. However, in Melucci's view, despite the way in which RMT postulates the construction of collective action as a necessary process for social movements, it too takes the unity of social movements for granted and fails to examine it as a process. Furthermore, it is seriously limited in its capacity to do so in so far as Resource Mobilization Theorists tend to see opportunities and constraints as "objective" realities. Melucci is opposed to what he calls dualistic thinking which emphasizes either the objective or the subjective dimensions of social life: for him the goals of action, the means to be used, and the environment within which it takes place are all defined by collective actors in the ongoing process of constructing a social movement. In this respect his work is in sympathy with those who have used Goffman's model of frame analysis, arguing that the motivation to participate in collective action is produced in interaction (although, as far as I know, he nowhere refers to RMT's appropriation of Goffman's work). However, unlike Resource Mobilization Theorists, Melucci follows the logic of this "cultural turn" through to its conclusion, arguing that the reasons for becoming involved in a movement and the calculations of cost and benefits are *only* developed in interaction. Although he thinks – perhaps somewhat inconsistently – that structural explanations of the objective conditions in which social movements have recently risen to prominence are of value, they are relevant to collective action itself only in so far as they enter into actors' perceptions and evaluations and so into the processes of interaction in which it is constructed (Melucci, 1988).

Finally, Melucci breaks with Touraine and with RMT by reject-ing the view that it is committed militants or social movement organizations who are the principal actors in collective action. For Melucci, social movements are above all sustained in "invisible submerged networks" in which experiments in life are carried on, new experiences created, and collective identities forged in everyday life. In his view, movements appear relatively infrequently as publicly visible phenomena in comparison with their existence in the practices of a largely part-time and floating membership in which they are formed and gain and maintain strength. The consciousness-raising groups of the early women's movement would no doubt be good examples of Melucci's "submerged networks," as would the health food shops, walking groups, conservationists, and self-help building programs of the green movement. Although movements may be invisible to the point where it seems as if they have altogether collapsed, the practices of networks of groups and individuals nevertheless develop alternative ways of living and thinking which quietly challenge society's dominant codes and which are ready to be mobilized for public protest if the occasion arises.

Despite these crucial disagreements with Touraine's work, Melucci does build on his understanding of social movements. Most impor-tantly, like Touraine he sees social movements as primarily engaged in cultural challenges to the logic of "post-industrial" society. Infor-mation as the key resource in contemporary society, the reflexivity of individuals and the society as a whole has been massively increased as a result, and global processes impinge on individual awareness in an unprecedented way. In view of this new social situ-ation, social movements should also be seen as "new," in Melucci's opinion, because the problems to which they respond are different from those of the social movements of the nineteenth and early twen-tieth century – the main point of comparison being, of course, the labor movement – and so, too, are the responses they make to those problems (Melucci, 1995a).

For Melucci, post-industrial societies are above all concerned with "signs;" even the production and distribution of economic goods are symbolically mediated, through design, advertising, the media, and so on. As a result, according to Melucci, unlike their nineteenth-century counterparts, "new social movements" are not concerned with struggles over the production of material resources, nor with their distribution or control through the state in citizenship rights, but rather with access to information (about the hazards of nuclear testing, for example) and the contestation of symbolic resources (such as sexist advertising or the aestheticization of violence in the media). They are, above all, concerned with contestation in the cultural realm. This is also the case, according to Melucci, because, again unlike working-class politics, contemporary movements are concerned with forms of organization and lifestyle which are ends in themselves rather than the means to realize an end in the future. In particular, the split between public and private spheres is lived more as a complementarity than an opposition, as it was in the past: the experiences and meanings of private life are directly linked to publicly expressed commitments and vice versa. The women's movement would again be a good example of Melucci's point here because of the way in which it has provoked the revolutionizing of relations between men and women in the private domestic sphere and, to a lesser extent, in the private realm of the economy, as well as in legislation and social policy.

In Melucci's view, the struggles of new social movements are struggles over identity: "to push others to recognize something which they themselves recognize; they struggle to affirm what others deny" (Melucci, 1989: 46). Although any conflict might be characterized in this way, he argues that the issue of identity has become more central with the increased reflexivity of complex societies. In Melucci's view, there is an ever-increasing control over every aspect of our lives in such matters as health, sexuality, and our relations with the natural environment. In this respect, he sees Foucault's understanding of power as important. On the other hand, however, the organizations which regulate our behavior also facilitate individual autonomy because they thereby put resources of knowledge and communicative skills at our disposal: without the development of capacities for learning and action, individuals would not be capable of the self-regulation required by the system. Increasingly, therefore, there is a greater emphasis on the capacity to act on action itself; to intervene in the biological and motivational structures of human beings in order to change oneself as an individual. In this respect, Melucci sees Foucault's model of power as one-dimensional: power does not simply involve the administration of subjects since networks of actors in complex societies may use the resources provided by powerful organizations in ways which were not intended by bureaucrats and managers (Melucci, 1989: 208–9).

According to Melucci, the emphasis on individual identity in complex societies is linked to new forms of collective action in social movements. This is most directly evident in the fact that individuals are motivated to participate in movements only in so far as it "makes sense to them," meeting, as they see it, their own personal needs. As Melucci sees it, however, it is relatively rare that this leads to narcissistic inward-turning groups since work on oneself is generally seen in these movements as the way to change the world by creating meaningful alternatives to the existing state of affairs. For example, the questions raised by the ecology movement concerning human relations with nature are immensely important for society as a whole as the destructive potential of technological intervention increases. Similarly, women's mobilization raises the general issue of how to recognize and accommodate biological and historical difference without repression (Melucci, 1989: 62). In fact, for Melucci, the definition of such questions as meaningful and the negotiations between individuals which link them to concrete ways of life are precisely the ways in which collective action itself is constructed in interaction. All the cultural innovations made in the process of individuals working on themselves in negotiation or in conflict with others – on the language they use, their sexual customs, affective relationships, dress, eating habits, and so on – constitute collective action which modifies the social order. Moreover, in so far as individual identity requires recognition by others, it is in itself intrinsically social: by its very nature, identity cannot be constructed outside relationships which give it meaning (Melucci, 1996: 29).

For Melucci, as for Touraine, social movements have a tangential relationship to established institutional politics; they cannot be assimilated to the political process because the conflicts they engender break the bounds of the current system (Melucci, 1989: 29). Melucci uses the term "politics" in a narrow sense, defining a political relationship as "one which permits the reduction of uncertainty and the mediation of opposing interests by means of decisions" and arguing that it takes place wherever interests are represented and decisions taken: in national political systems, but also in educational, administrative, and regional institutions (Melucci, 1989: 165). Social movements are principally concerned with solidarity and conflict in the cultural realm, as we have seen, and for Melucci their most important political function is as signs, or messages, which highlight hidden conflicts and problems and make visible the power used to resolve them in apparently rational, technical, decision-making procedures. As he points out, some of the dilemmas of contemporary society cannot be definitively resolved; for example, neither the elimination, nor the free use of nuclear energy is possible. Social movements publicize these "meta-political" dilemmas and Melucci argues that as a result they are necessarily ill suited for, and highly suspicious of, the conventional political process. Those, like Resource Mobilization Theorists, who look only at the effects they have on politics in this sense will, therefore, gain a wholly distorted view of their importance in contemporary societies.

In Melucci's view, social movements point the way beyond the limits of the present system, toward a new form of democratization appropriate to complex societies. They embody the need for new public spaces between civil society and the state in which movements can articulate and publicize themes and dilemmas to the rest of society and to the political actors who make the final decisions about how they will be dealt with. Such public spaces already exist to some extent, as Melucci sees it, in knowledge-producing institutions such as universities and cultural foundations, but they should be strengthened in the field of collective consumption – in relation to housing, transport, health, and so on – and also in relation to communications and the media in order to allow public confrontation and negotiation between the various actors involved (Melucci, 1989).

Melucci's work is evidently important for the new political sociology. It draws our attention to the new forms of cultural politics in contemporary society in which social movements are engaged, even if he himself uses a much narrower definition of politics. Melucci has been influenced in this respect by Touraine's re-thinking of Marxism, particularly by the way in which Touraine puts historicity at the center of his analysis. Both theorists have clearly taken seriously Marx's dictum that "Men make their own history, but not under circumstances of their own choosing." Melucci, however, is clearer than Touraine that it is the contestation of collective identity which is the key activity of social movements in cultural politics; there is no "objective" definition of the stakes of the conflicts in which they are engaged.

This understanding also brings Melucci's work within the "postmodern turn." His opposition to dualism means that he has much in common with discourse theory. In both cases, identity is seen as constructed by the manipulation of symbols which are effective in particular social contexts. There is no clear separation to be made between the way in which social life is defined and understood and the way in which it is lived, since both are implicated in ongoing social practices. In fact, in his more recent work, Melucci makes the connections between his work and the "postmodern turn" in sociology more explicit, putting forward the view that it is the development of post-industrial society which increasingly makes symbols effective in reality. He argues that to see information as mirroring or representing reality is now simplistic; information encoded in language and images increasingly contributes to the construction of social reality:

> Technological power has been accompanied by an exponential growth of symbolic possibilities, by an increase in self-reflective activity: by the heightened capacity to reflect and represent reality through a multitude of languages. This capacity seems to be gradually replacing reality itself, so that we are in the process of coming to inhabit a work constructed out of the images that we ourselves have created, a world where we can no longer distinguish reality from the reality of the image. (Melucci, 1996: 43)

What was previously implicit in Melucci's work – that it is in the manipulation of symbols and signs that collective identity is forged through the production of common meanings – is now made explicit. The question for social movements in contemporary society is, he suggests, "How and for what purpose should we use the *power of naming* which allows us to fabricate the world and to subsume it to the signs with which we express (or do not express) it?" (Melucci, 1996: 131).

Melucci's understanding of the cultural politics of social movements as taking place in everyday life is an important contribution to our understanding of contemporary society. There is no doubt that the way in which he sees social movements as active in civil society, rather than as oriented toward politics at the level of the state, has encouraged the development of his theory in these respects. However, there is an element of dogmatism in Melucci's refusal to consider how "new" social movements as well as "old" have been concerned with politics at the level of the nation-state. As we have seen, his theory illuminates the activities of social movements in civil society in ways which are completely neglected by RMT, focusing as it does on formal political activities. In this respect, it has been deservedly influential. However, social movements have always also engaged with the state to a greater or lesser extent. In particular, emerging in the context of an interventionist welfare state in Western liberal-democracies, "new" social movements have generally been involved in demanding the extension of citizenship rights in various ways. (We shall look at this in detail in chapter 4.) This aspect of social movement activity is ignored by Melucci, doubtless because of his utopian view of social movements as "breaking the limits" of existing society.

However, it is not clear that Melucci's theory of cultural politics *need* commit him to ignoring the activities of social movements in this respect. On the contrary, given his emphasis on the internal plurality of social movements and the way in which they work at different levels, his theory would seem to be well designed to encompass the range of political activities in which they engage. It should be possible, as Melucci himself argues, to see social movements working *between civil society and the state*, as engaged in the democratization of everyday life and also in extending citizenship rights. In the next section we will look at a synthesis of RMT and NSMT to see whether, given the prejudices of each tradition and the way in which they have developed, such a balanced perspective on social movements is now possible.

3.4 TOWARD A SYNTHESIS: THE DEFINITION OF "SOCIAL MOVEMENT"

In discussing the two main traditions of the study of social movements, we have seen that there has been a convergence between them in terms of the importance they give to culture in shaping participants' perceptions of aims and strategies. In fact, despite the very different premises of each tradition, those currently studying social movements are more likely to try to draw on both rather than to see them as incompatible (Klandermans et al., 1988; Johnston and Klandermans, 1995). One of the most thorough attempts to combine them is that of Mario Diani, who argues that the two traditions are now so close that it is possible to begin to synthesize them without doing injustice to either.[1] It is clear that the basis of Diani's synthesis is a sympathy with the work of Melucci, who has already tried to incorporate some elements of RMT's understanding of the importance of mobilizing structures and political opportunities. Here we will look at Diani's synthesis with a view to drawing out the importance of cultural politics to both major traditions in social movement theory.

Diani begins his task by laying out a working definition of "social movement," pointing out that it is striking how little work has been done on actually identifying social movements as distinct from other types of collective action. A social movement is a:

> specific social dynamic . . . It consists in a process whereby several different actors, be they individuals, informal groups and/or organizations, come to elaborate, through either joint action and/or communication, a shared definition of themselves as being part of the same side in a social conflict. By doing so, they provide meaning to otherwise unconnected protest events or symbolic antagonistic practices, and make explicit the emergence of specific conflicts and issues . . . This dynamic is reflected in the definition of social movements as consisting in networks of informal interaction between a plurality of individuals, groups and/or organizations, engaged in a political and/or cultural conflict, on the basis of a shared collective identity. (Diani, 1992: 2–3)

It should be noted that Diani's definition differs in one crucial respect from the understanding of cultural politics developed here. According to this understanding, there is no distinction between "political" and "cultural" as different kinds of conflict in the way Diani suggests. All conflicts necessarily take place in culture and, in so far as they involve struggles to realize only one of various possible courses of action in practice, they are political. It is, however, the case, as we have noted, that social movements engage in cultural politics in civil society and also at the level of the state, contesting exclusionary definitions of citizenship. It is no doubt in this sense that Diani intends his distinction between "political" and "cultural":' the first term referring to conventional forms of politics aimed at mobilizing political parties and lobbying to change legislation and the latter referring to the politics of everyday life. He apparently does not recognize both as cultural, although this is clearly the implication of the terms on which RMT and NSMT converge. This will become clear as we work through the synthesis he has constructed.

According to Diani, his definition of social movement emphasizes at least four aspects of their dynamics:

(1) "A social movement is a network of informal interactions between a plurality of individuals, groups and organizations" (Diani, 1992: 8). Both Resource Mobilization Theorists and New Social Movement Theorists see the mobilization of social movements as occurring in informal interactions involving individuals, groups, and organizations. This is made explicit in the case of Melucci's definition of collective identity as formed through interaction in "submerged networks," but it is also important among Resource Mobilization Theorists for whom "micromobilization" is a key component of social movement activity. There is a difference in emphasis, however, as those in the RMT tradition tend to see networks as providing the preconditions for mobilization which is then orchestrated by social movement organizations, while, for Melucci, they provide the settings for social movement activity proper – the contestation of identities and the practicing of alternative lifestyles. Arguably, this difference of emphasis is rather important, suggesting that the convergence between the traditions has distinct limits. Nevertheless, Diani is clearly correct to point out that both now recognize the importance of informal interactions to social movements.

(2) "The boundaries of a social movement network are defined by the specific collective identity shared by the actors involved in the interaction" (Diani, 1992: 9). According to Diani, writers in both traditions again acknowledge what is emphasized in Melucci's work: that a social movement requires a collective identity, including both a shared set of beliefs and a sense of belonging. Resource Mobilization Theorists have tended to focus on the former to the neglect of the latter: Zald and McCarthy, for example, see social movements as "sets of opinions and beliefs," which does not necessarily imply shared feelings of belongingness. However, Diani sees the more recent work in the RMT tradition on "micromobilization contexts" and "frame alignment processes" as emphasizing the collective negotiation of individual commitment, as opposed to individuals' solitary reflections on their reasons for joining collective action, and so as at least implying the construction of solidarity. He therefore insists on the importance of the process of symbolic definition

and redefinition of events, issues, activities, and other social actors in both traditions.

In Diani's view, both Resource Mobilization Theorists and New Social Movement Theorists must now take the terms within which social actors themselves see the movements in which they participate seriously: the collective identity of a social movement *is* that movement – it is nothing but a meaningful construction created in social action. It is clear that in so far as Diani is correct in his view that this is the consensus among social movement theorists, cultural politics is crucial to the understanding of social movements in both traditions. Structural or causal explanations of members' participation have been ruled out as inadequate: the negotiation of individuals' reasons for participating and the collective identities which are constructed as a result are what creates social movements as such.

(3) "Social movement actors are engaged in political and/or cultural conflicts, meant to promote or oppose social change either at the systemic or non-systemic level" (Diani, 1992: 11). As Diani notes, the idea that social movements aim at social change through conflict is central to NSMT. For Touraine especially, but also Melucci, one of the core components of a social movement is that it is engaged in conflict with an adversary who interprets the same values in a different way. However, Diani argues that, although the RMT tradition is ostensibly more concerned with processes of social change, conflict is implicit in their understanding of social movements in so far as they acknowledge that social change is achieved only through conflict with other actors, whether institutions, other social movements, or counter-movements.

The main difference between the two traditions is, as we have seen, that while RMT is concerned above all with the way in which social movements effect change through the mainstream political process, New Social Movement Theorists see activity at this level as that of a "public interest group" or even a political party, not of a social movement. They see social movements as active in culture, as engaged in challenging shared meanings and, in the case of Melucci, in self-transformation. Diani plays down this difference, clearly seeing it in terms of the difference between formal political activities and conflicts in civil society and arguing that it is a matter of emphasis rather than of fundamentally incompatible understandings of social movements. However, his reading of both traditions is rather selective on this point. In order to reach consensus on the different orientations of social movements, adjustments have to be made both to RMT and NMST.

RMT has, above all, been concerned with political change at the "non-systemic" level, that is, through the institutions of the state. In order to engage fully with cultural change, it would be necessary for Resource Mobilization Theorists to give less emphasis to social movement organizations as the principal actors in social movements and more emphasis to the negotiation of collective identity and social action in processes of interaction. It is true that this is possible within the terms of RMT but, as we have seen, it would also mean giving up the commitment to objectivity and scientific neutrality on which the tradition has been based. It would mean RMT following the implications of the more cultural understanding of politics it has developed to a conclusion which would bring it much more fully within the "postmodern turn."

NSMT, on the other hand, has been exclusively concerned with cultural change at the "systemic level." This is explicit in Touraine's work, and also in Melucci's: both see social movements as "breaking the limits" of the existing social system. For a complete synthesis between the traditions and an integrated social movement research program to be possible, New Social Movement Theorists would have to drop their commitment to complete "systemic" transformation.

In fact, the idea of "system" is inconsistent with other aspects of Melucci's social theory. First, as we saw in chapter 2, the transnational flows of globalization undermine the idea of a strictly bounded society with distinct limits. Secondly, in so far as collective identities are seen as nothing but unstable composites of different meanings continually in the process of renegotiation, it is again difficult to see society as having fixed limits. Melucci's commitment to the idea of system is at odds with his idea of increased reflexivity in contemporary society which is more readily understood as giving rise to a permanent state of flux rather than the transformation of one "system" into another. (In chapter 5 we will discuss more extensively the problems of the functionalist idea of "system" from the point of view of an understanding of cultural politics as central to contemporary social life.) As we have noted, Melucci's understanding of social movements as inherently pluralist and working on several levels would otherwise allow him to accommodate the way in which they engage in formal political activity, without compromising his understanding of the ways in which they engage in the democratization of everyday life in civil society. It would seem quite reasonable to adopt such an understanding, while giving up the romantic commitment to "systemic" transformation. Melucci's theory is potentially the more comprehensive in this respect, then, allowing an understanding of the way in which social movements engage in cultural politics both to realize social change through the state and also in the practices of civil society.

(4) "A social movement is a network of informal interactions between a plurality of individuals, groups and/or organizations, engaged in a political or cultural conflict on the basis of a shared collective identity" (Diani, 1992: 13). As Diani sees it, it is important to distinguish between social movements and other types of social and political action, such as interest groups, political parties, or religious movements. This is sometimes difficult given that social movements involve such a wide range of practices. However, he argues that it is precisely in this way that we should see social movements as distinctive forms of collective action: they are not simply organizations, however informal and non-hierarchical, but rather networks between different actors in which more or less formal organizations may sometimes play a part. Such citizens' rights groups as Common Cause in the US and interest groups such as the Child Poverty Action Group in Britain are not social movements. Nor are religious sects such as Nichiren Shosh (studied as such by Snow et al., 1980, in terms of their recruitment techniques). The unique characteristic of a social movement, according to Diani, is a collective identity which exceeds the boundaries of any single group of organization, while nevertheless maintaining a limited specificity. This definition would seem to be acceptable from within the terms of both the RMT and NSMT traditions, although it is the case, as Diani points out, that surprisingly little work has been done in either on precisely what makes social movements distinct from other forms of collective action.

Diani's analytic synthesis is useful for the way in which it clearly brings out the important insights of both the major traditions in the study of social movements. In particular, it brings out the importance of cultural politics to both RMT and NSMT. The understanding of social movements as involving the negotiation of collective identity, the contestation of definitions and meanings in conflict with other social actors, and social action carried out in accordance with those shared meanings are all aspects of cultural politics which both traditions theorize.

However, Diani himself does not entirely acknowledge this importance in so far as he seems to suppose that some social movements are engaged only in political action narrowly defined. In this respect he fails to acknowledge what NSMT theory has always insisted on, and what the appropriation of Goffman's ideas on "framing" in RMT is designed to illuminate, that the conflicts in which social movements engage are always, at the most general level, conflicts over cultural meanings. Social movements are often engaged in activities designed to influence governments, political parties, and policymakers, and it is possible that some may not be concerned with politics in this sense but solely with conflicts in civil society. They are, however, always engaged in the politics of cultural contestation. It is the understanding of social movements as continually engaged in cultural politics which makes them so central to the new political sociology.

3.5   SOCIAL MOVEMENTS AND GLOBALIZATION

Finally, the assumption of most social movement research is that mobilization, organization, and action take place within a bounded national territory, even if it is not necessarily addressed to the nation-state. This assumption is now increasingly called into question as a result of the explosion of interest in globalization in recent years.

It remains the case, however, that relatively little work has been done on social movements and globalization. In RMT there has been a recent growth of comparative work which attempts to "account for cross-national differences in the structure, extent, and success of comparable movements" on the basis of differences in the political characteristics of national organizational and state structures and also in national cultural frames (McAdam et al., 1996: 3). One of the most interesting findings of this work is the way in which some of the theoretical differences between the US-based RMT and the European NSMT are related to local differences in social movement activity. Historically, politics in the United States has been much less dominated by the labor movement than European politics; it has been characterized by a more open, non-corporatist style of politics in which movements tend to try to adapt to and influence the political process through organized lobbying. It has also been preoccupied with constitutional interpretation and litigation so that social movements have been very much concerned with legal contestation in the US. In contrast, Western European politics has been characterized by a more rigid corporatism to which movements have tended to respond in a more radical, anti-systemic way. As we have previously noted (p. 111), corporatism is now breaking down, but social movements in Europe are still more likely to organize outside the political process and to be opposed to the bureaucratic and hierarchical organizational forms of mainstream politics, as well as to its aims and values (Crook et al., 1992: 158–9).

Setting US movements against European ones in this way is clearly rather a crude dichotomization and much work has also been done comparing social movement activity in countries within Western Europe, as well as with the dramatic success of "anti-political" revolutionary social movements as a response to exceptionally rigid political structures in Eastern Europe. However, it does suggest that the focus of RMT on social movement mobilization through professional organizations and its assessment of the impact of social movements in terms of their direct influence on the political process has been influenced by the fact that most theorists in the tradition work in the US. This is not to deny the validity of the criticisms of RMT discussed above – the neglect of politics in civil society must be seen as a serious deficiency in any analysis of social movements – but only to point out that areas of contention between RMT and NSMT are at least partly due to significant differences in the political contexts in which each one was developed.

In terms of the issue of globalization, however, the comparative work currently being undertaken on social movements is extremely limited. Comparisons are made only in terms of cross-national differences so that social movements continue to be seen only in relation to national context. This is defensible in so far as the nation-state remains the principal actor in global governance, mediating the impact of international and transnational processes on national populations and shaping the issues on which people mobilize, how they organize and act, and the outcomes of that mobilization (Della Porta and Kriesi, forthcoming). However, it is clear that global processes also impact directly on social movements so that to focus only on the national context in which they operate is inadequate. Furthermore, transnational social movements are themselves an important aspect of globalization so that it is also important to consider how they work in the context of the global politics in which they operate.

An excellent illustration of these points is Sasha Roseneil's (1997) study of the women's peace movement based at the United States airforce base at Greenham Common in England in the 1980s. This was a transnational movement in several senses. First, and most importantly, participants in the movement defined it as such. The nuclear weapons sited at the base were seen as posing dangers for worldwide peace and security which the women's peace movement was organized to defend. Secondly, it was constructed specifically as a women's movement on the grounds that it is men who have power over the planet, since men make up the political and military elites which control nuclear weapons. This radical feminist identity was elaborated largely on the basis of writings which were particularly prominent in the US at that time, so that the ideas on which the movement was initially based were the result of transnational communication. Thirdly, especially as the peace camp became established, women came from all over the world to visit it, contributing to the identity of the movement as a worldwide women's peace movement. In fact, Roseneil makes the point that the missiles were specifically sited at Greenham Common because road communications were good there; this also enabled support for the women's peace camp from elsewhere in Britain, and also from other countries. As a result of these connections, women's peace camps were set up in Australia, Canada, Denmark, Germany, Italy, and the USA. As Roseneil points out, the women at Greenham Common challenged processes of globalization – military, political, and environmental dangers – which they experienced as intensely personal; they feared for their safety and that of their friends and family. But the challenge was itself bound up with processes of globalization, and dependent on them for its operation. In this way, her study shows how the personal, local, and global are inter-related in a transnational social movement (Roseneil, 1997).

There are at least four ways in which social movements should be theorized in relation to globalization. First, as Roseneil's study shows, many social movements are already mobilizing in relation to global problems. The most notable are the environmental movement, the peace movement, and the women's movement. In fact, as Sidney Tarrow points out, social movements have long been transnational: the anti-slavery movement, the women's suffrage movement of the nineteenth century, and the international labor movement were all involved in campaigns and exchanges which aimed at nation-states but which were not themselves confined within national borders (Tarrow, 1994: 52–3).

The possibilities for these exchanges and for the awareness of global problems has, however, been enormously increased by the second aspect of globalization that is relevant in this respect, the growth of transnational communication. This not only brings individuals and groups news of distant events, increasing awareness of problems in other places, and of interconnections across the planet, but also facilitates co-operation between local sections of a movement, tightening transnational links within it. This is again clear in the case of Roseneil's analysis of the support the women's peace movement at Greenham Common received, and also the way in which the repertoire of action they elaborated then spread across Europe and North America.

Thirdly, drawing on work by Benedict Anderson, Tarrow argues that the style of mass migration in the twentieth century is also conducive to the stimulation of transnational social movements. Again linked to the increased facility of communication, and to the development of international transport, migrants to the industrial West tend to keep close contact with those they leave behind in their country of origin. From this position they may contribute to nationalist struggles for liberation from religious, national, or political persecution within those countries as part of a transnational social network. Examples Tarrow gives include Palestinians in New York, Turkish Kurds in London, Irish in Massachusetts, Algerians in France and Punjabis in Toronto. As Tarrow (1994: 197) puts it, "By more or less covert financial contributions, by fax and e-mail, by letter bombs and discrete arms purchases, these long-distance nationalists are disturbing the neat symmetry between national states and national social movements that the world has inherited from the last century."

Finally, the displacement of the nation-state as the sovereign political institution is important to the study of globalization and social movements. This is the case even if the nation-state remains the principal focus of social movement activity, given that the national context itself is increasingly affected by international relations and supranational institutions. Transnational social movements may be seen as contributing to a global civil society in which they bring pressure to bear on internationalized states, supranational political institutions and transnational organizations, including multinational corporations. We will look at the possibilities of global civil society in more detail in chapter 5.

Note

1 Diani's schema actually includes four main trends which he sees as important within social movement analyses since the 1960s: collective behavior (Turner and Killian), RMT (Zald and McCarthy), political process (Tilly), and new social movements (Touraine, Melucci). The collective behavior approach has not been considered here because it has not been very influential in recent years, and the "political process" approach has been categorized with RMT, as is more usually the case. These differences do not affect our assessment of Diani's synthesis.

CHAPTER 4

Contesting Rights: Contesting Universalism

The cultural politics in which social movements are engaged has greatly contributed to the understanding of citizenship in the new political sociology. The study of citizenship is relatively recent in sociology, although as a concept, social status, and set of political practices it goes back to the ancient world. The model of citizenship outlined by T. H. Marshall in the late 1940s, and now regarded as the classic starting point of any discussion of the topic, did not achieve widespread influence until the 1960s (Rees, 1996: 1). It is since the 1980s, however, that citizenship has become a topic of extensive debate in political sociology. This is undoubtedly linked to the growth of social movements which challenge the traditional form of citizenship as it has developed in liberal democracies. In particular, social movements have responded to the neo-liberal development of that model in the politics of the New Right, especially in the US and Britain.[1]

The older sociological understanding of citizenship took class as the principal axis of inequality. As we shall see when we examine Marshall's model of citizenship in more detail in section 4.1, his account of the historical development of citizenship focused on the extension of citizenship rights as a feature of the progress of modern society. He represented this extension as the achievement of universal citizenship, of identical rights for all citizens regardless of socio-economic class. He neglected dimensions of social inequality other than those of class, notably of gender, "race," and ethnicity. This is unsurprising as Marshall was writing in late 1940s' Britain, when society was seen as stratified in terms of occupation, and the labor movement was prominent in campaigning for the expansion of citizenship rights, particularly the social rights of the welfare state. Class inequalities were the main focus of attention in society as well as in sociology. Increasingly, however, as "new" social movements like feminism, the gay liberation movement, and the civil rights and antiracist movements gained in strength and directed campaigns at inequalities in the rights of different categories of citizens, both Marshall's optimistic model of "universal" citizenship rights and the idea that social inequalities are essentially class inequalities have come under attack.

The main theme in the cultural politics of citizenship inspired by social movements is that of "difference." This is, in turn, associated with the postmodern "responsibility toward Otherness" which we looked at in chapter 1. In challenging the exclusion of social groups who do not conform to the norm of the white, heterosexual, male head of household, social movements also challenge the idea of a single universal citizenship conceived of as the same set of rights for all citizens. Challenges to exclusion rarely involve the simple claim that members of particular social groups are not treated like "normal" citizens. It is rather that what is "normal" should be displaced to become just one of a range of possibilities. In this respect, social movements challenge the idea of citizenship as consisting of individuals enjoying identical rights and imply a more open, pluralist model of society.

In liberal democracies the rights of citizens are ostensibly to civil freedoms, political participation, and social well-being *as* individuals. In fact, as the cultural politics of citizenship conducted by social movements makes clear, only *some* citizens have full entitlement to individual rights. Citizenship rights are actually the rights of a particular social group, white, heterosexual, male heads of households, and not simply of individuals as such. Those who do not fit the characteristics of "individuals" are produced as "Other," as inadequate or unsatisfactory citizens. Social movements show up the way in which "individual" citizenship rights are actually those of a particular social group by explicitly demanding different rights for different groups. This is especially the case with regard to some demands for rights for women and multi-cultural rights for ethnic minority groups. Claims on behalf of lesbians and gay men tend to be for the rights already enjoyed by heterosexuals, although they are made on behalf of homosexuals as a minority group and they do displace "normality."

However, claims for group-differentiated rights themselves risk the production of "Otherness." The identities and positions represented by social movements are not homogeneous. It is impossible, for example, to simply be a woman; one is always also socially positioned in terms of a particular ethnic background, sexual orientation, marital status, occupation, age, geographical location, and so on. Furthermore, contemporary society changes fast, partly as a result of the activities of social movements themselves. Social groups contain within them, therefore, a range of more or less traditional or "de-traditionalized" identities. This is evident, for example, where young people have been brought up in a society that is quite different from that of their parents – whether as a result of migration or simply of social change. The heterogeneity and fluidity of social identities is very important to a consideration of citizenship rights intended to promote more progressive and egalitarian ideals. The difficulty is – how can more inclusive sets of citizenship rights be achieved which do not privilege certain identities over others, nor constrain the development of new ways life? We shall discuss these issues in relation to sex and sexuality in section 4.2, and "race" and ethnicity in section 4.3.

The lack of interest in class and the concern with "difference" of the "postmodern turn" in sociological studies of citizenship need not lead to a neglect of gross inequalities of wealth and poverty, though it is true that they have not been as central as they once were. In fact, as we shall see in section four when we look at citizenship and poverty, it is not well understood in terms of class. The majority of those in "the underclass" or who are "socially excluded" are women and men from racialized minority groups, so that the production of "Otherness" is relevant in this case too. Furthermore, the terms used to categorize the poor and define poverty are both highly contentious and effective in structuring flows of power and resources. They are, therefore, an object of cultural politics and should be an important topic in the new political sociology.

The study of globalization is beginning to have an impact on sociological analyses of citizenship. Marshall's model of citizenship is again exemplary of traditional sociological concerns in that he treats it as one of the chief ordering features of a capitalist society clearly occupying a given territory and organized around a nation-state. In accordance with this conventional understanding, he supposed cultural homogeneity among the citizens of the nation. In fact, the ideal of the nation-state as consisting of a singular, unified, and self-determining nation has rarely been realized historically; there have almost always been large cultural minorities in nation-states. With the extensive labor migrations into the West in the late twentieth century, however, the discrepancy between ideal and reality has become ever more apparent. Citizenship is now being considered as multi-cultural and post-national as a way of ensuring rights for migrants and other minorities within states. We shall look at these issues in section 4.3, on multinational citizenship rights, and in section 4.5, on post-national citizenship rights.

Finally, the issue of state sovereignty, and the possibility of guaranteeing citizenship rights at all, comes into question where economic, social, political, and environmental processes cannot be controlled at the level of individual states. Again, changes are already beginning to take place in citizenship itself as a result of such processes. The recent creation of citizens of the European Union is an example. At the same time, new ideals of citizenship as global rather than national are also emerging, most notably in work informed by the concerns of the environmental movement. We shall look at both these dimensions of global citizenship in section 4.5. Global citizenship is no more than an aspiration, but as an ideal it is perhaps closer to being realized in contemporary society than at any other moment in history.

4.1   T. H. MARSHALL: CITIZENSHIP, SOCIAL CLASS, AND THE NATION-STATE

The classic starting point for a discussion of citizenship is the historical-sociological analysis of Thomas Humphrey Marshall. It is very much a product of its time and place, written at the peak of optimism concerning the post-war welfare state in Britain, and it is therefore of limited relevance for an understanding of contemporary society. Nevertheless, the analytic framework Marshall provides, in which citizenship is seen as comprising civil, political, and social rights, is useful and widely adopted. Furthermore, a number of the deficiencies of Marshall's model clearly illustrate the directions in which the new political sociology of citizenship has developed in relation to the cultural politics of social movements and processes of globalization.

Marshall analyzes citizenship as consisting of three types of rights: civil, political, and social. Civil rights involve the protection of individual freedoms, including "liberty of the person, freedom of speech, thought and faith, the right to own property and to conclude valid contracts, and the right to justice" (Marshall, 1992: 8). Associated with the modern institutions of the civil and criminal courts of justice, Marshall sees civil rights as developing in the eighteenth century. Political rights involve the right to "participate in the exercise of political power as a member of a body invested with political authority or as an elector of the members of such a body" (1992: 8). Already existing for some, according to Marshall, they became citizenship rights only in the twentieth century with the extension of universal suffrage to all adults. This established the principle that they depend on personal status rather than on economic means. In terms of institutions, they involve the development of parliament and the councils of local government formed in the nineteenth century. Social rights Marshall sees as developing in the twentieth century in their modern form, with the institutions of the welfare state, including the national system of compulsory education and those of health and social services. Marshall's definition of social rights is more abstract than his definition of civil and political rights, reflecting the wide view he takes of them:

> By the social element I mean the whole range from the right to share in a modicum of economic welfare and security to the right to share to the full in the social heritage and to live the life of a civilised being according to the standards prevailing in the society. (1992: 8)

Marshall linked the historical development of citizenship to the development of capitalism. In particular, he was interested in the coincidental development of citizenship rights as a system of *equality* with capitalism as a system of *inequality*. In conjunction with civil and political rights, he saw the slow development of social rights as contributing to the development of a parallel system of substantive equality which mitigates, and is in contradiction to, the economic inequalities of capitalism. As Marshall (1992: 33) puts it:

The extension of the social services is not primarily a means of equal-
ising incomes . . . What matters is that there is a general enrichment
of the concrete substance of civilised life, a general reduction of risk
and insecurity, an equalisation between the more and the less fortu-
nate at all levels – between the healthy and the sick, the employed and
the unemployed, the old and the active, the bachelor and the father
of a large family. Equalisation is not so much between classes as
between individuals within a population which is now treated for this
purpose as though it were one class. Equality of status is more important than equality of income.

Although the only existing inequalities Marshall pays attention to
are class inequalities, at the same time it is clear from his understanding of the inter-relationship of capitalism and citizenship rights
that he actually sees class conflict displaced with the development of
citizenship. In fact, Marshall goes so far as to predict that citizens
will become less interested in earning high wages, not only because
of high levels of taxes in a welfare state, but because money will itself
become less relevant where the essentials of life – including pensions,
unemployment benefit, good education, health care, and so on – are
provided equally, by right, to all citizens (1992: 47–8).

The details of Marshall's prediction have not been borne out, but
arguably the development of citizenship rights is one of the factors
that has contributed to the decline of class politics. Citizens orient
their political struggles and claims for greater equality toward the
state, while workers' struggles with employers have become less
important. Of course, class inequalities in welfare provision could
have remained the main object of citizens' concern, as they were in
Marshall's time, but in fact this has not been the case. It is not only
that class struggles at the economic level have been displaced by
the system of status equality constructed in terms of citizenship
rights which Marshall analyzed; it is also that class is no longer the
principal identity around which demands for greater equality are
organized.

Limits of Marshall's account of citizenship

There are several problems frequently identified with Marshall's
account which are relevant to our consideration of citizenship in

relation to the cultural politics of social movements and the consequences of globalization. We will deal explicitly with these topics in
following sections, but for the moment we will look at the deficiencies of Marshall's theory of citizenship more generally.

First, Marshall's model is criticized for the way in which it tends
to ignore politics. It is argued, notably by Anthony Giddens, that
Marshall's treatment of the extension of citizenship rights is implicitly evolutionist: it is as if there is a natural progression from civil to
political to social rights as part of the development of modern industrial society. Giddens argues that Marshall fails to give enough
consideration to how each of the three sets of rights has only been
achieved after protracted struggle (Giddens, 1982: 171). Not all
commentators on Marshall's work agree with Giddens. As Barbalet
(1988) notes, some actually take quite the opposite view, arguing
that Marshall's model shows how citizenship rights are extended
through conflict. Such divergent understandings stem in large part
from Marshall's own ambivalence on the question. He is certainly
much more interested in the sequence of development of citizenship
rights than in how this development has been achieved, and he gives
an unresolved and even contradictory account of it. In *Citizenship
and Social Class*, he says that the growth of citizenship "is stimulated both by the struggle to win those rights and by their enjoyment
when won," but then almost immediately goes on to say that "the
familiar instruments of modern democracy were fashioned by the
upper classes and then handed down, step by step, to the lower"
(Marshall, 1992: 24–5). Barbalet's interpretation seems the most reasonable: although Marshall does speak of conflict, what he means
by it is the conflict of principles between capitalism as a system
dependent on inequality and citizenship as a system of equality rather
than struggles between actual social groups. Barbalet argues that it
is not possible to judge from Marshall's sparse comments on the issue
whether he saw the working out of this conflict as a matter of
bargaining and conciliation or of struggle and violence. However, as
he notes, an emphasis on the development of new sets of rights
out of existing ones, combined with Marshall's lack of interest in
the actual conditions of their development, does incline his model
toward evolutionism (Barbalet, 1988: 30–1).

From Marshall's point of view, on the crest of the wave of post-
war welfare state creation in Britain, evolutionism would presumably not have seemed as inadequate as it does to most sociologists

in these less expansive times. In the wake of neo-liberalism, citizenship rights have been withdrawn as the welfare state "retreats." From our vantage point in the late twentieth century, it is clear that citizenship rights are an important object of cultural politics. Continually contested, they can never be finally secured and they certainly do not develop according to an inherent logic. In particular, they are what is at stake in many of the ongoing struggles between the New Right, especially in countries like Britain and the United States where it has been in government, and the variety of social movements which have been attempting to extend or protect citizenship rights.

The implicit evolutionism of Marshall's account is linked to another problem: its implicit universalism as an account of the development of citizenship rights in all countries. Marshall's history of the development of citizenship rights is a description of British society. However, he is at the same time proposing a general model of the development of the relation between citizenship and class in capitalist societies. It is implicit, therefore, that the British case is not unique, but representative of all capitalist societies. As a number of sociologists have pointed out, this is an unwarranted assumption which is not borne out by the development of citizenship in other countries. In the case of the US, for example, Michael Mann argues that because political rights were granted to the working class much earlier than in Britain, before the labor movement was strong enough to offer a real challenge to the ruling class, workers formed interest groups within the political constitution and party system. As a result, social rights remained undeveloped. As Mann puts it, "The most powerful capitalist state has not followed Marshall's road. It shows no signs of doing so" (Mann, 1996: 131).

From the point of view of social movements, there is a still more important aspect of Marshall's universalism: he assumes that citizenship rights within a society are themselves universal, that all citizens are equal as individuals. Probably the most theoretically elaborated challenge to this view has come from feminists. It is not that Marshall ignores the differences between the sexes altogether; in his account of the historical development of rights he does mention the way in which women's citizenship advanced at a slower rate than men's – in relation to winning the vote, for example. However, as Sylvia Walby (1994) has argued, Marshall's analysis of citizenship rights is so imbued with gender-specific assumptions that he fails to notice that the development of women's rights has actually followed quite a different trajectory from men's, even in the British case. As an example, she points out that women had very few civil rights until they were gained as part of the wider struggle for political rights in the nineteenth and early twentieth centuries: the right to own property, to professional employment, not to be beaten by a husband, to terminate a marriage, and so on. Some were not won until after political rights, thus reversing the development Marshall proposes for all citizens. Furthermore, Walby (1994) argues that some have still not been won today; the right to abortion, for example, she sees as the right of control over one's own body. Such cases are necessarily ignored by a model of citizenship which takes men as the norm and assumes that all citizens are alike. Similar points may be made in relation to all those who do not conform to this norm. A striking example is the black civil rights movement in the US, campaigning for freedom of the person, equality before the law, and economic freedom for Southern blacks about a hundred years after they had been formally accorded American citizenship with the ending of slavery (Morris, 1993). It is arguable that the lack of seriousness with which the judicial system treats racial harassment means that black citizens still do not have freedom of the person. We will look at the issue of the exclusion of different social groups from citizenship rights in detail in the next section. For the moment, it is important to note that on Marshall's model the question of differences between citizens does not arise.

Finally, Marshall's model is often seen as problematic now because of the way in which he limited his view to the nation-state. For the most part, this criticism is aimed at his economic theory. It is argued that he failed to consider how far the social rights he celebrated were dependent on the expansionary post-war economy. In fact, although Marshall himself saw citizenship and capitalism as conflicting, he was optimistic about their compatibility. In the light of the long recession since the 1970s, however, this conflict seems much more serious. State investment in welfare is now seen to be problematic because it undermines private profitability by high levels of taxation. Economic globalization adds a further dimension to the problem: in order to create a buoyant national economy, governments may need to offer incentives to attract multinational companies and so keep rates of business tax, and even wages, as low as possible. Clearly, this economic argument is an important element of the neo-liberal critique of the welfare state and as such it is open to challenge, but many sociologists are also pessimistic about the compatibility of capitalism and citizenship in this respect (Turner, 1986). It is necessary, therefore, to give more consideration to the issue than Marshall does. It may be that economic globalization means that citizenship, and in particular political and social rights, can no longer be secured by the nation-state, but require international and even supranational regulation.

4.2 CITIZENSHIP, SEX, AND SEXUALITY

The women's movement and the gay and lesbian movement have been among the most prominent of social movements contesting the traditional model of citizenship rights and trying to work out more inclusive models. Although, as social movements, they developed quite separately, the issues they raise are analytically linked. Both women's citizenship and rights in relation to homosexuality problematize traditional roles for the sexes and demonstrate how existing citizenship, far from affording rights to individuals as such, depends on the position people occupy in relation to the nuclear family.

The women's movement

The most important point of the recent feminist critique of liberal citizenship is that, developed from a male perspective, it has institutionalized a male norm. Contemporary feminists see women as incorporated into liberal democracy in a paradoxical and unjust way. As a result, they are continually faced with what is known as "the sameness–difference" dilemma. Should the women's movement focus on rights for women to be treated the same as men or on gender-specific rights, enabling women's differences from men to be valued and taken into account as the means of gaining genuine equality between the sexes?

As it is, there are three, quite contradictory ways in which women are excluded from full citizenship rights. First, women are discriminated against when they should have the same rights as men. Secondly, on the other hand, they are treated the same as men when only differential treatment would make genuine equality possible. In such cases, physical and historical differences are ignored which prevent women from actually participating in institutions and practices developed to suit men, even though they have the formal rights to do so. Thirdly, however, some citizenship rights, notably social rights, are accorded differently to women and men, and in such cases women are treated as inferior citizens. As feminists see it, the paradoxes and inconsistencies of women's citizenship are linked to the way in which they have developed secondarily to men's. Historically, until very recently, citizens have been male heads of households and women's citizenship has developed within the framework set by rights developed on this basis.

The first and second cases are exemplified by civil rights. In the past, feminists have put a good deal of energy into campaigns for equal rights for women to be treated as identical to men, to remove the barriers to women's participation in public life and to try to ensure their protection in the private sphere. In the US in particular, many feminists continue to see equal rights as the most important aim of the women's movement. An example is maternity rights. Until the 1960s, many American employers had rules which compelled a pregnant woman to leave her job at a set time and forbidding her to return to work before a certain date. Maternity leave with pay was not provided and the right to return to work was not guaranteed. The initial impetus of feminist campaigns was to overturn such rules as discriminating against women. In the 1970s, they were found to be unconstitutional on the grounds that they infringed freedom of personal choice; it was decided that women should not *have* to go on maternity leave when pregnant. The current situation is that employers are bound to treat pregnancy and maternity no less favorably than any other illness or disability, states of ill health which may also be suffered by men. Many feminists see this as unsatisfactory: pregnancy is specific to women and to describe it in such terms in order to make it gender-neutral is to capitulate to the male norm. Furthermore, in most states, paid maternity leave is covered only by insurance schemes which employers are under no obligation to provide, so that women who get pregnant are being discriminated against as women. However, "equal rights" feminists support the ruling, against "difference" feminists, on the grounds that to insist on special treatment for women would prevent them competing on equal terms in the labor market and force them into economic dependence on men (Bacchi, 1990: ch. 5).

As Bacchi (1990) argues, the position of "equal rights" feminists in the US often seems extreme to feminists elsewhere. To a large extent it is due to a lack of social rights; where women have a statutory right to paid maternity leave the same problems do not arise. In such countries, the "difference" feminist position is much less risky for women, and it has become increasingly important. Feminists are now concerned that treating men and women as the same in law is ineffective as a means of realizing real equality between the sexes. The anti-discrimination rights gained in Europe and North America in the 1960s and 1970s, for example, now tend to be seen as ineffective precisely because they fail to take into account women's particular embodiment and the way in which their historically specific circumstances differ from those of men. Equal pay legislation, for example, which stated that all workers should get equal pay for doing the same jobs, was of little use because men and women tend to do different kinds of jobs. In the British case, the European Court of Justice ruled against this law and it has now been changed: comparison must now be made between work of equal *value*. However, it remains the case that the basis of comparison is the male norm in so far as women must show the work they do to be of equal value to the better-paid work done by men. Unsurprisingly, perhaps, the job evaluation surveys on which judgments of equal worth are based generally reproduce the undervaluation of women's work which already exists in society (Frazer and Lacey, 1993: 86).

The third case is exemplified by gender-differentiated social rights. Women are disproportionately represented in all welfare states, both as beneficiaries and also as workers in the health, social, and education services. Because they have less access than men to market-provided services, women are more often dependent on welfare than men. However, the benefits women receive, and the jobs they do, are different from men's. Benefits are two-tiered in all systems: one tier consists of benefits to which citizens are entitled by virtue of insurance contributions paid on the basis of waged work; men are predominantly entitled to this type of benefit. The other consists of benefits which are not directly paid for by insurance contributions and these are predominantly received by women. They include benefits to which citizens are entitled by virtue of being the dependants of insurees, means-tested benefits for those in poverty and, in rare cases, benefits paid to those who have the main responsibility for the care of children or others who cannot care for themselves in the home. The type of welfare benefits which have greatest legitimacy and financial value are those received through work-related insurance; the other type is somewhat stigmatized, since it may be seen as unearned, and involves lower sums of money (Walby, 1994).

According to feminists, women's inferior social rights are again the consequence of taking men as the norm. Social rights are linked to a male norm of continuous, full-time employment in the labor market, interrupted only by the unfortunate accidents against which the worker insures himself. However, this type of work depends on unseen and unpaid work in the domestic sphere, mainly done by women. The work of wives and mothers is unrecognized by the welfare state, since the sexual division of labor is treated as natural. Citizenship in contemporary society is premised on a model of the family as consisting of a male breadwinner and a female who cares for the children and the home. In actual fact, relatively few households now conform to this model. Some of the growth in poverty in recent times is, of course, related to the growth in male unemployment: to a large extent men also now receive inferior, means-tested benefits. However, much is related to what is sometimes called "the feminization of poverty," the way in which many women, no longer dependent on men but unable to participate fully in a labor market constructed for male breadwinners, have to rely on the small amounts of money the state allows them. This is particularly the case for single parents, usually women, who cannot afford child-care, and older women who often do not have occupational pensions and who have outlived or separated from their husbands (Pierson, 1991: 73–5).

Feminists have linked women's inferior social rights to their inferior political rights. Women, it is argued, have less power in society than men. It is for this reason that some feminists argue that the welfare state is patriarchal. A number of Scandinavian feminists in particular, writing in a context in which social rights for women are more extensive than anywhere else in the world, have argued that women's inferior citizenship is due to their lack of decision-making power, both within welfare institutions themselves and also in the institutions of representational government. Although women are employed in large numbers in the public sector, they occupy positions similar to those they occupy in the private sector, low in the bureaucratic hierarchies, so that they do not make decisions about how institutions are organized. It is also argued that, although women have the same formal political rights as men to vote and to stand for election, in practice very few women participate in "high politics." This is seen as due to straightforward discrimination, on the part of political parties who propose members for election and of electors themselves, and also to the fact that it requires long hours which are incompatible with women's domestic responsibilities. It is argued, therefore, that although good social rights are valuable in allowing women to escape subordination from individual men in the home, if women then become dependent on a state over which they have no control, they have done little more than exchange private patriarchy for public patriarchy (Hernes, 1984; Siim, 1988).

In recent years, then, the focus of the women's movement has been on political rights, both on the part of feminist theorists and movement activists. This represents a significant shift on the part of the second-wave feminist movement which, unlike that of the nineteenth century, has been rather suspicious of the state. The movement has been dominated by socialist and radical feminists who have tended to see the state in functionalist terms as reproductive of capitalism and patriarchy, and who have preferred to direct their activities elsewhere. In many respects, this strategy has proved very fruitful. The success of the slogan "the personal is political" is indicative of the politicizing of subjectivity and personal relations, for example, and many of the institutions set up by the movement, such as the centers dealing with rape and domestic violence, have had a significant impact on perceptions and practices. Arguably, as we saw in chapter 3, these forms of politics are as important to women's citizenship as formal rights to political participation. It has, of course, also been the case that some second-wave feminists have been engaged with issues of law and public policy, often working through trade unions in Europe, or through interest groups such as the National Organization for Women in the United States. It is, however, relatively recently that the issue of women's representation as such has been raised.

The discussion of political rights for women, however, exemplifies another prominent dilemma in recent feminist thought and action: that raised by the issue of essentialism. It is useful to distinguish two different types of essentialism used in this debate. Following Diana Fuss (1989), the first may be identified as "real essentialism." Derived from Aristotle, it indicates that the essence of something or someone is what is irreducible and unchangeable about it or them. It is also the most common use of the term in feminist theory. It is used to describe the belief that women are intrinsically and unalterably different from men. The most obvious difference in this respect is in reproductive capacities and there is considerable discussion concerning the intrinsic importance of this aspect of sexual difference. However, the term is also applied – pejoratively – to those who agree with Carol Gilligan (1993) that women have a "different voice" from men in relation to moral issues: context specific and relationship oriented rather than based on adherence to universal moral principles. The second use Fuss calls "nominal essentialism." The essence of someone or something here consists in what remains the same across the different uses of a term, a classification made in language. She argues that social constructionists, those who take as their starting point the anti-essentialist view that there are no intrinsic differences between women and men, may also be nominal essentialists. They focus on historically and socially specific differences between the sexes, on "the production and organization of differences" (Fuss, 1989: 2). In relation to reproductive capacities, for example, they argue that what is important is the way in which perceived differences are used to make a *social* difference between the sexes as stereotypical mothers and fathers of children. Furthermore, social constructionists contend that there are social differences between women in this respect which are as important as those between men and women. Linda Nicholson (1983), for example, discusses how white women in nineteenth-century America were excluded from public activities and confined to the home in order to maximize their capacities to bear children, while, as soon as they were no longer commodities to be bought and sold, black children were much less valued and black women were socially positioned as menial workers. As a result, she argues, the orientation toward care analyzed by Gilligan as specific to women would more appropriately be applied to white women in a particular, historically specific situation; women *as such* do not have a "different voice," since women do not speak with a single voice at all (Nicholson, 1983). Nevertheless, as Fuss argues, although social constructionists oppose real essentialism, the perspective retains a degree of – unacknowledged – nominal essentialism in so far as they continue to classify the world as divided into "men" and "women." As she puts it, "Some minimal point of commonality and continuity necessitates at least the linguistic retention of these particular terms" (Fuss, 1989: 4). Although "women" are treated as a heterogeneous social group, rather than as a "natural kind," there is nevertheless the assumption that such a group can, and should, be seen as sociologically relevant.

The importance of Fuss's distinction becomes evident when we look at the issue of political rights. It has recently been argued by feminists that, given the under-representation of women in political institutions, women need special rights in order to achieve equality with men in this respect. Anne Phillips, one of the most prominent proponents of this view, puts forward the widely accepted argument that there should be quotas to increase women's presence in the political process in order to enable them to influence policies affecting women (Phillips, 1991, 1995). Phillips actually explicitly rejects essentialism on the grounds that women are not all the same and do not share the same interests. Furthermore, her argument is not that women in political institutions should be seen as *representing* women. As she points out, representation in liberal democracies is based on geographical area or, in the case of proportional representation, on promises of action, not on the direct representation of social groups. In fact, such representation is impossible if the category "women" is seen in pluralist terms, as a heterogenous group of cross-cutting and even conflicting identities: speaking in the name of "women" could only mean favoring some and excluding others. Nevertheless, her most compelling argument for the presence of women in the political process is that women share certain experiences so that they will articulate views which would not otherwise be heard. This argument makes little sense without the assumption that women share a certain perspective which makes them different from men, even though Phillips qualifies her argument by saying that there are no guarantees that this is the case (Nash, 1997). She is, then, arguing for special political rights for women on the grounds that there *may* be a real, though not necessarily natural, difference between the sexes.

The essentialist assumptions of Phillips's argument for political rights are clear in contrast to the more resolutely anti-essentialist position of Judith Butler (1993). In her view, *any* use of the term "women" to designate a social group is misguided. In terms of the distinction articulated by Fuss, she argues against real *and* nominalist essentialism. Butler maintains that "women" does not exist outside performances which bring the identity into practice. Any representation of women as an existing social group, in feminist debates and in the campaigns of the women's movement, just as much as in more obviously repressive instances of the use of the term, is actually productive of that categorization rather than the representation of a given reality. Butler is very much influenced by Foucault, and her arguments are close to those of the discourse theorists we looked at in chapter 1. She distances herself from discourse theory, preferring to think of identities as produced in "performance" – in embodied social practices – rather than in "discourse" with its linguistic connotations, but in taking practices rather than language as the object of analysis she adopts a similar perspective to that of the self-identified discourse theorists, Laclau and Mouffe (Butler, 1993).

According to Butler, the reification and regulation of gender relations produced in discourse are precisely what feminists should militate against. Far from arguing for political rights for women, since "the feminist subject turns out to be discursively constituted by the very political system that is supposed to facilitate its emancipation . . . an uncritical appeal to such a system for the emancipation of 'women' will be clearly self-defeating" (Butler, 1990: 2). Feminists should be concerned rather to disrupt and problematize the use of the term "women" wherever possible in order to overturn the "heterosexist matrix" which requires the duality of the sexes. Butler's work has been as influential in queer theory as in feminist theory and we will return to this point in the following section. For the moment, however, it is important to note that, for Butler, and for other post-structuralist feminists, the invocation of "women" for political purposes makes such a goal impossible. It contributes to the rigidity of the sexual division by foreclosing in advance the emergence of new identities which could transform or expand existing sexual differences. In this way, feminism is part of the problem because it contributes to the reification of sexual difference rather than to the dissolution of the problem itself.

Phillips's proposals and Butler's arguments against any feminist representation of women as a social group illustrate the polarity of feminist views in the current debates on essentialism. There is no obvious resolution to the conflict. However, in practical terms, it is also the case that the women's movement is, and arguably always has been, involved in politics of both kinds. Not only in Scandinavia but in other liberal democracies like Britain there have been campaigns for quotas for women MPs, for example. At the same time, there has been continual resistance on the part of women to be subsumed under a particular categorization of "women." This resistance may sometimes result in demands for rights to "sameness," but if this is done in a context in which there are institutional structures allowing for differences between the sexes in specific contexts – such as the right to maternity leave, for example – while there may be a tension between the two strategies, they are not necessarily incompatible. Group rights for women may be necessary in specific cases, but it is also necessary to disrupt assumptions about how individual women live as individuals who happen also to be identified as women. Otherwise group rights will "freeze" identities and prove too constraining, both for those who do not easily fit the group identities available, and also in terms of the wider social change for which the women's movement has always aimed (Riley, 1988; Nash, 1998a).

The gay and lesbian movement and queer politics

There is an obvious connection between campaigns for rights for women and rights for sexual minorities in so far as both challenge the way in which citizenship has historically been rooted in patriarchy. Both the feminist movement and the lesbian and gay movement demand rights for individuals to live on equal terms outside the traditional nuclear family which has structured citizenship rights in the past. It might be expected, therefore, that feminists and lesbians and gay men would have a common cause against "compulsory heterosexuality" which relegates those who do not conform to inferior citizenship rights. However, although both movements have used the term to analyze society, in practice the relationships between the three groups have been much more complex. There have been conflicts between gay men and radical feminists who have opposed what they take to be a masculine, libertarian lifestyle; gay men and lesbians, who often have very different lifestyles and sexual practices; and between "political lesbians," who see themselves as the vanguard of feminism, and other lesbians, who may or may not be feminists and who resist the de-sexualizing of lesbianism by political lesbians (Edwards, 1994). These differences have meant that it has generally proved impossible to present a united front. In recent years, however, feminists and those who identify as "queer" have come together to some extent, at least theoretically. Paradoxically, however, what makes it possible for individuals to unite under the "queer" banner is the way that queer politics challenges the very identities on which the older movements were based.

The struggle for gay citizenship rights began in the 1960s, alongside other social movements of the time. The gay liberation movement was founded in the United States in 1969, following the Stonewall riot, in which the regulars of a gay bar in New York fought back after years of being raided by the police. Similar movements were established a little later in most Western European countries. Proposing a revolutionary anti-capitalist, anti-family, and anti-medical analysis of gay oppression, the movement was short-lived and soon gave way to more moderate organizations campaigning for reform. Campaigns for the extension of citizenship rights enjoyed by the majority to be extended to sexual minorities began to be well supported (Evans, 1993: 114–17; Weeks, 1993a: 198). Lesbians, often involved in the initial impetus of the gay liberation movement, were less involved in the campaigns for legal rights and against police harassment which became the main themes of the gay movement. Historically, lesbians have suffered more from invisibility than from legal repression, since lesbianism has never been illegal, though it has been stigmatized. They have, however, participated in the important cultural politics of the movement which have made gay and lesbian lifestyles visible and viable. There is no doubt of its success in this respect. Every city now has gay bars, many have a gay neighborhood, and the impact of the movement on the media, popular culture, and fashion is evident everywhere. "Lipstick" lesbianism, in particular, has been seen as contributing to the recent fashion for gay images. However, with less disposable income than men, women have not been able to exert "consumer power" to the same extent as men and lesbians tend to be less visible in commercial spaces too.

In terms of citizenship rights, for the most part the gay movement has focused on equalizing civil rights between heterosexuals, gay men, and lesbians (to the extent that they share the same legal interests). The age of consent to sex, different everywhere but consistently higher for gay men in most countries until recently, has been targeted as blatantly discriminatory. Following a European Union ruling against Britain in 1997 the age of consent is now equal in most countries of Europe. In the US it varies across different states. There have been campaigns to legalize gay marriages. The refusal to recognize gay partnerships in law is particularly problematic because so many rights and benefits still depend on marriage in contemporary society. Gay partners continue to be denied immigration rights, pension benefits, and tax breaks. Nor can they adopt children since only married couples may adopt jointly. Scandinavian countries are the only ones in which same-sex partnerships with the legal weight of marriage are possible. Another continuing injustice is employment rights. In Britain and elsewhere, there are no laws protecting against discrimination for sexual orientation. This leaves gays open to hiring and firing discrimination, harassment or unequal pay and dismissal for reasons of sexual orientation. In the US this issue has recently come to the fore with the question of whether gay men and lesbians should be allowed to serve in the armed forces. The highly unsatisfactory solution of "don't ask, don't tell," while admitting that there are gays and lesbians in the military, gives them no legal rights should they ever publicly affirm their sexuality. Finally, among the most serious cases of the continuing exclusion of gay men from civil rights is the harassment by the police to which they are subject, and the failure of the police to protect them from harassment and violence by other men. There are laws, for example, to which only gay men are subject, although they are supposed to be applicable to all citizens, regardless of sexual orientation. Only gay men, for example, are prosecuted for sodomy, as an "indecent act."

Andrew Sullivan (1995) neatly summarizes arguments for equal citizenship rights for lesbians and gays. It would mean, he argues, quite simply extending the same civil rights to homosexuals as those enjoyed by other citizens:

an end to all proactive discrimination by the state against homosexuals. That means an end to sodomy laws that apply only to homosexuals; a recourse to the courts if there is not equal protection of
heterosexuals and homosexuals in law enforcement; an equal legal age
of consent to sexual activity for heterosexuals and homosexuals,
where such regulations apply; inclusion of the facts about homosexuality in the curriculum of every government-funded school . . . ;
recourse to the courts if any government body or agency can be proven
to be engaged in discrimination against homosexual employees; equal
opportunity and inclusion in the military; and legal homosexual marriage and divorce. (Sullivan, 1995: 171–2).

It is probable that no gay activist would disagree with such a list
of rights. However, there is considerable debate about the compatibility of campaigning for citizenship rights with other, potentially
more radical, aims to which the gay and lesbian movement might,
and arguably should, aspire. Again, as in the case of the women's
movement, the question turns on the issue of essentialism.

The problem is that in order to gain citizenship rights, gays and
lesbians have, quite reasonably, adopted the strategy of describing
themselves as a "sexual minority." This is seen as the only realistic
way to gain a hearing for the extension of citizenship rights in liberal
democracy. They are claimed as "minority rights," to be granted to
those who are not responsible for their sexual orientation and who
should not, therefore, be persecuted and oppressed for it. This strategy depends, then, on the essentialist view that homosexuality is an
innate disposition. It fits with the conservative, medicalized view of
gays and lesbians as born, not made. Although this is certainly the
belief of most self-identified gays and lesbians, it is at odds with the
arguments of sociologists on the topic. They are much more likely
to see homosexuality, like heterosexuality, as a historically and
culturally specific identity rather than an innate disposition: we learn
to see ourselves as having a "sexuality" only when such a view is
socially available (Weeks, 1986). This anti-essentialist view is also
more likely to be held by the younger generation of "queer" activists,
who reject the fixity of the "sexual minority" claim in favor of a
more disruptive challenge to the status quo.

From a queer perspective, claims for "minority rights" actually
contribute to the dominance of an understanding of different
sexualities as "normal" or "abnormal." This means that, at best,
gays and lesbians can only ever be tolerated, since they will always

be the abnormal minority (Herman, 1993: 251). What queer activists agitate for is rather the disruption of all fixed identities: lesbian, gay, bisexual, transsexual, and "still searching." This challenge extends to the naturalized links between reproductive capacities, gender identity, and sexual desire prescribed as normal by "the heterosexist matrix" in which masculine males must desire feminine females and vice versa. Queer practices may disrupt, as Judith Butler (1990) argues, by parodying and subverting gendered sexual identities, showing that they are not the expression of innate, natural tendencies but are nothing but performances. To quote a letter from a debate in the San Francisco *Bay Times*, "There is a growing consciousness that a person's sexual identity (and gender identity) need not be etched in stone, that it can be fluid rather than static, that one has the right to PLAY with whomever one wishes to play with (as long as it's consensual), that the either/or dichotomy ('you're either gay or straight' is only one example of this) is oppressive no matter who's pushing it" (quoted in Gamson, 1996: 406).

In practice, queer activism is associated with "in your face" demonstrations such as "kiss-ins" which "mimic the privileges of normality" (Berlant and Freeman, quoted in Gamson, 1996: 409), the return of camp styles and other forms of irony, "mixed" venues for men and women, and "gender-fuck" aesthetics like the photography of Della Grace in which lesbians are shown using the paraphernalia of gay male desire (sometimes even including facial hair) (Mort, 1994). Older self-identified gays and lesbians who find "queer" problematic are concerned about the blurring of boundaries it promotes. The inclusion of bisexuals, transsexuals, and even heterosexuals who feel confined by conventional sexual expression, as "queer" removes the solid political ground they have struggled to mark out as a minority, and which provides the basis from which rights claims are made. This is indeed a problem as liberal democracy accords right to groups only if their membership is clear. A recent judgment in Colorado, for example, found that there was no case for outlawing discrimination against gay men, lesbians, or bisexuals since "We don't have a group that is easily confinable" (the Colorado solicitor-general, quoted in Gamson, 1996: 410).

As Steven Seidman (1993: 132) has argued, anti-essentialist queer activists tend to see identity itself as the main axis of domination.

This is problematic in so far as the assertion of collective identity is necessary to militate against institutional forms which exclude lesbians and gays from full citizenship, so perpetuating violence and injustice. In this sense, the conflict between essentialist and anti-essentialist strategies is similar in the case of feminist and queer politics. However, it is not so easy to see how the two strategies can be reconciled in practice. If, as Sullivan (1995) argues, equal citizenship for lesbians and gays requires nothing more in principle than the extension of existing rights to all individuals, it is not clear that this commits those individuals as individuals to any particular sexual identity indefinitely. It is clear, then, that it is possible to affirm the stable identities with secure boundaries the political system requires, without individuals necessarily feeling bound by such identities. However, it is also clear that the public disruption of fixed identities is problematic so long as citizenship rights have not been extended to gays and lesbians. So while both strategies are currently being pursued in practice, given the dangers each one presents for the other, the outcome is far from assured.

4.3   CITIZENSHIP, "RACE," AND ETHNICITY

The themes of exclusion and inclusion in relation to a citizenship model premised on a white male norm are continued in debates around citizenship, "race," and ethnicity. In these debates, however, the social identities in question are highly contested and the very terms used to discuss the issues are controversial in contemporary society.

In this text, and commonly elsewhere, "race" is in "scare quotes" because it is so closely implicated in racism. Developed in a quasi-scientific biological discourse in the nineteenth century, it referred to different species of persons, hierarchically ordered as naturally superior and inferior. This use of the term is now discredited. It is generally held, among sociologists and biologists at any rate, that humans are of the same genetic stock and that there is a continuum of individuals in terms of any of the features used to distinguish them – color, size, intelligence, and so on – rather than distinct groups which exist as "natural kinds." Nevertheless, claims about "race" are still used to distinguish people in social life more widely. It is therefore important to study how individuals are assigned to different "races" and the inequalities which are produced as a result. The difficulty then becomes how to avoid confusing the concept "race" with its referent while studying groups distinguished in this way. A common solution for sociologists is to think in terms of "racialized" groups, to which characteristics are socially attributed on the grounds of race. It is then possible to examine differences between groups of citizens in terms of common social position and treatment, without supposing that the individuals who make up such groups actually possess the racial characteristics attributed to them.

The term "ethnicity" is somewhat less commonly used, though its contestation in cultural politics is increasing. Although it is therefore less "dangerous" than "race," the two terms are often closely connected. In Europe, "ethnicity" is used to denote cultural difference but only those groups distinguished by color are normally referred to as "ethnic groups." Italians, Poles, and Ukrainians are rarely designated in this way (Mason, 1995: 15). In this respect, ethnic minorities are racialized groups. In North America, where immigration is much more established as the norm, this is not always the case: it is more common to refer to white people as belonging to ethnic groups. The question of the inter-relation of "race" and ethnicity is further complicated because what is called "new racism" calls for the exclusion of minorities from the nation on the basis of their unassimilable cultural difference, without grounding this in biological difference. At the same time, "ethnicity" is increasingly mobilized in political struggles as a self-descriptive term to represent cultural identity. In many countries, arguments concerning the need for culturally differentiated citizenship rights are now made as the only way in which racialized ethnic minorities can be assured of respect on the part of the majorities with whom they must live.

In this section we will briefly analyze the history of citizenship with regard to "race" and ethnicity, charting in particular the shift from assimilation to differentiated citizenship rights. It is not that the older model of integration is now obsolete. On the contrary, it is still very much favored by policy-makers in some European countries. The point is rather that it now co-exists alongside the demand for group rights in the name of equal respect for all citizens in multicultural societies.

Immigration, assimilation, and "new racism"

"Racial" or ethnic minority groups take many different forms in relation to the majority society of which they form a part. Some societies define themselves as multi-cultural. In India, for example, the
criminal law is uniform, recognizing only individuals, while each religious community is governed by its own civil laws. The Indian
citizen has, then, a kind of dual identity as a member of a religious
community and as an individual (Parekh, 1993). In the West,
however, the mono-cultural nation-state is the dominant model. In
such societies, citizens are supposed to enjoy identical rights as
members of a common national culture. Marshall certainly saw citizenship rights in this way: on one hand, they enable citizens to participate in the common standards of civilization; on the other, they
contribute to social solidarity, unifying the nation in a shared sense
of community (Marshall, 1992). As Will Kymlicka (1995: 236)
points out, Marshall's understanding of citizenship rights is somewhat paradoxical: he sees them not only as fostering a common
culture, but also as presupposing it. In fact, many European countries have always contained large cultural minorities: Bretons in
France, Catalans in Spain, and so on. Some Western European countries, such as Britain, Belgium, and Switzerland, may well be
described as multinational, where "nation" means "a historical community, more or less institutionally complete, occupying a given territory or homeland, sharing a distinct language and culture"
(Kymlicka, 1995: 11). New World nations, such as Australia,
Canada, and the United States, are undoubtedly multi-cultural since
they are made up of immigrants from different cultural and linguistic backgrounds, and, since they all contain native First Nations, they
are multinational too. Despite the fact that it has virtually never been
realized, however, the dominant model of a culturally homogeneous
nation has nevertheless posed problems for the minorities who live
and work in these countries.

In Western Europe the largest, and most visible, minority groups
have resulted from the labor migration which has taken place across
the world since the 1950s. The very issue of whether or not immigrants are entitled to citizenship is linked to the homogenizing
nation-state. There are two ideal-typical ways of attributing citizenship rights at birth. Some states traditionally grant citizenship to all

those born within the state's territory (*jus soli*). Others grant it according to the citizenship of the baby's parents (*jus sanguinis*). In practice, as we shall see, countries now use complicated procedures for granting citizenship, so that these ideal-types are not so clear cut. It is also possible to achieve citizenship as an adult through naturalization. All countries allow naturalization, though some encourage it, while others actively discourage foreigners from applying for citizenship and decisions are discretionary. In all cases, applicants have to prove their commitment to the country of choice. As a minimum this almost always involves real or effective residence in the state's territory (*jus domicili*). Residence in a country is, therefore, a necessary but not a sufficient criterion for full citizenship of that country (Hammar, 1990: 72–7).

European countries differ in their attribution of citizenship according to the model of the relation between nation and state that they embody. Colonialism has also been an important factor in relation to post-war labor migration since many people have come from ex-colonies to the over-developed metropolitan centers. In the British case, those who arrived before 1962 from ex-colonies had the full citizenship rights attributed to all those born on British territory. Since then, however, British citizenship has moved closer to *jus sanguinis* and it is now limited to those with a parent or grandparent born in the country – mostly whites. Immigrants who arrived after the 1970s have a status closer to that of migrant workers in other European countries: short-term contracts as workers and no long-term rights of settlement. Citizenship in France, although still based on *jus soli*, has also become relatively more closed. France has traditionally been a more inclusive nation, with citizenship based on legal rights attributed by the state, particularly in comparison with the more romantic *Volkish* German nation. As in the British case, many early migrants arrived in France from colonies with full citizenship rights, granted as a result of being born on French territory. There are also large numbers of migrant workers from Southern Europe without citizenship rights, however, and, in this respect, it is closer to other European countries than to Britain. Until recently, second-generation migrants were all attributed French citizenship at birth and naturalization was actively encouraged as a policy to assist assimilation and to increase the French population. In recent years, however, rights of automatic citizenship have been brought into question in relation to second-generation Algerians, apparently because of the difficulty of assimilating Muslims into a secular society (Oommen, 1997: 165). In contrast, German citizenship has been traditionally based on *jus sanguinis*. Naturalization is only possible under very strict criteria and, even though policies have been liberalized in recent years, the political culture does not support it. The link between the German nation and the state is not as close as in the French case; traditionally, it is blood rather than the law that makes the German nation. This has led to the anomalous situation in which Eastern Europeans of German descent are legally citizens of the Federal Republic of Germany, while people of Turkish descent born and bred in Germany have to apply for naturalization. Even where this is possible, they must give up their Turkish citizenship in order to become German citizens. Both Germans and immigrants see becoming a German citizen as akin to becoming ethnically German, with the consequence that even second-generation migrants born in Germany often remain foreigners. Combined with the large numbers of refugees it has accepted from Eastern Europe, this means that Germany has the highest proportion of non-nationals in the European Union (Brubaker, 1992).

Citizenship is always more than simply a matter of legal rights. In homogenizing nation-states, it is supposed that to participate fully in the opportunities and benefits to which citizens are entitled it is necessary to be integrated into the national culture. Assimilationism as a "race relations" policy has two inter-related elements. The first is that it has been closely linked to the restrictions on immigration which have been a feature of the recent histories of all European countries. In the words of Roy Hattersley, a British politician, speaking in the 1960s, "Integration without control is impossible, but control without integration is indefensible" (Solomos, 1993: 84). The rationale behind this view is that the national majority will not accept large numbers of immigrants, so that in the interests of racial harmony there must be restrictions. Secondly, the latter half of Hattersley's phrase makes clear the further connection between assimilationism and race relations policies in legislation against racism. Many European countries, though not all, have laws banning discrimination against individuals on the basis of race, color, or ethnic origin. They were passed with the explicit aim of defusing conflicts between white and black and to promote the integration of immigrants into the fundamental institutions of the wider society. However, where such legislation exists, it has not ended racial discrimination, nor the systematic disadvantage suffered by racialized groups (Wrench and Solomos, 1993).

Individuals in racialized minority groups in European countries consistently have inferior rights in comparison with those from the majority groups. Interestingly, the distinction between citizens and migrant workers who are not citizens but who are long-term residents – now the majority of migrant workers – is not as sharp as might have been expected in this respect. Denizens, as these long-term migrants are often called, have virtually all the rights of citizens, except full political rights (Hammar, 1990). We shall look at how this situation has arisen and its consequences for citizenship models organized in terms of the nation-state in section 4.5 below. It is important to note, however, that even where citizens identified as black have identical rights to those seen as white, they are often substantially inferior.

Here we will briefly compare the civil, political, and social rights of black and white people in European countries. Civil rights are guaranteed for all by the rule of law and by human rights conventions signed by nation-states. In effect, however, what this means is that, although all members of racialized minorities have the same formal civil rights as majority citizens, in practice they are not equal. The lack of seriousness with which the police tend to treat racially motivated attacks, and the greater likelihood of black citizens rather than whites being on the receiving end of police brutality, are well documented. Political rights to vote in national elections are not granted to denizens (in The Netherlands and Sweden they may vote in local elections), though they have organized and campaigned through unions and pressure groups and have sometimes achieved quite effective political influence in this way (Hammar: 1990: 137–9). Again, however, there is a discrepancy between formal and substantive rights. Those citizens who are black often feel that their views and interests are under-represented in mainstream political parties. The issue is somewhat complicated by the fact that different minority groups may have few common interests apart from their racialized identification. This is the case in Britain, for example, where Afro-Caribbeans and Asians have quite different priorities (Layton-Henry, 1992). Nevertheless, it is also the case that political parties in Britain have resisted setting up specifically "black sections," fearing a split in the vote. In terms of social rights, denizens and black citizens are similarly placed with regard to the provision of welfare services and social security benefits. The similarity tends to be, however, that of inferiority to white citizens. Although the position of black people in education, housing, and the health services varies according to sex, age, class, geographical location, and so on, it is nevertheless the case that they are consistently subject to poorer provision of welfare services than whites across Europe. This is particularly important because they are also more likely to find themselves unemployed or in low-paid work than whites since they also have an inferior position in the labor market.

The unequal citizenship rights of members of racialized minority groups in Europe are not exclusively a result of racism on the part of the majority population. There are important structural factors at work too. Economic recession and the decline of manufacturing has resulted in job losses in those areas in which male migrant workers were employed, and the location of racialized minorities in decaying inner cities means that they are likely to be exposed to the worst effects of government cuts in welfare spending, including poor educational provision. In the case of older, first-generation immigrants, there may also be difficulties of language (Cross, 1993). Nevertheless, racism is undoubtedly also important. Discrimination is notoriously difficult to identify, but explicitly racist violence has increased in most European countries in the 1980s and 1990s. In some cases it is organized and has been stimulated by the rhetoric of right-wing parties, articulating and reinforcing xenophobia; in other cases it seems to be more closely associated with territoriality and youth culture (Merkl, 1995).

At the very least, then, the assimilationist model of immigration has failed to ensure equal rights for all citizens of the nation-state. However, the more serious charge against it is that it may actually contribute to racism. In supposing that racial harmony can only be achieved by absorbing minority groups into the wider society, it contributes to the view that each nation has its own cultural values and way of life such that it cannot tolerate sharing its territory with those of another culture. This "new racist" doctrine is prominent in the literature and speeches of the New Right and of neo-fascist groups across Europe. Unlike older versions of racism, it is not premised on the supposed biological superiority of one race over another. What is at issue is cultural difference: it is held that all ethnic and racial groups are equal, but it is "natural" that members of different cultures should feel threatened if they have to share their territory with those who live according to incompatible cultural norms (Barker, 1981). In practice, "new racism" legitimates violence against members of racialized groups who do not belong to the majority nation and may lead to calls for their repatriation – a genuine, if impracticable, possibility where minorities are not citizens. Although the assimilationist model differs from "new racism" by calling for tolerance on the part of the white majority, it mirrors it by supposing that it is only in so far as members of ethnic minority groups are few in number and indistinguishable from the white majority that they can be tolerated. Like "new racism," the assimilationist model thereby makes racialized minorities the "problem" in race relations, not white racism.

Multi-culturalism and group-differentiated citizenship rights

The conclusion of those who reject the assimilationist model of immigration on the grounds that it contributes to "new racism" is that multi-cultural societies require multi-cultural citizenship rights. In many countries, especially those of the New World – the USA, Canada, Australia, and New Zealand – but also some Northern European countries like Britain, Scandinavia, Holland, Belgium, and Switzerland, the assimilationist model of citizenship is actually currently being displaced by multi-culturalism. As a prominent advocate of multi-culturalism, Will Kymlicka (1995) has argued that it is the only justifiable liberal policy. This is important since citizenship rights in the West are based on the liberal tradition. It is also surprising since liberals have generally held that the public sphere, including state institutions and the law, should be value-neutral and that cultural identity should be relevant only in the private sphere. However, the presence of significant cultural minorities makes it obvious that this is, in fact, not the case: legal rights, assumptions concerning appropriate welfare provision, the language of public institutions, and so on are all culturally specific. This suggests that it is not possible to be neutral in such matters and that supposed universality is a mask for the dominance of one culture over others. As Kymlicka sees it, there is an impeccable liberal argument for individual freedom which follows as a consequence of acknowledging the cultural specificity of liberal institutions. The central liberal tenet is that individuals should be free to choose their own lifestyles. It is this premise that makes liberals view cultural rights with suspicion, since they are opposed to forcing any individual to conform to a set of group values. However, as Kymlicka points out, in order to make choices, there have to be valuable ways of life to choose from. It is culture – traditions, history, and language – which gives choices meaning, makes them comprehensible, vivid, and desirable to us. Therefore, in the name of individual freedom, cultural differences should be upheld and protected (Kymlicka, 1995).

Kymlicka analyzes multi-culturalism into two kinds, each of which is now a somewhat different issue with respect to group-differentiated rights in liberal democracies. The first he calls "multi-nationalism." Multinational societies contain within them minorities which, under different circumstances, might have retained or established their own sovereign governments, but which have been incorporated into a single state, either voluntarily through federation, or as a result of conquest. The United States, he argues, is of this kind, containing American Indians, Puerto Ricans, the descendants of Mexicans (Chicanos), Hawaiians and others (Kymlicka, 1995: 11). Typically demands for rights from these groups are for rights to some kind of self-government as a separate nation. Quebec has achieved such status in Canada, for example, through the federal division of powers which gave the province extensive powers over language, education, culture, and immigration. Native peoples in North America have also gained considerable rights to self-determination through the system of reserved lands within which they have increasing control over health, education, family law, policing, criminal justice, and resource development (1995: 29–30). Legitimate multi-nationalism, in Kymlicka's view, results in virtually parallel sets of citizenship rights which overlap only to some extent in common rights for all.

The second type of multi-culturalism he calls "polyethnicity." Societies into which there has been migration are of this type. Poly-ethnic societies are those in which immigrants participate in the public institutions of the dominant culture, but maintain some distinctive ways of life in terms of customs, religion, language, dress, food, and so on. Again, the United States is a good example. Immi-grants have been expected to conform to the English-speaking insti-tutions of the public sphere and, although tolerated in private, it is only since the 1970s that the expression of different cultural heritages has been encouraged. Kymlicka argues that these groups do not require such extensive group-differentiated rights as nations. Their main aim is to be integrated into the multi-cultural society of which they are a part and to enjoy equal respect with other citizens. Minority groups in a polyethnic society will generally enjoy those rights common to all citizens, in his view. They should also, however, have some distinctive rights, in order to avoid disadvantages suffered as a result of their difference from the dominant culture and to combat racism (Kymlicka, 1995: 30–1).

To a limited extent, some group-differentiated rights have been instituted in many countries. In Britain, for example, Jews and Muslims are exempt from laws which would make it impossible for them to slaughter animals in accordance with their traditional methods, and Sikhs may wear their turbans instead of the crash helmets required by law. Recently, Muslims and Seventh Day Adventists won the right, already enjoyed by Catholics, to government funding for schools in which the curriculum will be organized around these religious faiths. Multi-culturalism in education is perhaps most highly developed. It involves the recognition of the history, literature, and religion of cultural minorities, and often the celebration of different festival days. Although it is not actually a legal right as such, multi-cultural education is seen as offering children from minority groups genuine equal access to educational opportunities, as well as encouraging tolerance, if not understanding, from the majority population.

There are important exceptions in Europe to the development of multi-culturalism. Despite its relative openness to immigrants, there is strong resistance in France to the recognition of a plurality of communities with respect to citizenship rights. Interestingly, this is the case among anti-racists as well as on the part of those who are sympathetic to the anti-immigrant rhetoric of the National Front Party, the largest of its kind in Europe. French citizenship is strongly universalist; to be equal, individuals must have identical rights. This assumes, however, the truth of the assumption that liberal institutions are culturally neutral. There have been clashes between the state and Muslims in France as a result; for example, schoolgirls who cover their hair in accordance with Muslim customs have been excluded from schools. Although the situation is complicated, since it is not necessarily the case that racism in France is more acute than elsewhere and there are particular political reasons for the rise of the National Front, it is difficult not to conclude that the supposed universalism of citizenship contributes to what has been described as French "Muslimphobia" (Lloyd and Waters, 1991; Wieviorka, 1993). Germany is another important exception with regard to the development of multi-culturalism. In fact, Germany does not officially recognize itself as a country of immigration at all. Migrant workers were not intended to take up residence there, and there is little space to think in terms of multi-culturalism where naturalization is seen as changing one's cultural identity. Again, the situation is complicated, but it is likely that there is a connection between the status of the members of racialized minorities as "foreigners" in Germany, even if they were born there, and the growing incidence of racial violence across the country (Wilpert, 1993).

As multi-culturalists see it, recognizing cultural differences in group-differentiated polyethnic citizenship rights enables genuine integration, while the assimilationist model results in exclusion for those who do not fit, or who are seen as not fitting, the dominant culture. Kymlicka (1995) argues that, far from encouraging the fragmentation of society, as assimilationists fear, demands for culturally specific rights enable minorities to participate fully in a multi-cultural society. Furthermore, it is rare for ethnic minority groups to demand "internal restrictions," the legal power to impose cultural norms on their members. Such demands are unacceptable from a liberal point of view, since they undermine individual freedom rather than protecting it. The enforcement of any cultural norms which impose traditional restrictions on women and children that are not legal in liberal democracies, such as arranged marriages which violate existing laws regarding informed consent, clitirodectomy, and so on, are to be refused on Kymlicka's theory.

Despite its current popularity with many policy-makers, multi-culturalism is not without its critics. The most general criticism is that it is necessarily ineffective as a way of addressing inequalities because the inferior position of minority groups is not cultural but structural. It is a matter of socio-economic inequality, not of psychological feelings of cultural inferiority or oppression, nor ultimately of the acceptance of minority groups by the majority white population. Although multi-culturalism may be of some relevance in addressing the exclusion of certain historical experiences, cultural, and religious practices from the mainstream, in this view it is ineffectual and even insulting to address the disadvantage suffered by racialized groups in this way (Williams, 1989: 92–5).

However, the socio-economic inequalities suffered by racialized groups are not necessarily as unrelated to culture as this criticism suggests. If culture is thought of as discourse, as embodying practices rather than simply as ideas and symbols, it will be recognized that the assumptions of a dominant national culture concerning particular ways of life may have important effects at the socio-economic level. This is evident, for example, in cases of what may be called "institutional racism." The term itself is highly contested. Initially developed to challenge the idea that racial inequality is a product of nothing more than the prejudice of white individuals, it is often used very loosely to refer to any pattern of disadvantage affecting non-whites (Mason, 1995: 9). It is also used, however, more precisely, to mean the application of institutional rules which work to the advantage of those who conform to a cultural norm. In gaining access to good public housing, for example, those who live in the small nuclear families currently normal in the West have an advantage over those who live in larger households or extended families. This type of racism has nothing to do with the prejudices or ideas of the individuals who provide welfare benefits; it is built into the rules of the provision itself, in this case, the assumption that there are few large households needing accommodation. Although the prejudices of individuals are certainly a problem in administering the provision and protection of rights, arguably "institutional racism" in this sense is a more significant source of socio-economic disadvantage for certain groups. The criticism of multi-culturalism as "idealist" and ineffectual in relation to material inequalities relies on an absolute distinction between ideas and material reality which is not tenable from the perspective of discourse theory. Group-differentiated rights are not a matter of preserving superficial cultural differences; they are also relevant to the equal participation of all citizens in the opportunities of a pluralist society.

Nevertheless, it is important also to recognize that "culture" itself is a term which may be used to different effect in different discourses. There are certainly cases where it is inappropriate to think of unequal citizenship as primarily a matter of cultural differences. In some cases, indeed, this may be a way of de-legitimizing claims for greater equality. Perhaps the best example of the difficulty of thinking of citizenship in this way is the position of African-Americans in the United States and the way in which the New Right has suggested cultural differences as the reason for their predominance in "the underclass."

Since the civil rights movement of the 1950s and 1960s, the chief issue for African-Americans in terms of citizenship has been integration through desegregation. The striking separation of black and white in the US invariably works to the advantage of whites: poor housing, neighborhoods with high rates of crime, poor schools, low pay, and limited job opportunities restrict the realization of full citizenship rights for black Americans in comparison with whites. The role of culture in segregation is, however, far from clear. As Kymlicka (1995) notes, African-Americans fit neither the category of multinational nor that of polyethnic group. They were brought to the continent involuntarily, from different African cultural and linguistic backgrounds, and for a long time they were actively discouraged and even prohibited from trying to develop a common culture. They have no homeland nor distinctive social forms in America as national minorities do, and yet they have been kept physically segregated from the mainstream white culture (Kymlicka, 1995: 24). Multi-culturalism has played some part in the movement against segregation, challenging the ethnocentrism of the liberal arts canon in American education, for example, with black history, literature, and so on. But the main claims for cultural difference have come from those who argue that poor black Americans reproduce their poverty as a result of inappropriate attitudes to work and family life. In this case, a discourse of cultural difference reinforces segregation and legitimates inequalities rather than articulating claims for more equal citizenship rights and the genuine participation of all. We will look at the claims of the New Right with respect to the racialized underclass in more detail in section 4.4 below.

Nevertheless, it is also important to note that the movement against African-American segregation, although not calling for group-differentiated rights on the basis of cultural differences, has called for "special rights" for blacks in order to redress historic disadvantage. According to Kymlicka and others, such arguments are also justified in liberal terms in so far as they are designed with the aim of bringing about a color-blind meritocracy. The best known of these involves the use of quotas in universities, companies, and the public sector to bring the prospects of employment for black Americans closer to equivalence with whites than they would otherwise be as a result of imposed historical segregation, poorer living conditions, and disadvantage in the labor market. "Affirmative action" takes many forms, from "active non-discrimination" in which the employer tries hard to recruit minority applicants before deciding which candidate to employ for the job, to "reverse discrimination" in which preference is given to applicants from minority groups which have been discriminated against in the past. Affirmative action programs have always been extremely controversial and highly politicized. They have been criticized from the left on the grounds that they have benefited some black people while failing to address the problem of black poverty as such. However, it is the right-wing criticism which is currently dominant: that affirmative action is unfair to white individuals who may not be chosen for jobs or university places in competition with black people. The counter-argument that white people have only lost what they gained through past discrimination no longer has the resonance it once had. While affirmative action continues in the United States, it is increasingly under threat and has been outlawed in recent well-publicized court cases involving selection for university places. In the case of "special rights" for African-Americans in US, it is individual rather than group-differentiated rights which are in the ascendant (Omi and Winant, 1987).

"Special rights" remain important, however, with regard to rights to representation in the political process. Multi-culturalists, like feminists, are concerned with the way in which minority groups are under-represented in the legislatures of Western liberal democracies. Claims for political representation take different forms according to the group in question. As Kymlicka (1995) notes, claims for political representation are not synonymous with demands for self-government nor for group-differentiated rights on the grounds of cultural difference. It is rather that they involve giving minorities a fair hearing in a situation in which their views would otherwise be systematically ignored. This is consistent with liberal understandings of democratic representation in which, as a bare minimum, it should provide for the protection of individual interests. In a more elaborated liberal version of democratic participation it does more than this, facilitating citizens' individual development in accordance with their recognition of the common good. In either case it is unfair that individuals who are members of minority groups are not represented. Increasingly group-differentiated political rights are an important issue in multi-cultural liberal democracies.

In the US, the most prominent attempt to reform systematic imbalances in representation has been "re-districting" – redrawing the boundaries of electoral districts to create black-majority or Hispanic-majority districts. Ironically, however, although instituted as part of the campaign against segregation, it is only effective in so far as residential segregation is the reality. In response, the Supreme Court has ruled that re-districting involving "segregating" races for the purposes of voting is to be regarded with suspicion. Like other affirmative action programs designed to redress systematic disadvantage, it should be seen, Kymlicka (1995) argues, as a temporary measure. In fact, it is reviewed regularly to assess how well it is working and whether it is still required.

However, there are cases where societies seem to be divided more permanently, along religious or cultural lines. In such cases, it may be argued that requirements for group representation are not temporary. This is clearly the case where there are claims for a degree of self-government, as in federal systems, or where groups live on their own land, as Native Americans do. In other cases, however, group political rights are designed to accommodate differences within common decision-making procedures. This is, for example, the case in what is known as "consociational democracies," like those of Holland and Belgium, in which religious cleavages are represented by different political parties. In such cases, political stability is supposed to depend on sharing decision-making power so that the cabinet will be composed of leading figures from all parties, there will be minority veto over socially divisive issues, and so on (Phillips, 1995: 14–5). The system in New Zealand is similar in that Maoris select candidates from a specific electoral list so that they are guaranteed representation in parliament as a group, though there is no Maori party. However, there are no examples of special political rights for racialized minority groups in Europe. Although consociational democracies are apparently more open to the possibility of fitting Muslim representation into the existing pluralist framework than other political systems, this remains no more than a possibility at present (Phillips, 1995: 15). In Britain, unusual in Europe because of the high proportion of black citizens with full voting rights, there is resistance to the fragmentation of the left of center vote that black electoral lists are seen to represent. In European countries in which immigrants do not have citizenship, they have no right to vote in general elections at all. However, with the establishment of settled minority communities and the articulation of systematic differences in interests, it seems likely that the discussion of fair representation will be increasingly important in the future.

The whole issue of group-differentiated rights might be considered highly contentious in relation to the critique of essentialism which has been so important, as we have seen, in relation to citizenship for women and "sexual minorities." It is, however, less well developed than in these cases. In some respects, this is surprising. The anti-essentialist case against the concept of ethnicity as a way of distinguishing actual groups of persons *is* highly developed. Anti-essentialists argue strongly that we should see culture as *process* rather than as a set of attributes possessed by a particular group. Culture is not fixed in eternal forms, it is constantly being made and re-made in historical processes. It is on these grounds that Hall (1991a, b) and others see cultural identities as "hybrid;" they are always constructed by drawing on a multiplicity of cultural symbols and identifications which are re-combined in ways such that they do not "authentically" belong to any particular ethnic group as such. Multi-culturalism might, therefore, be seen as problematic on the anti-essentialism account in so far as it contributes to what Gilroy (1993a) calls "ethnic absolutism," the construction of rigid and supposedly unchanging distinctions between cultures in ways which constrain creativity, individuality, and challenges to the status quo.

Furthermore, as many writers have pointed out, minority groups are not homogeneous and different experiences, according to sex, sexuality, age, and so on, mean that there are many different ways of living ethnicity. In particular, it should be noted that women sometimes have quite different citizenship rights from men; for example, concerning their rights to enter a country or bring in their partners and families. Even where citizenship rights are identical for both sexes, the very different family and employment situations of women, and their marginalized participation in political organizations, means that their citizenship status is actually very different (Yuval-Davies, 1991; Brah, 1992). One of the difficulties of categor-

izing the world in terms of ethnic groups is that it tends to emphasize differences between groups at the expense of considering the
diversity within them.

Although the concept of "ethnicity" is, then, highly dubious on
the anti-essentialist account, the idea of "cultural differences" is
central both for anti-essentialists and multi-culturalists. For this
reason, Hall argues that it is necessary to re-think the concept of
"ethnicity" rather than abandoning it, as a step toward understanding the construction of racialized identities. As he puts it:

> If the black subject and black experience are not stabilized by nature
> or by some other essential guarantee, then it must be the case that
> they are constructed historically, culturally, politically – and the
> concept which refers to this is "ethnicity." The term ethnicity
> acknowledges the place of history, language and culture in the con-
> struction of subjectivity and identity, as well as the fact that all dis-
> course is placed, positioned, situated, and all knowledge is contextual.
> (Hall, 1992b: 257)

This re-thinking of "ethnicity" as part of an anti-racist strategy
also requires a re-thinking of "nationality." With the rise of "new
racism," there has been a growing interest in the ways in which
nationalism and racism are intertwined in the relations between
white majority populations and the communities that have resulted
from immigration in Europe. As a form of "ethnic absolutism,"
multi-culturalism may be seen as potentially contributing to "new
racism," to the view that cultural differences are immutable so that
ways of life which are incompatible may not be able to share the
same national territory and institutions. On the other hand, group-
differentiated citizenship rights may be seen as a practical way of
calling into question the "naturalness" of constructed national identities as part of a wider transformation of citizenship rights in a post-
national, globalized world. They represent a dislocation between
state and nation in that they ensure the rights of avowedly non-
national minorities. Although such citizenship rights as have been
achieved for cultural minorities may be seen as inadequate because
of their limited impact on the unequal position of racialized groups,
they may also be seen as representing the beginnings of a commitment on the part of the state to those citizens previously ignored or
even seen as illegitimate in a mono-cultural nation. Writers like
Gayatri Spivak (1987) have argued that the "risk" of essentialism,

of freezing mutable and contested identities in particular historic forms and treating them as if they were outside history, is worth taking where that risk is formed from the vantage point of a dominated group. Although this is a controversial and complicated issue, multi-cultural citizenship rights may be an example of a justified "strategic essentialism" where they contribute to the development of more egalitarian post-national rights in the place of the exclusion of racialized minority groups from full citizenship rights in the countries in which they live and work.

4.4 CITIZENSHIP AND POVERTY: THE "UNDERCLASS" AND "SOCIAL EXCLUSION"

Before we look at the question of post-national rights, however, it is important to give some consideration to citizenship and poverty, since Marshall's optimistic view that the welfare state would lead to greater equality between citizens has not been borne out by subsequent developments. However, his intuition that equality of citizenship status is now more important than socio-economic inequalities is a useful one for understanding contemporary poverty (see pp. 160–1). Poverty is now seen as the problem of the state, despite attempts by the New Right to free it from this responsibility, in as much as the majority of the very poor are on welfare benefits. References to the poor as an "underclass" are not references to "class" in the sense in which it would have been understood by Marx or Weber. It is not a group characterized by its position in relation to the labor market. It is more a collection of disparate groups defined principally in terms of "race," ethnicity, and gender and linked together by their status as "inferior" citizens, whether or not that status is seen as deserved.

In Marshall's conception of citizenship, social rights are related to the idea that all citizens should be able to participate in a common standard of "civilized" life. Citizenship in a welfare state society is not simply a matter of formal, legal rights; it is also about material goods and the possibilities they afford for social life. On this understanding, citizenship and poverty are antithetical. In fact, in the years following the institution of the welfare state in Britain, it was assumed that poverty had been virtually eliminated; only poverty among the old, sick, and disabled remained a problem and it was understood that it would soon be remedied by continuing economic expansion. Notoriously, poverty was re-discovered in the 1960s by Peter Townsend. He opposed the definition of poverty on which previous assessments had been made, the "absolute" or "subsistence" definition according to which those who do not have enough for the necessities of life are in poverty. In Townsend's view, this definition was too restricted: the necessities of civilized life go beyond those required simply to meet animal needs. He defined poverty in relative terms, as the lack of goods which enable people to participate in everyday life:

> Individuals, families and groups in the population can be said to be in poverty when they lack the resources to obtain the types of diet, participate in the activities and have the living conditions and amenities that are customary, or are at least widely encouraged or approved, in the societies to which they belong. Their resources are so seriously below those commanded by the average individual or family that they are, in effect, excluded from ordinary living patterns, customs and activities. (Townsend, quoted in Scott, 1994: 78–9)

Although Townsend does not use the term "citizenship" in his work, his definition of poverty is complementary to Marshall's view of citizenship rights: the poor are excluded from citizenship because they are excluded from full participation in society.

Following the beginning of the world recession in the 1970s, it is to be expected that poverty in the West would have increased. This is confirmed by studies of poverty, though the exact extent of the increase is controversial. Townsend's definition of poverty as relative deprivation, although undoubtedly plausible conceptually, is quite difficult to use as a measurement of poverty. It is necessary to decide exactly how much money is needed to live according to customary standards and then to measure the number of those who have incomes lower than this figure. Townsend himself set the figure at 150 percent of the British unemployment benefit rate, after taking housing costs into account, and this was confirmed by a subsequent large-scale study of poverty in Britain in 1985. This means that all those on welfare benefits or state pensions in Britain are in poverty, as is a high proportion of those on low incomes. Evidently, then, since the numbers of unemployed and those employed on low wages have increased, so too have rates of poverty.

The official British measurement of poverty is lower than Townsend's; it is at the level of the lowest welfare benefit. Even on this less generous measure, however, the percentage of the population living in poverty in Britain rose from 6.4 percent in 1968 to 19 percent in 1987 (Scott, 1994: 92). It is difficult to compare rates of poverty cross-nationally because different countries use different definitions and measurements. However, there is now a measure for countries in the EU, the European Poverty Line (EPL), set at 50 percent or more below the national average. On this measure, from the mid-1970s to the mid-1980s, there was little change in the level of poverty, except in Ireland, Portugal, and Britain where there were large increases. The largest were in Britain. In the United States, poverty continues to be defined in terms of "subsistence." The official poverty line is an income which would allow for the provision of the necessities of life. On this measure, poverty has not increased since 1968. However, the $12,092 a year which is supposed to meet the needs of a family of four is popularly believed to be too low to do so. Taking the more realistic figure of $15,017 as the poverty line, there were 45 million in poverty in the US in 1988, rather than the 32 million measured by the official line (Scott, 1994: 127–8).

Townsend's definition of poverty as relative deprivation is not, then, accepted everywhere. However, in contemporary social research, the "subsistence" definition of poverty is mainly used by those influenced by the New Right. It is also, in this way, linked to a much more restrictive model of citizenship than that outlined by Marshall. The neo-liberalism of the New Right has been significant in the re-shaping of citizenship rights in Britain and the United States. There has been a drive to end what is seen as a damaging dependence on the welfare state. The welfare state is seen as actually contributing to poverty from this perspective, rather than alleviating it, by reducing the incentive to work and by interfering with "natural" market-based economic processes. The social aspect of citizenship is redefined as more a matter of *obligation* than of rights. The citizen has obligations to society and the family, which should be expressed through work (King, 1991; Roche, 1995).

In the US, the New Right understanding of poverty and citizenship has been developed into a theory of how poverty is reproduced by the behavior of the poor. It is argued that there is now an "underclass," made up of single mothers dependent on welfare and semi-criminal men who do not work. The term "underclass" is heavily racialized. It is associated conceptually with a supposedly black lifestyle in which women have children by many fathers who do not provide for them, and empirically with the large numbers of black people living in poverty in the ghettos of American cities. It is also feminized. In the US, young, unmarried or childless men have no automatic right to state benefits; they have the right to insurance-based unemployment benefit, but growing numbers do not qualify for it because they have worked too little and made too few contributions. It is practically only single mothers who are eligible for the means-tested welfare benefit, Aid to Families with Dependent Children. Charles Murray, one of the most important proponents of the New Right view of the "underclass," argues from a rational choice perspective that welfare benefits make dependence on the state a more attractive possibility for many women than marriage or paid employment. As a result, families are growing up in a "culture of poverty" in which there is no ethic of responsibility toward work or family (Lister, 1996). As a number of writers have commented, the underclass is seen as "the undeserving poor," a term from the nineteenth century which links poverty to morality rather than to economics.

William Julius Wilson (1987) has contested the New Right understanding of the "underclass," arguing that it should be seen as an economic and social phenomenon, rather than the result of rational individual choices. As such, it is indistinguishable from the formation of the ghetto itself. The "underclass" is the result of the black middle-classes moving out of the inner cities and the worsening economic prospects for the deprived African-Americans who remain there. In Wilson's view, the most important problem for members of the "underclass" is social isolation: many families in poor areas of the city experience long-term unemployment, and, because they have few contacts with those in steady jobs, welfare dependence becomes a way of life (Wilson, 1987). However, Wilson's thesis has received little support on the left. He has been criticized for underestimating the effects of racism in segregating blacks in the ghetto and for over-emphasizing pathological behavior among the poor. Despite his stress on "structural" causes, his use of the term "underclass" is seen as too close to that of the New Right to challenge their interpretation of urban poverty. Few researchers use the term as a result, and Wilson himself now prefers "ghetto poor" (Silver, 1996). Norman Fainstein (1996) has challenged the premises of the ongoing debate about urban poverty still more fundamentally, arguing that, in fact, the great majority of the poor in the US do not live in black ghettos: statistically, two-thirds are white; one-third lives in rural areas; and, far from being confined to the long-term unemployed, poverty is increasing among those who are employed.

Many of the criticisms made of the term "underclass" apply also to "socially excluded," the more commonly used term for the poor in Europe. "Social exclusion" came to prominence in France in the mid-1980s to refer to "the rise in long-term and recurrent unemployment and the growing instability of social relations . . . family break-up, single-member households, social isolation, and the decline of class solidarity based on unions, workplaces and social networks" (Silver, 1996: 113). Although not as strongly racialized, it has been used alongside "underclass" in Britain, to describe much the same phenomena. It is now widely used in EU policy documents.

Fainstein's (1996) substantive point is that the poor are not qualitatively different from the rest of the population; it is not their characteristics as a group we should consider in order to understand growing poverty. He argues that the whole family of terms "underclass," "ghetto poor," and "excluded" work "to deflect attention from the dynamics of economic and political processes which generate and reproduce the very populations and places which appear to lie under or outside of capitalist systems" (Fainstein, 1996: 154–5). Similarly, Giovanna Procacci (1996) has argued that "social exclusion," suggesting as it does that the poor are "outside society," displaces and contains the problem of inequality. While "exclusion" suggests a static division of social space, with citizens inside and the poor outside, the idea of inequality points to the possibility of achieving equality. It therefore implies a more dynamic analysis of social institutions and the way in which they produce poverty (Procacci, 1996).

Lydia Morris (1996) fleshes out such an analysis in terms of the gender and "race" dimensions of the "underclass" or "socially excluded." She argues that separating out the poor as essentially different obscures the wider social changes which mean that work, family, and welfare have become dislocated. Citizenship in the welfare state was premised on full, male employment and the nuclear family, consisting of a male breadwinner and female carer at home. The family is now breaking down and there is a high rate of unemployment, particularly, she argues, among migrant workers who are employed in the most insecure and poorly paid jobs. In the US, the largest group of this kind is Mexican men, but the same argument would also apply to African-American men. In such circumstances, Morris (1996) argues, it is unsurprising that it is single mothers and men in racialized minority groups who are over-represented in poverty statistics. To stigmatize women for dependency on welfare in a context in which they have been constructed as dependent is unjust. Similarly, black men tend to be unemployed because in depressed economies they find it impossible to get work. In the case of migrant workers, it is only because the indigenous population refused to do badly paid and precarious jobs that they were initially allowed into expanding Western economies. In more depressed times, even these jobs may not be available to men or women from racialized minorities. In Morris's (1996) view, poverty is linked to the structural position of particular groups in the labor market and to actual, not just formal, citizenship status, on which real access to social support depends.

The importance of the social context of poverty is particularly clear in relation to the New Right solution to welfare dependence, the introduction of "workfare." Following Lawrence Mead's influential book, *Beyond Entitlement* (1986), workfare was introduced in the US to inculcate in poor citizens an obligation to work corresponding with the right to receive welfare benefits. Mead argued that they should be provided with incentives to free themselves from dependence on the state by making them engage in some activity in exchange for benefits. The receipt of benefits is now conditional on participation in a "work program." In practice, the compulsory aspect of workfare tends to focus on developing the skills needed to get a job, but states have the power to make work programs more punitive (King, 1991). Some elements of workfare have been introduced in Britain under the Blair government, in particular the emphasis on getting single parents off welfare and into paid employment. As a policy, then, it has moved from the domain of the New Right to become more mainstream. It is still, however, extremely controversial as a way of dealing with poverty.

Workfare is premised on the assumption that jobs do exist which welfare recipients refuse to take. There are undoubtedly some jobs, but they are unlikely to be the kind of well-paid, secure jobs which enable people to escape poverty. Furthermore, if those who argue that we are now moving toward a post-Fordist society are correct, the workfare solution is quite inadequate to the long-term problem. From this perspective, society is now undergoing changes which mean that there is a need for relatively less work in relation to productivity. There is, therefore, the possibility of permanent structural unemployment (see p. 237). If this is the case, it is certainly necessary to re-think citizenship and the relation between the market and the state in welfare, but in refusing to consider the possibility of such far-reaching changes the proponents of "workfare" contribute more to the problem than to the solution (Roche, 1995). Finally, in so far as workfare is designed to force single parents into paid work, it involves a conflict for women between being the breadwinner and the traditional carer in the home. Although in some states and in Britain, the emphasis has been on providing child-care to enable women to participate in paid employment, workfare is one-sided in forcing women to meet their family obligations in a traditionally masculine way. This is especially the case in so far as policy-makers and employers fail to address the way in which the labor market is structured to make it difficult for either sex to combine care for dependants with paid work.

The emphasis of the New Right on paid work as the basis of citizenship is not new: it is a feature of all insurance-based systems in which welfare is tied to employment status. However, in a context in which paid work is secondary for a large section of the population, whether for traditional reasons, as in the case of many single mothers, or because it is no longer as central to the reproduction of society as it was in industrial society, this emphasis is increasingly problematic. In such a context, it may function more as a policy for containing and disciplining the poor than as a way of alleviating poverty.

A useful way of understanding how the poor might be better integrated into citizenship is that proposed by John Scott. He argues that if poverty is seen in Townsend's terms as relative deprivation, it is by definition related to privilege. If people can be deprived by being excluded from public life, they may also be *privileged* in relation to public life. He suggests that a privilege line could be drawn, at an income level above which it is possible to exclude others from advantages by withdrawing into private benefits unavailable to the public (Scott, 1994). It is then possible to measure poverty in relation to wealth, constructing it as a relationship between citizens rather than as either a moral category or a purely economic one. Citizens may be excluded, but they may also exclude. This understanding of citizenship returns us to Marshall's conception of citizens as participating in a common standard of life, but, like the arguments of the New Right, it puts the emphasis at least as much on obligations as on rights. In this case, however, the obligations are on everyone to participate in the public status of the citizen, not just on the poor to perform according to expectations they may find impossible, or even undesirable, to attain.

4.5   POST-NATIONAL CITIZENSHIP

As we noted in section 4.3 on "race" and ethnicity, citizenship in the West has developed as an aspect of the mono-cultural nation-state. However, partly as a result of processes of globalization, and partly as one of those processes itself, it seems that in contemporary society citizenship is being extended beyond the nation-state.

In chapter 2, on globalization, we saw how nation-states are increasingly compelled to co-operate with others in international organizations and political institutions as a result of transnational economic and social processes which they cannot control within their borders. The European Union is the best example of this development since it has the most wide-ranging powers, sharing sovereignty to some extent with the member states which make it up. Initially based on international co-operation for economic purposes, it is now developing some of the features of a supranational state. This includes guaranteeing the rights of citizens of the European Union, although individual member states retain control over important aspects of conferring citizenship rights. The EU, then, is both a response to other processes of globalization and is itself contributing to globalization as such.

Other examples may be cited of international political bodies which are both a response and a contribution to globalization. Military alliances, such as NATO, and economic trading agreements, like GATT, G7, and so on, indirectly affect the rights of the citizens of nation-states in a very general way in so far as they constrain states' abilities to direct their own affairs. However, international organizations and institutions may also have a direct effect on human rights within nation-states through international law, backed up by economic sanctions and, on rare occasions, with military force. The growth of international regulation concerning human rights, particularly with regard to the increase in "spontaneous" transnational migration to the West due to worsening conditions in the developing world, has affected states' obligations toward citizens, non-national residents and asylum-seekers. As a result, it is now possible to think of rights as post-national. No longer the province of the nation-state which ensures rights for its own nationals to the exclusion of those who fall outside this category, even if they happen to reside in the territory of the state in question, it is argued that more genuinely universal, human rights are superseding the narrow particularistic citizenship rights of nation-states. Again, this is not an absolute change. As noted in chapter 2, nation-states remain the principal actors on the world stage. International law is agreed on by nation-states who are then responsible for implementing human rights in their own territories and who must also co-operate to compel those states which do not comply with international agreements to do so. Nevertheless, the fact that many states have incorporated human rights conventions into domestic law suggests that, even under these conditions, what has been called the "global rights regime" is having some effect.

Finally, potentially the most far-reaching vision of global citizenship is that of the environmental movement, which calls for a radical re-thinking of citizenship in the light of continuing environmental degradation. A response to globalization, as yet it has made little progress in bringing about the global citizenship it envisages. This is not to say, however that it has had no effect. Environmental concerns have been raised as an issue for public awareness and they are now on the international political agenda. Far from a reality, global citizenship is nevertheless a real possibility for the future.

Migration and rights across borders

Section 4.3 of this chapter, on citizenship, "race," and ethnicity, was mainly concerned with settled populations of migrants to the West.

Until the 1980s there was a general belief that mass migrations had ended and debates over citizenship rights in relation to discrimination, racism, and multi-culturalism took place on the basis of this assumption. In fact, while immigration into the US was restricted from the 1920s, and European countries ended systematic labor migration from the mid-1970s, migration continued in other forms. There were the families of migrant workers who were granted rights of settlement on the grounds of "family reunion." This form of migration was particularly important in European countries like Germany with its "guest-worker" system. In the US, it actually led to an *increase* in immigration in the 1960s and 1970s, and it also meant more visible immigration with the entry of Asians and Latin Americans rather than the Europeans who had previously made up the majority of migrants. There was also a significant migration of managerial, professional, technical, and scientific workers, a category of privileged workers which is usually ignored, who moved between advanced capitalist countries. Similarly invisible is the increasing rate of intra-European migration, both of skilled and unskilled workers. However, in the late 1980s and into the 1990s, there was political alarm in all Western countries about new forms of migration: the increase in the numbers of illegal immigrants and political asylum-seekers.

These "spontaneous" forms of migration lead to political alarm because they suggest that nation-states have lost control of their borders and so of the administration of the territory and population under their jurisdiction. It is also likely that they are seen as particularly problematic because they involve Third World immigrants. In the US, it is over the increase in illegal immigrants from Mexico that the alarm has been raised. In fact, restrictions on entry to Mexicans have never been closely enforced and US employers have long made use of low-skill, low-wage, agricultural workers from south of the border. However, due mainly to worsening conditions in the Caribbean Basin, there has been an increase in illegal immigration in this region since the 1970s. In Europe, it is in relation to the opening up of national borders within the European Union that illegal immigration is seen as a problem. Unskilled manual labor has been recruited to build up service industries in Spain, Italy, Portugal, and Greece, until recently providers of migrant labor for elsewhere and now the destination for illegal immigrants from North Africa. Other European countries are concerned because they see the opening of national borders as allowing the spread of illegal immigrants throughout the Union. Asylum-seekers and refugees have increased in number until there is now an estimated 23 million worldwide (Richmond, 1994: 115). While the number of individuals applying for political asylum in any single country is relatively small in comparison with its existing population, and in comparison with numbers of other migrants, a great deal of political anxiety is generated in all Western countries concerning what is seen as a "massive influx" of potential immigrants (Castles, 1993; Miles, 1993; Jacobson, 1996).

As a result, all states have taken measures to discourage new forms of migration. In the US, there have been attempts to control illegal immigration, mainly by penalizing employers who knowingly hire unauthorized aliens. In Europe, measures have been linked to the new institutions of the European Union. While the Schengen Agreement will eventually allow unrestricted travel within the EU (subject to limitations imposed by individual member states), increased resources have been made available for surveillance of the external borders and the policing of migrants and asylum applicants, including a computerized database of criminals, deported, and unwanted persons. There is also growing international co-operation between the countries of Europe, North America, and Australasia to facilitate harmonization of immigration policies and to combat illegal immigration. Such measures are often described as constructing "fortress Europe" and "fortress America," political units which put up insurmountable barriers to those outside. On the grounds that these are at the same time barriers to maintain racial segregation, Anthony Richmond (1994) has described this new world order as "global apartheid." He argues that immigration controls involving work permits, segregated housing locations, restricted travel and deprivation of political rights are used against illegal immigrants and asylum-seekers in order to protect privileged access to health, education, and welfare services, just as the South African government used such measures to control and exploit the black population when apartheid was enforced.

There is, however, an alternative, and much more optimistic, assessment of global migration processes which sees them as significant for the way in which they have prompted a form of post-national citizenship. It is important to note that in dealing with residents who are not citizens, including guest-workers and "denizens" as well as illegal immigrants and asylum-seekers, states are often bound by human rights conventions and international law rather than by national government legislation. Treaties and covenants based on the Universal Declaration of Human Rights, and signed and ratified by states, explicitly require them *not* to distinguish between persons on the grounds of nationality in civil, social, and political rights. It is under such agreements that states are obliged to allow the admittance of the family members of guest-workers as a basic human right. Furthermore, they are obliged by the International Covenant on Economic, Social and Cultural Rights to provide a range of rights to health care, education, housing, and welfare to all those resident within their territories in so far as resource capacities allow. In fact, as noted above, legal aliens generally now have the same rights as citizens in the West, except political rights to vote and stand for election. In relation to political asylum-seekers, nation-states are bound by human rights conventions which mean that no individual who has "a well-founded fear of being persecuted for reasons of race, religion, nationality, membership of a particular group or political opinion" may be turned away (Jacobson, 1996: 68). As Jacobson points out, this erodes the principle that a state should above all be concerned to protect its national interests, including enforcing foreign policy and ideological distinctions in immigration policies. Human rights also govern the position of national minorities within nation-states. Under the International Covenant on Civil and Political Rights, a state is bound to protect the rights of minorities on its territory, even against its own nationals. Even illegal immigrants have some rights – to appeal against deportation, to be treated humanely and, in the US, to receive education and some social services. Furthermore, many countries have accepted the difficulty of deporting large numbers of people who are thoroughly integrated into local communities, and have periodically granted amnesty to what are then known by the more neutral term of "undocumented aliens" rather than "illegal immigrants."

According to Yasemin Soysal (1994), these changes point toward an emerging form of post-national citizenship. As a result of global migration processes and the regime of international human rights which has grown up to deal with it, rights are now based on universal personhood, not membership of a particular nation. Nationality and rights are disarticulated as the absolute distinction between "citizenship" and "foreigner" is eroded within nation-states, at least in terms of formal legal rights (Soysal, 1994). Similarly, David Jacobson (1996) argues that individual rights are no longer directly tied to nationality; the individual now has a status in international law, and in many cases, rights attached to this status are equivalent to the rights of citizens guaranteed by nation-states.

Jacobson and Soysal are much more optimistic than Richmond because they do not see the state as acting in a singular and unified fashion with regard to migration processes. Nor do they see a homogeneous global order emerging. It is rather that there is a void in national law with respect to non-national residents and asylum-seekers, that individuals (and to a lesser extent minorities) are becoming the object of international law, and that the state is now accountable to its residents in terms of international law. Under these conditions, associations, organizations and individuals maneuver to try to gain a measure of security and well-being for those who would otherwise be without rights – with some degree of success. As Soysal argues, states are caught between competing claims to legitimacy: bound on one hand to respect human rights, and, on the other, to regulate immigration as an expression of sovereignty, their activities are not always consistent (Soysal, 1994: 7–8).

It is not, then, that international human rights law is seen as replacing the sovereignty of the state. On the contrary, in some respects it may be that the legitimacy and scope of the state is strengthened by recourse to international law. It is states which are called upon to guarantee human rights. In the case of refugees, for example, it is because states have the duty to protect and further the well-being of the population residing within their territories that asylum-seekers may legitimately claim to be stateless when they are in danger of persecution in their homeland.[2] Furthermore, the state itself is the critical mechanism in advancing human rights: information must be gathered, monitoring carried out, and measures implemented to ensure that rights are properly instituted. Finally, although international financial institutions, such as the World Bank, now consider human rights, and aid may be refused where violations are apparent, it is nation-states who are primarily responsible for the enforcement of international law through the UN, NATO, and other military alliances. There is, therefore, as Jacobson puts it, a dialectic between the growing transnational authority of human rights organizations and legislation and the extension of the state in order to engage with that authority (Jacobson, 1996: 112–13). Nor is it the case that post-national citizenship replaces nationalism. On the contrary, as Soysal argues, claims to nationality, cultural distinctiveness, and self-determination which were previously linked together in nation-states are themselves disarticulated and re-articulated as core elements of what it is to be human. They thus reappear in individual and collective strategies in relation to universal human rights. As she notes, "The universalistic status of personhood and postnational membership coexist with assertive national identities and intense ethnic struggles" (Soysal, 1994: 159). Nowhere are these dialectics more evident than in the most advanced set of political institutions to which post-national citizenship rights may be attributed, the European Union.

European citizenship

The word "citizen" has only recently been used to refer to those who live and work in the countries making up the European Union. Before the Maastricht Treaty was ratified in 1993 the main reference was to "workers," economic co-operation being the chief concern. The language of citizenship represents a further step toward a supranational European state with an explicit focus on political union. The Maastricht Treaty created citizens of Europe, stating that "Every citizen holding the nationality of a member state shall be a citizen of the Union." It further stated that the four fundamental freedoms – of movement of goods, persons, services, and capital – previously attached to citizenship of a member state were to be rights of citizens of the Union. They remained the same as they were before in virtually every other respect, though the treaty also created some new citizenship rights. The most important are undoubtedly political rights; those citizens of the Union who are resident in a member state of which they are not a national now have the right to vote and stand for election in local elections and for the European Parliament. Significantly, they still have no rights with regard to national elections. There are also new rights for all residents of the EU, including non-citizens, to petition the European Parliament concerning maladministration of its institutions (Guild, 1996). Social rights remain minimal at the EU level. Previous attempts to standardize benefits and rights for workers across nations are continued in the Maastricht Treaty, but social rights are extended very little beyond participation in the labor market. The emphasis on ensuring the free movement of workers remains and there is no attempt to harmonize national welfare systems (O'Leary, 1995).

The question of the extent to which citizenship of the European Union may be described as post-national is not a simple one. Citizenship rights remain clearly national in some respects. EU citizenship is granted only to those who are nationals of member states and the decision about who to include is made at the national level. Nation-states retain the power to divide those who are resident in their territories into European citizens, with all the freedoms of the Union, and non-citizens, who will not have the automatic right to travel or work in other countries within Europe. The link between nationality and citizenship is reproduced rather than undermined in the current conception of European citizenship (Mitchell and Russell, 1996: 63). Furthermore, rights will continue to be assured by nation-states, and the European Union has only limited power to make member states comply with its rulings. The European Union has an integrated legal system but, as Elizabeth Meehan (1997) has pointed out, there is a plurality of legal instruments within the common legal order, each of which works differently at different levels. The European Parliament, Council, and Commission act jointly to make regulations which are directly applicable in member states. However, most common policies are not the object of regulations but of directives which "direct" states to act to bring about a common objective expressed quite abstractly and without detailed instructions. Directives are intended to allow divergences in national procedures with respect to policy implementations, resource allocations, and so on. Furthermore, new directions in policy cannot be made without the consent of the Council of Ministers, an inter-governmental body made up of representatives of member states rather than a supranational institution. In some cases, states are permitted to opt-out of commonly agreed objectives on the basis of distinctive national traditions. The UK, for example, is exempt from introducing workers' rights to consultation in the workplace. The rights of the citizens of the European Union continue to be determined to a large extent, then, by the nation-state within which they happen to reside (Meehan, 1997).

On the other hand, it is also clear that in some respects the new citizenship rights instituted by the Maastricht Treaty are post-national. They are, however, post-national in two rather different ways. First, a number of the rights ensured by the European Union are post-national in the sense that they are universal human rights, attached to persons rather than to citizens. For many years the European Court of Justice (ECJ) has been guided by the European Convention on Human Rights (ECHR) in order to make its judgments. In this respect, it works something like a European Constitution and Bill of Rights (Jacobson, 1996: 81). In most of the member states of Europe the ECHR is not only recognized as international law but is directly incorporated into domestic law-making. Furthermore, the judgments of the ECJ are binding on all member states. The nation-states which make up the European Union have, therefore, been incorporating international law into their statutes for up to 25 years before the Maastricht Treaty created European citizenship. In this sense, at least, post-national citizenship in Europe was not created by the explicit declaration that Europeans are citizens of the EU.

Secondly, however, European citizenship may be said to be post-national in that the European Union is increasingly a supranational state sharing the sovereignty of member states. This is already evident in the fact that, as we have noted, law is made in the institutions of the Union which over-rides that made by the member states. The main issue that arises with respect to post-national citizenship of this type is what is called "the democratic deficit." In so far as contemporary citizenship at the level of the nation-state involves civil, political, and social rights, post-national citizenship of the EU is seriously inadequate in terms of political rights. At the level of the nation-state, democratically elected governments are losing the power to make policies and legislation which are binding on their citizens as member states give up sovereignty to the institutions of the EU. At the level of the EU, however, elected officials have very little influence over the legislative process. The European Parliament is the only democratically elected institution of the EU and it has only a consultative role in policy-making. The European Commission draws up legislation which is then debated by Parliament and voted on by the Council of Ministers before it becomes law. Officials on the Council are chosen by their respective national governments, not elected. The Maastricht Treaty took certain measures to address the "democratic deficit" of the EU by strengthening the powers of the European Parliament; for example, the Commission and its president are now subject to Parliamentary approval. However, it is clear that in order to prevent a lack of democratic accountability as a result of the transfer of powers from the member states to the EU, all the political institutions of the EU need reform (Newman, 1996).

Although Europeans have a form of post-national citizenship assured by the EU as an emerging "supranational state," it is problematic in so far as it has eroded some of the political rights they enjoyed as the citizens of sovereign nation-states. This is not to suggest that the EU is necessarily undemocratic. On the contrary, lack of democratic accountability at the supranational level must presumably be weighed against the potential gain in control by national governments over economic processes which cannot be contained within national borders. Nevertheless, the EU vividly illustrates the general problem for the democratization of global political institutions. Until recently, it has only been nation-states which have been represented at the international level, not individuals and social groups. This has changed a little in the institutions of the EU in so far as individuals have some political rights. There is now some discussion of further developments in this direction, but it seems unlikely that nation-states would willingly concede still more sovereignty to allow the creation of a federal Europe in which decisions were made by elected bodies at the supranational level and power was devolved to state parliaments, rather than the other way around. In the case of nation-states, the extension of political rights and democratization followed the mobilization of workers' and women's groups in civil society. It may be that the democratization of the European Union requires a similar mobilization to create a transnational civil society (Goodman, 1997).

Citizens for the environment

The most recent social movement to challenge the limitations of conventional citizenship is the environmental movement. Above all, its challenge is to citizenship organized around the nation-state. Citizens sensitive to the environment must be global citizens: as we noted in chapter 2, environmental processes do not respect the artificial boundaries of nation-states. At the moment, such a model of citizenship is no more than the aspiration of the environmental movement. As such, the question of what environmental citizenship might eventually involve is necessarily highly speculative. There are, however, a number of suggestions concerning how environmentalists should aim to go beyond Marshall's model to develop a global, environmental citizenship.

First, there is the issue of citizenship rights and who should be included as citizens. As we have noted, citizenship rights have been extended by social movements, and environmentalists now argue that they should be extended still further. In the first place, future generations should be included as having citizenship rights. In some ways, this is not as controversial a proposal as it might initially seem. To some extent, the rights of future citizens who are now children are considered, rights to education and welfare, for example. Furthermore, there is the expectation that citizenship will be awarded to those as yet unborn in so far as the relevant conditions are expected to continue in much the same way. The Norwegian Constitution seems to have formalized such an expectation in relation to the environment in an amendment which states that:

> Every person has the right to an environment that is conducive to health and to natural surroundings whose productivity and diversity are preserved. Natural resources should be used on the basis of comprehensive long-term considerations whereby this right will be safeguarded for future generations as well. (quoted in Christoff, 1996: 165)

More controversially, animal rights activists argue that rights should also be extended to animals, on the grounds that they too suffer, and also that they have moral value equal to that of human beings and so they are owed justice on an equal basis (Van Steenbergen, 1994). There are obvious difficulties with this argument, however, since animals, unlike humans, will never be able to exercise citizenship rights on their own behalf, nor respect the rights of other citizens, nor carry out the duties expected of citizens. It therefore seems more reasonable to think of the protection of animals and other non-human species as a matter of *responsibility* on the part of citizens, rather than as a matter of citizens' rights.

Secondly, then, global environmental citizenship is often seen in terms of responsibility for nature, or "environmental stewardship" as it is sometimes called. This emphasis on responsibility rather than rights marks a difference between environmentalism and other social movements, and perhaps even a conflict of interests. It is not that the idea of responsibility is new; in fact, it has always been intrinsic to citizenship. For example, the right to vote implies also the responsibility to elect political leaders, and in some countries citizens are legally required to participate in local and general elections. Social movements have, however, generally campaigned for the extension of citizens' rights, not their duties and obligations. There may be a tension between environmentalism and other social movements over this issue since the extension of rights to welfare has depended on the expansion of the capitalist economy. While some representatives of the green movement see concern for the environment as compatible with capitalist reproduction, others argue that economic growth is unsustainable in the long-term interests of the environment. There is, then, uncertainty over whether states can meet demands for social rights to welfare and social security and at the same time environmentalist demands to curb capitalist exploitation and despoliation of environmental resources.

Thirdly, citizens' responsibility for the environment is often linked to greater participation in political life. The suggestions for increasing this participation are varied. Steward (1991) suggests that citizens should be involved with experts in assessing the environmental risks which affect them and what should be done to counteract them. Christoff (1996), directing his attention explicitly toward the transnational and international level, suggests regional parliaments, like a democratized European Parliament, or referendums of populations in regions of ecological significance which cross national borders. At the moment, however, participation in environmental politics tends to be much more informal, involving mobilization on the part of such organizations as Greenpeace and Friends of the Earth. The politics of the environmental movement mainly involves lobbying state and international bodies to legislate on environmental standards, media campaigns to influence individual consumer choices and corporate investment decisions, the provision of environmental education and information, and so on. In other words, it is a politics which is conducted outside conventional political institutions and which aims mainly to foster a new political culture of environmental awareness. In this way, the networks of the environmental movement may contribute to a growth in transnational practices and orientations which mean the emergence of a global civil society (Falk, 1994b).

Writers on environmental citizenship tend to see the emergence of global civil society as offering the greatest hope for its future. Evidently, globalization in the widest sense – the growth of transnational economic and social processes and the setting up of international political institutions – does not necessarily mean an increase in environmental awareness. On the contrary, up to a point, economic globalization may simply result in a more extensive and effective exploitation of the Earth's resources and more widespread environmental degradation. Of course, environmentalists believe that the planet's inhabitants will, by the same token, be increasingly exposed to ecological disasters as a result. However, this will not necessarily lead to informed measures to safeguard the environment. People may choose to ignore "nature's warnings." Nor will a greater degree of democratic participation lead automatically to a greater sensitivity to the environment. Indeed, it might equally well lead to greater destruction if citizens embrace a productivist, consumer identity. Global environmental citizenship requires an increase in public awareness of the issues and the construction of the will to act in such a way as to ensure a healthy and flourishing environment in the long term. Hence, the importance of cultural politics in a global civil society.

In fact, the environmental movement is beginning to see some success in its contribution to the formation of a global civil society. The activities of environmental organizations are contributing to the growth of public awareness and some consideration has been given to environmental issues on the part of international political institutions. There is now a system of international laws, conventions, and treaties covering such cases as protection of the North Sea, the elimination of CFC gases, and so on. However, in comparison with environmentalists' views of the seriousness of environmental destruction, and the importance of changes needed to deal adequately with it, such measures are extremely limited. Global citizenship remains an ideal. It need not, however, be seen as a mere ideal. Richard Falk prefers to see global citizenship as aspirational in the sense that it involves a political project oriented toward the future, encouraging activities oriented toward creating a community which does not yet exist, that of global citizens. The cultural politics of global citizenship involves the creation of a new collective identity. As Falk (1994b: 138–9) puts it:

> traditional citizenship operates spatially, global citizenship operates temporally, reaching out to a future-to-be-created, and making of such a person "a citizen pilgrim," that is, someone on a journey to "a country" to be established in the future in accordance with more idealistic and normatively rich conceptions of political community. (Falk, 1994b: 138–9)

In accordance with this sentiment, we turn to the question of how the potentials for more pluralistic, egalitarian, and globally oriented citizenship developed in the activities of social movements might be realized in the future political communities of Western liberal democracies.

Notes

1 There are important terminological differences between the US and the rest of the world in relation to the terms "neo-liberalism" and the "New Right." In the US, the "New Right" tends to mean the Protestant religious right, while elsewhere it means the movement connected to political parties, such as the Conservative Party in Britain under Mrs Thatcher's leadership, consisting of those committed to neo-liberal economic policies and divided between moral libertarians, on one wing, and moral "fundamentalists." Liberalism in the US is associated with those who advocate the extension of the welfare state, while elsewhere it refers to those who prefer "market forces" to state intervention (Giddens, 1994: 23). Here we shall use the more widespread definitions.

2 My thanks to David Owen for this point.

CHAPTER 5

Democracy and Democratization

"Democracy" is the term which legitimates political regimes across the world in the late twentieth century. However, while thinkers such as Fukuyama (1992) trumpet the triumph of liberal democracy with the fall of communism, it is widely acknowledged in the West that "really existing" representative democracy does not work as well as it should. Indications include the declining numbers of voters who participate in national elections in countries where voting is not obligatory, the increase in the volatility of party political allegiances, and the rapidity with which media-led issues come to prominence and are just as quickly forgotten. The democratic public in the West is generally seen to be apathetic, cynical and unstable. On one hand, then, democracy is celebrated; on the other, there is growing concern about how it works in practice.[1]

This ambivalence is also a feature of recent sociological accounts of democracy, which treat it as a normative ideal, while criticizing "really existing" liberal democracies. As we noted in chapter 1, political sociology is concerned above all with the study of the empirical conditions within which power is exercised and constrained. It may be distinguished in this way from political theory and political philosophy, concerned above all with conceptual analysis and normative justifications. However, identifying potentially progressive alternatives in existing conditions and considering how they might be realized is an important aspect of the new political sociology. In this respect, it is both empirical and normative.

In this chapter we will give detailed consideration to three models of democracy. The first two represent the most prominent models of democracy in contemporary sociology: deliberative democracy and post-structuralist radical democracy.[2] In particular, we shall look at the work of Jürgen Habermas as exemplary of the first, and that of Laclau and Mouffe as exemplary of the second. We will look at them in the context of the sociological literature to which they are related, on complex societies and postmodernity respectively, to avoid the tendency of most discussions of democratic theory to treat it as political philosophy rather than political sociology. The third model is that of David Held, the theorist who has contributed most to the sociological understanding of the implications of globalization for democracy.

Laclau and Mouffe's theory of radical democracy is the only one of the three which explicitly deals with cultural politics. As a post-modern theory of democracy, it is usually opposed to Habermas's model of deliberative democracy, which he sees as a contribution to "the unfinished project of modernity" (Habermas, 1981). As we shall see, it is certainly the case that there are important differences be-tween them. However, in relation to traditional political sociology, they also share certain features.

In his influential book *Political Sociology* (1993), Tom Bottomore describes the field as traditionally organized in terms of two princi-pal traditions concerned with the significance and consequences of the emergence of liberal democracy. The first is represented by Tocqueville, writing in the first half of the nineteenth century, and, at least in some respects, continued by Weberians in the early twentieth century. Tocqueville was a French aristocrat, somewhat alarmed, but also fascinated, by the modern society being shaped by the democratic movement of his time. Above all, he saw the social equality developing as a result of democracy as both good and bad: good, because it would lead to greater well-being for all and a more stable society; bad, because, in the process of levelling out existing social hierarchies, it would undermine individual freedom. As Bottomore points out, in analysing "democratic societies" as such, Tocqueville does not restrict himself to the analysis of a form of gov-ernment; he is concerned with what would later be called "a demo-cratic way of life" (Bottomore, 1993: 12–3). However, he does see the political regime of democracy as the prime mover in modern society: it gives value to the well-being of the population as a whole, destroys hierarchies, and encourages the new industrial society based on trade and manufacturing. In contrast to that based on Marxism, the tradition in political sociology founded on Tocqueville's work takes politics to be an independent and highly significant factor in determining social and economic life. In this respect, he is followed by Weber, concerned, as we have seen, with the concentration of the means of administration as a parallel development to that of the means of production. Like Tocqueville, Weber was pessimistic about the long-term effects of mass democracy for individual freedom; hence his support for charismatic politicians to counteract the rationalizing effects of the bureaucracy required to administer it (see pp. 11–12).

The other tradition identified by Bottomore (1993) is that developed on the basis of Marx's analyses of capitalism and democracy. In this case, the democratic state is not seen as an independent force for social change, but rather as dependent on the capitalist mode of production. Marxists are more impressed than Toqueville by the emerging industrial society and its effects in producing social classes. Democracy on this account is a product of the emerging bourgeoisie. The major debate in Marxism concerning liberal democracy has, in fact, been over the extent to which it is merely a tool of the bourgeoisie or may be used by the workers to further their class interests, so leading to a genuine form of democracy in which social life is really governed by "the people" (Bottomore, 1993: 13).

From the perspective of contemporary sociological studies of democracy, these very different traditions have some common features. First, both traditions in some sense accept liberal democracy on its own terms in so far as they focus on the institutions of representative democracy as the site of democratic participation. Of course, Marxists are critical of liberal democracy since they see it as extremely limited; societies are not governed democratically since democratic institutions are nothing but a foil for economic interests. However, liberal democracy fails, on the Marxist account, in so far as its "officially" designated political institutions fail. The state is not, as it should be according to liberals, a neutral arbiter of conflicts in civil society, genuine interests are not represented in parliament, and so on. Weberians also restrict their criticisms of liberal democracy to its political institutions and their effects, however far-reaching and widespread such effects might be. In this case, it is the rigidities of state bureaucracy and the irrationality and ignorance of "the people" which mean that representative democracy does not live up to its own ideals. Secondly, both traditions tend to see society as relatively homogeneous, made up of large, fixed groups with stable interests. In the case of Marxists, society is divided (if not empirically then analytically) into the two classes of capitalism locked into conflict over their opposed interests. In Tocqueville's view, democracy itself produces social homogeneity as equality is extended into all areas of life. The point is more complicated in the case of Weberians. Although they do see rationalization as homogenizing, they also see a multiplicity of interest groups forming in capitalism, particularly in relation to the stratification of classes in the labor market. It is these groups which are represented by political parties. In neither tradition, however, is there scope for analyzing democracy under conditions of radical flux and fragmentation in which occupational positions are unstable and cross-cut by gender, sex, "race," and ethnic identities.

It is in such conditions that new political sociologists set about analyzing democracy. As a result of socio-economic instability and the influence of social movements demanding greater participation in a multi-cultural and "post-feminist" society, democracy is now more pluralist and fragmented than it was for the older traditions. The negotiation of identity and difference within and across social movements is one of the principal preoccupations of recent democratic theory. At the same time, taking the politics of social movements seriously also means that there are multiple sites of democratic contestation. While it is still true that only states have the power to pass legislation supported by force, a key consideration where citizenship rights are an issue, it is not the case that they thereby have a monopoly of power, even over those living within their territorial boundaries.

Democratic struggles in contemporary society take place in cultural politics distinct from those of the state in at least three important senses. First, as we have seen in the case of social movements, they are as much about changing practices in civil society as they are about policy-making and passing law. Secondly, they are concerned with redefining the remit of the state itself. In the case of citizenship rights, the scope and capacities of the state are contested and redefined in relation to the identity of citizens and what they may legitimately expect from it. While this type of cultural politics is conducted through the institutions of representative democracy as well as between civil society and the state, in so far as it is concerned with the practices through which the state itself is formed, it necessarily goes beyond existing institutions. Thirdly, democracy at the level of the nation-state is problematized in a way not considered by the older traditions as a result of processes of globalization. If the state can no longer control economic processes and national politics in the name of "the people," then democracy at this level is called into question even as an ideal. Political sociologists attempting to identify possibilities of enhancing democratic participation must consider the cultural politics in which international, transnational, and supranational political institutions are being formed.

In the late twentieth century, then, social processes and political activities from both "below" and "above" the state mean that political sociologists address quite a different situation from that faced by "the founding fathers." In this respect, although theories of deliberative and radical democracy are opposed in terms of their philosophical premises, they both attempt to deal with similar sociological conditions. Both theories try to show how democracy is possible in a context in which social identities are fragmented and where the nation-state is decentered as the site of politics. Habermas's model of deliberative democracy and Laclau and Mouffe's model of radical democracy both show an appreciation of the importance of politics outside the formal political institutions of the state and offer accounts of how this potential for greater democratic participation might be realized. They share a view of social movements as largely a progressive force in contemporary politics, offering the possibility of new forms of solidarity and co-operation. This is particularly important in that fairer and more fulfilling forms of social life are seen as possible only where the advancement of commodification and bureaucratic structures into every aspect of social life is made more democratically accountable, and this can only be achieved where progressive forms of social solidarity are realized. We shall look at these models in turn, in sections 5.1 and 5.2, critically examining each one as a response to the sociological conditions of complex societies and postmodernity respectively.

In section 5.3, we turn to David Held's model of cosmopolitan governance in order to consider the possibilities of global democratization. This has received very little attention in the other models, but it is clear that processes of globalization require forms of global democracy in order to regulate and deal with their effects. Held's pioneering work in this respect will be discussed in the light of the model of cultural politics developed throughout the book. It will be suggested that this understanding of cultural politics complements Held's theory and offers a way of understanding, in principle, how it might be realized.

5.1 COMPLEXITY AND DEMOCRACY

In so far as theories of complex societies are based on structuralist-functionalist theories of modernization, they are definitively outside the terms of the "postmodern turn" within which, as we have seen, most recent sociological work is situated. Structuralist-functionalism sees society as developing "behind the backs" of social actors, often despite their intentions; as an evolving system rather than as produced by social actors in meaningful engagement with their world. Such ideas are not necessarily adopted uncritically by theorists of complex society. As we shall see, Habermas in particular takes the view that not all social life can be understood in structuralist-functionalist terms. Nevertheless, in this respect, this body of work is different from that which we have been examining up to now. Habermas's work is also outside the "postmodern turn" in so far as he sees democracy as grounded in the necessary conditions of language. Such an understanding is assured only within a realist epistemology; the structures of language which give rise to the "validity claims" of speech acts are seen as existing independently of social construction. Habermas has, in fact, been one of the most prominent opponents of postmodernism for its lack of concern with scientific knowledge and universal values. Against postmodernism, Habermas advocates a renewed commitment to the Enlightenment ideal of reason, believing that to abandon its application to social life is also to abandon justice and the possibility of a more co-operative social order (Habermas, 1987c).

Here, however, we shall not be discussing the philosophical differences between Habermas and postmodernists, the usual basis of comparison between them. We will focus on sociological differences, and similarities, even though these cannot, of course, be neatly separated from philosophical questions. We will consider Habermas's model of democracy as a response to the conditions of complex societies, assessing it as an attempt to show how democracy is possible despite the breakdown of traditional social solidarities and the difficulties of controlling highly bureaucratized and commodified social systems.

Complex societies and the difficulties of democracy

Habermas is, in fact, the most optimistic of theorists of complexity and democracy. For others, notably Claus Offe and Danilo Zolo, complexity makes democracy virtually impossible. Although these political sociologists do not accept all the details of the functionalism on which theories of complex societies are based, they all take seriously its underlying thesis: that social groups tend to organize themselves to carry out increasingly differentiated tasks so that society develops into functionally specialized "subsystems" as it advances. As a result of modernization, society has developed into a highly differentiated and fragmented set of subsystems which mean that it is now impossible to bring it under the control of democratically elected representatives of "the people." While, historically, modernization made democracy possible, it is now making it impossible.

The most important characteristics of complex societies are as follows. First, they have a highly differentiated division of labor so that tasks are carried out in specialized subsystems. This makes for an increasingly fragmented society as events and experiences within one social environment are impossible to translate into the terms used in another. In the example given by Danilo Zolo (1992: 5), a religious experience cannot be conveyed in terms relevant to a sports club, office or nuclear research laboratory. More obviously, it is the case that technical language used in a particular sphere is simply inaccessible to those who are not familiar with it. Secondly, although there is discontinuity of understanding between subsystems, they are increasingly functionally interdependent. Again, to take an example from Zolo's (1992: 5) work, a political campaign is dependent on the media, which are dependent on legislation governing political use of the media, and often also on the advertising market. Thirdly, there is an increasing lack of social solidarity as a result of the rapidly changing, fragmented social and cultural formations of contemporary society. In particular, there has been a breaking up of the class structures, identities, and political organizations which underpinned the democratic welfare state. Fourthly, complex societies tend to have "weak" states. According to Claus Offe (1996), this is because lack of social solidarity means that an over-arching institution like the state which binds all citizens is no longer seen as legitimate, and also because, since it is undermined by processes of globalization, it is difficult to use the state to protect collective interests or introduce reforms for the common good.

Offe, a collaborator with Habermas in his early work, argues that contemporary societies should be seen as "complex" rather than modern, and certainly not as "postmodern," because they are characterized particularly by rigidity which militates against the opening up of possibilities supposed to be produced by modernization. Complex societies are faced with historically unique problems in that prediction and projection become virtually impossible. Specialized functional differentiation means that the unintended consequences of any action taken within one subsystem on the future possibilities of the others are extremely difficult to predict, especially given the understanding that benefits in modern societies should be universal. Once we actually suffer these consequences we see that often what was designed to enhance freedom of choice for everyone actually has the reverse effect. Offe gives the example of a transport system. If it were decided to facilitate the use of the car for everyone, it would thereby obstruct its efficient use by anyone (Offe, 1996: 13). In so far, then, as democracy involves both participation in forming the will of the people and also the execution of that will, complexity is a serious barrier to the realization of democracy. In Offe's words:

> "complex" societies have become rigid to such an extent that the very attempt to reflect normatively upon or to renew their "order," that is, the nature of the coordination of the processes which take place in them, is virtually precluded by dint of their practical futility and thus their essential inadequacy. (Offe, 1996: 12)

Since, in complex societies, it is impossible to conceive of projects embracing the society as a whole, the expansion of options generated by rationalized subsytems does not actually lead to more freedom for individuals.

Offe does suggest two, rather meager, sources of hope for democracy. The first is the rise of social movements in civil society. Here he agrees broadly with Habermas concerning their potential to influence political decision-making from outside the political system by deliberations in civil society (Offe and Preuss, 1991). Since this claim is more fully developed in Habermas's work, we will discuss it below. The second is his view that, to institute democracy, society must be simplified as much as possible without losing the gains of modernization, to make decisions more transparent and to increase control. In particular, Offe suggests, it is important to loosen the interdependencies between the different sectors of society. The main example he gives here is the independence of Norway, Sweden, Austria, and Switzerland from supranational political-economic alliances. He argues that the success of these national economies in comparison with those of other Western European nations is due to the greater control they exercise over social, political, and economic systems within their respective territories. The retreat from globalization would be a way of strengthening the steering power of the state by simplifying its social environment. To the same end, he argues, the state should "unburden itself," devolving power and responsibilities as much as possible to other institutions and groups in society. It should retreat in an organized way, providing the regulatory framework within which essential social functions could be carried out without becoming dominated by market considerations and private interests. Offe admits, however, that such solutions probably require just the conditions which no longer exist in complex societies: a "strong" state already loosely integrated into supranational institutions and processes, which can withdraw from society in an orderly fashion, and a culturally homogeneous nation with strong traditions and institutions on which such a retreat could rely (Offe, 1996: 68–70). Furthermore, it is simply impossible to "opt-out" of many processes of globalization: the risks associated with environmental damage are only the most obvious example.

Danilo Zolo is still more pessimistic than Offe about the possibilities of democracy in complex societies. He focuses more explicitly on the political process, arguing that the dominant model of democracy in political science is now out of date. This is the model of "competitive elitism," initially developed by Joseph Schumpeter in the 1940s as a corrective to what he called "classical democracy" which, taking ancient Athens as the ideal, saw democracy as requir-ing the full participation of all citizens in decision-making to realize the common good. According to Schumpeter, in modern societies this is impossible; democracy can only consist of the competition between political parties for citizens' votes. Individuals cannot participate in decision-making directly, but only through the selection of those professionals who will make expert decisions on their behalf (see pp. 13–14). Schumpeter's model has often been criticized for allowing only a very attenuated form of democracy, but Zolo argues that in complex societies even those minimal conditions he saw as provid-ing the possibility of democracy have been undermined. In particu-lar, there is no genuine competition between points of view from which electors might choose. Zolo sees several reasons for this. First, there is no genuine competition between parties; they all put forward much the same policies. This is a product of the way in which parties have themselves become integrated into the state. The "new class" of party professionals exercises influence in economic, administrative, and information systems and identifies the party with the public bureaucracy as a whole. Inter-party competition is less important, in Zolo's view, than the common interest shared by members of the "complex organism" created by all the parties together. Combined with the tendency to "converge toward the center" to attract volatile votes and to please the largest number of voters, parties no longer present different programs between which citizens might choose. Secondly, there is the risk of political paralysis with the fragmentation of interests acting on the political process from outside the political sphere proper, including those of economic, religious, and technological groups. Thirdly, most pol-itical negotiation takes place between such groups behind the scenes and is simply not visible to the average voter. Finally, the rise of the mass media has resulted in the decline of the public sphere in which citizens previously exchanged political views and issues were debated. According to Zolo, all personal experience and thought is now mediated through television, radio, newspapers, and so on, so that political agendas are set by those who control the arguments and images represented there rather than by the citizens themselves (Zolo, 1992).

Citizens have, then, been turned into poorly informed consumers without any real choice. Zolo sees this as a dangerous situation, pos-sibly leading to totalitarianism. His solution, in so far as he is willing to suggest one, is not, however, greater democratic participation, since this is unrealistic in complex societies for precisely the reasons he has outlined. Zolo argues that what is necessary to safeguard individual freedom is rather the protection of social complexity through the division of powers and the rule of law. He sees this as realistic because civil rights to private property, freedom of exchange, physical integrity, and so on, may be seen as a by-product of what is functionally necessary in complex industrial societies, the division between the political and economic systems (Zolo, 1992: 181–2). On Zolo's model, it seems that what the citizen should expect from democracy is minimal, amounting to no more than civil rights.

Jürgen Habermas: democracy, social movements, and the public sphere

Both Zolo's and Offe's recommendations concerning democracy are severe in comparison with those of the dominant figure in this tradition, Jürgen Habermas. He is more optimistic about the potential for democracy in contemporary life, in part because – unlike Zolo for whom political activity is confined to the state – he sees the mobilization of social movements in civil society as a significant contribution to its development. Nevertheless, for Habermas as for Offe and Zolo, the complexity of contemporary society does mean that democratic participation in government must be extremely limited.

Habermas also draws on structuralist-functionalism for his analysis of the evolution of society into contemporary complexity. He sees modernization as resulting in the functional differentiation of society into four principal spheres, characterized by two different types of orientation. The economy and the bureaucratic state are both seen as systems in which social actors orient themselves by thinking strategically on the basis of perceived self-interest. These systems produce their own media of communication, money and power respectively, which are used to steer society. Habermas sees these systems as functioning according to their own internal logic, and reaching a high degree of efficiency as a result. The other two spheres Habermas designates "the lifeworld," comprising the public sphere of civil society outside the state and economy and the private domestic sphere. Actors in these arenas orient themselves in terms of communicative action, toward understanding each other rather than toward bringing about objective, impersonal results (instrumental action) or influencing other actors (strategic action). Although modernization has produced efficiency, Habermas does not see it in benign terms. He is concerned that money and power are more effective than the influence produced by the public sphere and the commitment produced by the private domestic sphere. The lifeworld is continually threatened with domination through commercialization and bureaucratic administration which encroach into community and personal life, controlling and distorting human communication. According to Habermas (1987b), it is this "colonization of the lifeworld" which democratic social movements must resist.

Habermas argues that the potential for democracy developed as modernization progressed, but that the complexity of contemporary societies means that it is now extremely limited. In an influential early work, *The Structural Transformation of the Public Sphere* (1989), he made a historical study of the growth of societies and clubs in the eighteenth century which provided social spaces for the rational criticism of state practices by informed outsiders. It is something like this role that he has in mind for social movements, although he sees it as very much more difficult to fulfill in the twentieth century than in early modernity. Although he is critical of the early bourgeois public sphere as socially exclusive – composed as it was of educated, propertied men – Habermas's main concern in this book is with its degeneration. He sees this as a result of three main developments which, at the same time, made it less exclusive. First, as the public sphere expanded to include more participants, large-scale organizations such as political parties, with their oligarchic-bureaucratic tendencies, replaced individuals. Secondly, the clear distinction between public and private was undermined and public life became more a matter of negotiating interests between parties, administration, and special interest groups than attempting to reach agreement about the objective common good, however idealistic that might have been. Large organizations and the introduction of particular interests into the public sphere produced a fragmentation of the public and an unwillingness to step outside narrow interests in order to participate in discussion concerning the good of society as a whole. Thirdly, the growth of mass communications made citizens into the passive recipients of products of "the culture industry" and worked to manufacture consent without genuine deliberation. The degeneration of the bourgeois public sphere is, therefore, an example of the critical theme Habermas was to develop in his later work, the destruction of rational communication in the lifeworld by the encroachment of the economy and state. In *The Structural Transformation of the Public Sphere*, however, he made radical proposals concerning the possibility of revolutionizing society which he was later to retract. He argued that there is no possibility of reviving the public sphere in contemporary society, but that the organizations and institutions which have destroyed it may be democratized from within. Political parties and organizations, state agencies, and the media should be organized in such a way as to make them open to rational-critical debate, to counteract concentrations of power and money, and to realize the transformative potential of a reformed democratic public sphere (Habermas, 1989; Calhoun, 1992).

In his later work, Habermas's model of democracy became much less radical. He gave up the aim of influencing institutions from the inside: principally, it would seem, because he accepted the functionalist view that systems work according to their own logic and cannot, therefore, be transformed politically. In particular, against the socialism with which he was previously allied, he argued that the free-market economy cannot easily be directed by the administrative apparatus without losing efficiency, while the state must be kept within strict bounds if totalitarianism is to be avoided (Calhoun, 1992: 436).

Habermas does not fully endorse functionalism. He has engaged in debate with Niklas Luhmann, the principal contemporary exponent of this view, rejecting his systems theory of society as a self-referential totality on the grounds that it is unnecessarily conservative. It fails to take into account the development of the lifeworld in which resistance to the subsystems of the economy and state is not only possible but also desirable. Nevertheless, he does see the economy and state as self-enclosed systems. As a result, he accepts the functionalist view that the possibilities for democracy are limited. At some points he seems to suggest that the sole aim of citizens should be the protection of the lifeworld against these systems. He casts social movements in this role of defence here, but it is very doubtful that reaction against capitalism and bureaucracy is the only concern of social movements which, as we have seen, are often concerned to extend administration and the market into the "private domain" in order to ensure citizenship rights. This makes them rather different from the community-based, local groups critical of capitalist growth which Habermas seems to have in mind (Habermas, 1987b: 391–6). At other points in his work, however, Habermas is much more positive concerning the role of social movements and the possibilities for democracy, suggesting that it is possible to influence the state administration system, and so to reorganize the economy to some extent, but that this can only be done from outside the system, "in a siege-like manner" (Calhoun, 1992: 452).

Since *The Structural Transformation of the Public Sphere*, until his most recent work on law, Habermas has actually been little concerned with the institutional basis of democracy. He has been occupied above all with working out the grounds for normative ideals produced in communicative action. He sees this as necessary because the fragmentation of social interests and values in late modernity militates against the solidarity which is the only means of prevailing over money and administrative power. Habermas finds the grounds for normative claims in what he calls the "validity claims" of language. He argues that all acts of communication involve four validity claims: to comprehensibility, objective truth, moral correctness, and sincerity. We assume that anyone who speaks seriously could answer the questions: "What do you mean?," "Is what you say true?," "Are you entitled to say that?" and "Do you really mean it?" (Outhwaite, 1994: 40). While in everyday communication these claims are not generally questioned, Habermas maintains that if they become problematic, either because interlocutors disagree or because they misunderstand each other, it is possible to shift to another level – that of discourse ethics – in which claims may be explicitly discussed. Once the taken-for-granted agreement of the lifeworld is broken, it is possible to search for rational agreement by testing out the justification of claims in discussion. In fact, Habermas argues, communication presupposes the possibility of genuine consensus concerning validity claims and therefore the possibility of unrestrained discussion in an "ideal-speech situation" to which all speakers have equal access and in which only the force of the better argument prevails (Dews, 1986: 163). This, then, is the principle which grounds democratic deliberation. Furthermore, according to Habermas, validity claims are only justified in discourse ethics if they are shown to be generalizable; that is, if they are or could in principle be agreed on by everyone who might be affected by them (Habermas, 1990). For example, if everyone potentially affected agrees that it is right to tolerate religious groups even if some of the rituals in which they engage are found to be offensive to others, then it is right to do so. The justification of validity claims in democratic deliberation requires consensus on general principles which may then be taken to represent the community's common interests. In this way, democracy can serve to unite the fragmented groups of modern societies around common norms and understandings and enable citizens to present a united front against the colonization of the lifeworld and to influence the administrative power of the state.

In his most recent work, Habermas returns somewhat to the question of the institutions through which democracy might achieve such effects. He turns to constitutional law, arguing that it has a close connection with discourse ethics because both share the principle that the interests of each person affected should be given equal weight. The law and legal decisions must be non-partisan and therefore open to rational criticism and democratic deliberation; law-making is only legitimate in so far as it achieves the agreement of all citizens. This is only possible where the constitution itself is democratic; that is, where the basic individual rights of citizens are protected by law. As Outhwaite points out, the meaning of democracy should not be taken too literally here; it is not that everyone should actually participate in an actual assembly of citizens. As Habermas puts it: "popular sovereignty . . . draws back into the so to speak subject-less communication circuits of forums and association. Only in this anonymous form can its communicatively fluid power bind the administrative power of the state apparatus to the will of the citizens" (quoted in Outhwaite, 1994: 143). Habermas's model of democracy in conditions of complexity is a reconceptualization of the public sphere in which social movements are the principal actors in democratic will formation, working to define issues in less formal settings which are then dealt with through conventional political channels. More concretely, he proposes introducing more democratic procedures and participation into political parties, more plebiscitary elements into the constitution, and more regulation of the media to curb political and economic agenda-setting and to promote the freedom of critical audiences (Habermas, 1996: 442).

There are a number of common criticisms of Habermas's model of democracy. Here we will focus only on those which are relevant to the sociological aspects of his theory of democracy. First, there is the question of Habermas's adherence to at least some elements of functionalist theory, which seriously limits the possibilities of democratizing the institutions of the state and capitalist economy. As Thomas McCarthy (1991), Habermas's translator, argues, it is not entirely clear why he feels compelled to adopt functionalism. Habermas himself has been critical of functionalism in the past, mainly on the well-rehearsed grounds that, while it may provide good explanations for the self-preservation of biological organisms, where social structures are maintained, restructured, and destructured in the ongoing interactions of social members, and where self-preservation cannot simply be taken as physical, the very idea of a self-maintaining system is, at best, metaphorical. McCarthy (1991: 120) argues that he has subsequently made "a pact" with systems theory in which "certain areas are marked out within which it may move freely, on condition it keeps entirely away from others." He argues that this pact is unnecessarily restrictive for critical theory.

According to Hans Joas (1991), Habermas finds systems theory useful because it allows for the consideration of social processes which are not the product of intentional actions. However, as Joas points out, functionalism is not the only way in which unintended consequences may be taken into account (Joas, 1991). From the point of view of those working within the "postmodern turn" in sociology, like Anthony Giddens, unintended consequences provide the conditions within which action takes place which either sustains or disrupts existing social practices and their outcomes. As such, social processes are always to some extent amenable to collective action. In Giddens's view, functionalism leads to the neglect of situated practices and the way in which they are reproduced by social actors knowledgeable about the context in which they act (Giddens, 1984). Similarly, post-structuralists reject functionalist ideas of causality and totality. Functionalism, with its understanding of social life as subject to "quasi-natural" laws of development, is incompatible with post-structuralist theories of social reproduction. For Laclau and Mouffe, for example, the indeterminacy of social meaning results in inherently unstable social practices which, even as they are reproduced, are necessarily open to resignification in new ways. Though they may remain relatively constant over time, this is a contingent matter of historical relevance rather than the product of their causal interdependence with other social structures, as it is for functionalists. As we shall see in the next section, the understanding of social structures as relatively open to cultural politics makes Laclau and Mouffe a good deal more optimistic concerning the potential for the democratization of social institutions than Habermas, Offe, or Zolo, working largely within the terms of functionalist theory.

The second main criticism of Habermas's theory of democracy concerns the way in which he sees democratic deliberation as oriented toward consensus. The most celebrated argument in this respect is that elaborated by Lyotard in *The Postmodern Condition* (1984). In fact, as Outhwaite points out, there is actually a good deal of overlap between Lyotard's and Habermas's understanding of contemporary society as pluralized and fragmented, without belief in over-arching principles of moral reason and social progress (Outhwaite, 1994: 99–100). However, for Lyotard, Habermas's concern to generate solidarity through reasoned consensus is worse than the problem he is trying to solve. He describes the idea of consensus as "terroristic," doing violence to the heterogeneity of the language-games liberated by the postmodern incredulity toward meta-narratives. As he puts it, "Postmodern knowledge . . . refines our sensitivity to differences and reinforces our ability to tolerate the incommensurable" (Lyotard, 1984: xxv). As Lyotard sees it, consensus attempts to regularize and homogenize those differences, if not destroying, then, at least marginalizing local and specific cultural understandings. The postmodern theme of respecting differences also has resonance for some feminists and multi-culturalists who point out that, although difference is recognized in Habermas's vision of democracy, it is always to be overcome for the sake of common agreement, rather than cultivated and encouraged (Gould, 1996: 172–3). As we have seen in chapter 4, the theme of respecting difference is central to the cultural politics of citizenship in which social movements are engaged.

Finally, Habermas's model of democratic deliberation is seen as over-rationalist and therefore as potentially exclusionary of identities which are outside the norms of existing liberal democratic politics. Rather than cultivating the postmodern "responsibility toward Otherness" exemplified by post-structuralism, Habermas's model risks producing the marginalization of certain groups. As Iris Marion Young (1996) argues, even in highly controlled conditions of democratic decision-making, communication takes place as much through greeting, rhetoric, and storytelling as through rational argument involving "giving good reasons" and accepting only the force of the better argument. She maintains that to fail to recognize that there is a plurality of speaking styles is unwittingly to privilege the norms of formal, general, and assertive argument actually associated with dominant groups in society. In order to include everyone in democratic participation, especially women and those from subordinate cultural groups, Young argues that wider forms of communication must be given a place (Young, 1996). This criticism is particularly serious given that one of the aims of Habermas's model is to overcome the fragmentation of contemporary society by making deliberative democracy inclusive of everyone and therefore creative of new forms of solidarity.

It could also be argued that Habermas's over-rationalist model of democratic deliberation leads him to neglect certain aspects of the public sphere and the politics of social movements in relation to the mass media. In *The Theory of Communicative Action* (1987), Habermas does see the media as potentially contributing to rational debate, rather than as necessarily contributing to its degeneration as he argued in *The Structural Transformation of the Public Sphere*. He sees the media as embodying an "ambivalent potential" because they open up communication across time and space, as well as strengthening social control by channeling communication through administrative apparatuses and multinational corporations (Habermas, 1987b: 389–91). He acknowledges, too, the recent work in media studies which suggests that audiences are not simply the passive recipients of images, stereotypes, and simplified agendas, both because the interests of media owners and professionals are not so smoothly integrated as to present unified effects and also because audiences themselves are now seen as more active in their interpretation. Habermas's analysis is more consistent with this research than that of Zolo, who simply does not address it at all, a significant omission given the important part played by the mass media in creating an ignorant and docile electorate in his view. His commitment to rational debate would presumably, however, rule out the kind of "spectacular" contestation in which social movements have engaged as a serious contribution to democratic will formation. It is difficult to see how the incidents staged by Greenpeace specifically for the world media, for example, would fit Habermas's notion of the public sphere, or indeed, of communicative action. Social movements generally contribute to democratic debate in the public sphere by using the media strategically to negotiate aesthetic and moral meanings. In this respect, they are more easily understood as engaging in cultural politics than entering into rational deliberation.

5.2   POSTMODERNITY AND RADICAL DEMOCRACY

One of the most confusing aspects of debates around postmodernity is that those who see contemporary society as postmodern do not necessarily situate themselves within the terms of the "postmodern turn." On the contrary, sociologists tend to suppose that postmodernity can only be theorized "from the outside," as it were, rather than entering into what they see as the relativism and nihilism of postmodernism as a way of thinking. This is true, for example, of Zygmunt Bauman, one of the most prominent of those who have tried to establish the sociology of postmodernity. For him, as for others, postmodernism is the culture of postmodernity and as such it is characterized by skepticism about ultimate truths, the belief that values depend on one's perspective, and the uncertainty and indeterminacy of meanings. He argues that it is the task of sociology to analyze this culture as a whole and to understand its relationship to the social structures which underpin it, rather than to embrace the postmodern skepticism toward meta-narratives (Bauman, 1992; see also Featherstone, 1988). The extent to which it is possible, or desirable, for sociologists to remain or to get outside culture is, of course, questionable (see Crook et al., 1992: 231–9; Seidman, 1994b).

We shall not discuss this question here, however. Our topic is the understanding of democratic politics in the sociology of postmodernity. Politics is closely linked to culture in postmodernity. Theorists of postmodernity are all concerned to emphasize that one of its key features is the expansion of culture. While culture in modernity is seen as occupying an autonomous sphere, concerned with such aspects of life as art, self-expression, religion, and morality, in post-modernity it becomes part of every aspect of life. As Kumar puts it, culture takes over society until they both become "one, or at least, twin aspects of the same (insubstantial) thing" (Kumar, 1995: 119). For the most part, this expansion of culture makes sociologists of postmodernity as pessimistic as theorists of complex societies concerning the potential for democratization of contemporary society. For Marxists, in particular, it means that consumerism and the mass media have triumphed over radical political commitment. Alternatively, for Laclau and Mouffe, since politics is always cultural, the fluidity and instability of contemporary society open opportunities for political contestation and the transformation of social relations in radical democracy.

Postmodernity and politics

There are two main approaches to the sociology of postmodernity. The first, that of Marxism, focuses on the expansion of consumer and media culture as a result of the development of capitalism. The second focuses more on the development of knowledge, seeing it as a radicalization of modernity. In both cases relatively little attention has been given to the potential for democratization with which Laclau and Mouffe are concerned. For the most part, pessimism concerning the prospects for radical politics in postmodernity seems to preclude its consideration.

In the Marxist approach, concern with postmodernity is, for the most part, centered on the way in which it makes radical politics practically impossible. The best-known proponent of this view is Fredric Jameson, for whom postmodernism is "the cultural logic of late capitalism" (Jameson, 1984). For Jameson, capitalism is increasingly global, dynamic, and oriented toward the faster production of ever more "novel-seeming goods" for consumption (Jameson, 1984: 56). As a result culture has expanded beyond the semi-autonomous sphere it occupied in modernity and is increasingly integrated into commodity production, to the point where Jameson finds it pertinent to ask whether "everything in our social life . . . can be said to have become 'cultural' in some original and as yet untheorized sense" (1984: 87). Jameson sees postmodern culture as depthless and devoid of feeling; surface and textual play replace truth and value. He gives the Bonaventura Hotel in Los Angeles as an example: the central lobby is an enormous undifferentiated space – a hyperspace – in which it is only by chance that a person can find his or her way. The hotel has been forced to introduce color-coding and directional arrows to help visitors. Jameson takes this as emblematic of late capitalism in which we find it impossible "to map the great global multinational and decenterd communicational network in which we find ourselves caught as individual subjects" (1984: 84).

Jameson's fears that we have entered a new social landscape in which old maps may not be appropriate fit rather oddly with his commitment to Marxism. David Harvey (1989) is much clearer about the continuing usefulness of Marxism, seeing postmodernity as driven by the expansionist needs of the capitalist economy (see pp. 59–61 on Harvey's theory of global capitalism). In Harvey's work there is no doubt about the distinction between economic base and cultural superstructure as there is in Jameson's: postmodern culture is determined by "flexible postmodernity." Jameson and Harvey share, however, a pessimism concerning progressive politics. For Jameson, the problem is that political expression is necessarily made in culture, so that it becomes part of the problem rather than the solution. He gives the example of the music of punk band, The Clash. Overtly political, they were unable to achieve a critical distance from the culture of which they were a part so that they were necessarily reabsorbed by it (Jameson, 1984: 87). Harvey sees the only way out of the injustices and instabilities produced by global capitalism as "a new version of the Enlightenment project" in which there is social solidarity and a political project based on a historical materialist understanding of class struggle (Harvey, 1989: 359). He sees no possibility of a radical politics of the postmodern, despite the fact that his compelling portrayal of postmodern culture does not seem to give much hope of an easy exit from it.

The exception to Marxist pessimism concerning postmodernity is that of the "New Times" theorists of the British journal *Marxism Today*, summed up in their "Manifesto for New Times" (June 1989; see also Hall and Jacques, 1989). They see postmodernity in terms of post-Fordism, a new form of society structured by capitalism in response to the rigidities of Fordism. Where Fordism involved mass production for mass consumption, new technologies of "flexible specialization" make small-scale production for niche markets more profitable. An often-cited example is the firm Bennetton, which is said to be able to respond to market changes within ten days. It has a system of electronic cash registers which constantly transmit detailed information about sales to a central design and management team, complemented by flexible subcontracting firms who make the clothes (Kumar, 1995: 44–5). Post-Fordism involves the globalization of capitalism with an international division of labor and rapid and extensive flows of capital. There have also been significant changes in the occupational structure, with a growth in the service sector of the economy, associated with new technology and also the expansion of jobs connected with leisure pursuits, and a decline in manufacturing. The class division between manual and non-manual workers prominent in Fordism is being replaced by a workforce divided into core and periphery workers according to their value to capitalist organizations. Core workers are skilled, relatively secure, and well-rewarded, while peripheral workers are low-skilled, poorly paid, in insecure jobs, or unemployed.

In conjunction with these changes in the forces and relations of production, post-Fordists also see changes in culture and identity. The relatively stable class and status positions of Fordist industrial society have been undermined by changes in the economy and the growth of consumerism. In contemporary society, there is a fluidity of constructed identities, based on consumption and lifestyle choices as much as on occupation. There is also a breakdown of the links between class and politics mediated by national political parties, both because class identities no longer have the relevance they once had and also because the nation-state is no longer seen as capable of securing class interests as it was before rapid and extensive globalization undermined the Keynesian welfare state.

New Times theorists are relatively optimistic concerning the consequence of such changes for democratic politics. Addressing social movements, including the labor movement, the voluntary sector, pressure groups, and the left-wing Labour Party, they argue that society, far from being de-politicized as other Marxists suppose, is now increasingly politicized as personal issues, environmental concerns, and collective identities are contested. However, they argue that what is needed in order to institute new democratic politics is an alliance between different groups to reform the state, to make it more decentralized and enabling in order to meet the demands of a more pluralist and individualist society.

The New Times understanding of democratic politics has a good deal in common with that of Laclau and Mouffe, as we shall see, and they were, in fact, closely associated with the journal *Marxism Today*. The main difference is that New Times theorists remain clearly within Marxism, while Laclau and Mouffe see themselves as post-Marxists. Diagnosing social change principally as a consequence of economic change, New Times theorists continue to see the class struggle as central to radical politics ("Manifesto for New Times," p. 13), despite the emphasis they give to new identities and social formations which are not readily seen in class terms. Where concerns over economic security and conditions of work are combined, for example, with concerns over child-care or environmental risks, it is not easy to see such conflicts in terms of class, nor to see interests as necessarily divided along class lines. At the end of the 1990s, the New Times emphasis on class seems rather quaint, even in Britain, arguably one of the most class-conscious countries in the world. While *Marxism Today* has undoubtedly stimulated new political ideas – it has been credited with contributing to the re-making of the Labour Party in Britain – it now seems rather limited in this respect.

Like most Marxists, theorists working in the second main approach to the sociology of postmodernity also tend to be rather pessimistic with regard to radical politics. The chief exception is Lyotard, whose text, *The Postmodern Condition* (1984), may be seen as defining the whole area of research as such. Lyotard draws on Daniel Bell's and Alain Touraine's analyses of the fundamental transformation of industrial society into post-industrial society as the basis of his understanding of postmodernity (Lyotard, 1984: 3–5). In *The Coming of Post-industrial Society*, Bell (1976) argued that, while industrial society was characterized by the production of goods, in post-industrial society information will be the organizing principle of the economy and social relations. There has been a growth in the importance of knowledge with rapidly increasing technical innovation in industry and the need for management and problem-solving to control it and plan its use. Touraine's analysis is very much the same in its broad outlines, but where Bell anticipates better communication and planning as a result of the new technology, Touraine emphasizes new sources of conflicts between "technocrats" and those they manage in post-industrial society.

Lyotard does not engage with the details of the argument that we are now moving into a post-industrial society; he simply adopts the idea that knowledge is now the principal force of production (Lyotard, 1984: 3–5). The point he wants to make is that, far from representing progress, as both Bell and Touraine seem to suppose, the technological development of the "information society" destroys the notion of progress altogether. According to Lyotard, science, which in modernity was underpinned by reason and the promise of human emancipation, is no longer the legitimating meta-narrative of society. In postmodernity, society dissolves into a plurality of narratives in which science takes it place as one narrative among others, no more privileged as the site of truth or value than any other (see p. 38). Lyotard does not really explain this development. He boldly asserts that "we no longer believe in meta-narratives" (1984: xviv)) as an empirical fact, and links it to another – quite plausible – claim, that the new form of legitimation for knowledge is "performativity," the technical increase in power. The commercialization of information and research has replaced ideals of rational social improvement through science.

Lyotard's diagnosis of the possibilities of postmodernity released by the ending of the meta-narrative of reason and progress is quite ambivalent. On one hand, he clearly sees the commercialization of knowledge as regrettable, although, since there is no over-arching morality, it is not easy to condemn. On the other hand, Lyotard welcomes the pluralism released by the ending of meta-narratives and the way in which science itself is now producing uncertainty rather than knowledge. Lyotard sees such postmodern scientific developments as Gödel's undecidables, Heisenberg's uncertainty principle, and Mandelbrot's fractals as contributing to the possibility of creative playfulness, unconstrained by the need for over-arching legitimation. Similarly, he celebrates social "differences" and the creativity and enjoyment of multiple identities, now free to express themselves without the constraints of over-arching morality. It is this enthusiasm for relativist fragmentation and pluralism that has earned Lyotard the title of a "ludic" postmodernist; advocating "anything goes," his vision of postmodernity is seen as inviting playful resignation to the status quo rather the reconstruction of politics (Best and Kellner, 1997: 27; see p. 39).

Zygmunt Bauman endorses Lyotard's view concerning "the end of meta-narratives" and the fragmentation of society into multiple, and unconnected, language-games, though he is a good deal less positive about it. For him, the end of belief in over-arching meta-narratives of truth and value results in a retreat into small-scale communities in which there is a reassuring agreement on what is known and how to act. He sees this as dangerous, especially since the rejection of universals means that there is no common ground between different groups on which they might negotiate across their differences. Postmodernity potentially means the dissolution of social bonds altogether and the division into what Bauman calls "tribal communities" (Bauman, 1992: 133–9). He also agrees with Marxist analyses of postmodernity that commodification has extended to the point where the consumer is sovereign. In Bauman's view, the "seduction" of consumerism means that there is no longer any need for the "fictions" of modernity. Those who participate in the consumer society need no further motivation for conforming to what society requires, while those who do not are not needed and can be kept in their place by surveillance and repression (Bauman, 1987). Bauman sees politics as extremely limited in postmodernity. Political activities are dissipated because the nation-state is weakened, both by lack of legitimation in an over-arching meta-narrative, and also by globalization. It is, therefore, unable to draw social protest to itself as it did in modernity. The heterogeneous nature of social grievances also makes it difficult for groups to organize themselves into collective forms of protest to address the state (Bauman, 1992: 197).

However, Bauman is also critical of modernity. He sees it as a project, inaugurated by the Enlightenment, to impose rational order on nature and society through scientific knowledge and incontrovertible, universal moral principles. As a result it has often led to the imposition of homogeneity and order by force, as in totalitarianism. Postmodernity is the affirmation of the necessary failure of this project and the rejection of its premises. From this point of view, Bauman endorses the conclusions of the sociology of reflexivity. Following Giddens, he sees possibilities of greater reflexivity where there is no single truth and the individual is thrown back on him or herself as the only authority in his or her life (Bauman, 1992: 204). He does not, however, connect this to new collective forms of politics, nor to possibilities for democratization.

Finally, we will look at an account of postmodernity which is particularly interesting here as it starts from very similar premises to those of theories of complex societies. Stephen Crook, Jan Pakulski, and Malcolm Waters see postmodernity as a radicalization of processes of modernization. However, on their account, it is producing quite unexpected results. They prefer the term "postmodernization" to "postmodernity," arguing that it is not possible to delimit the outcome of far-reaching changes in advance, and that what might actually be emerging is the permanent destabilization of social structures (Crook et al., 1992: 2).

Like theorists of complex societies, Crook and colleagues see modernization as producing functionally specialized and interdependent subsystems as a result of the differentiation of tasks in society. For them, however, the modern differentiation of spheres has led to "hyperdifferentiation" and is now producing "de-differentiation." Crook and his associates see hyperdifferentiation as thoroughly undermining the modern differences between economy, state, community, and family. Modernization has proceeded to the point where bureaucratic power and money have entered into every aspect of social life. This means that the colonization of the lifeworld by the system feared by Habermas is already well established. However, the process is not ended. Modernization has also resulted in the impossibility of imposing centralized control, giving rise to hyperdifferentiation. Where modernity was characterized by large-scale organizations, production units, communities structured in class terms and nuclear families, in contemporary society the absence of centralized control around a unifying principle has resulted in a multiplication of social units. For example, in the case of production, the mass-production systems of modern capitalism now co-exist alongside units producing for market niches, co-operatives, segmented organizations, subcontractors, homeworkers, and so on. In the case of the family, nuclear families co-exist alongside single-parent families, step-families, gay and lesbian families, extended families, and so on. If lack of centralized control led to the explosion of differences, however, Crook et al. (1992) now see it as giving rise to their erasure, in de-differentiation. Each social unit attempts to generate media – of money or power, for example – in order to further its aims. In modernity this leads to functional specialization. Economic units, for example, are more able to generate money than religious units. In contemporary societies, however, each social unit tries to use as many media as possible. TV churches can generate money as well as value-commitments, while businesses attempt to generate a life-time commitment to the company on the part of their core workers.

Like other theorists of postmodernity, Crook et al. (1992) see it as involving the expansion of culture. Postmodernization means that culture itself is now de-differentiated as "postculture." Symbolic power, released from the "high/low" hierarchy of art in modernity, becomes a medium for the construction of identities through "style" and "taste" in every area of life. Cultural tradition is collapsed into "a postcultural emporium of styles" for consumption (1992: 37). The boundaries between social units collapse and determinate social identities are continually called into question so that unpredictability and chaos rather than control become the norm. In so far as there is any order, it is secured through the stabilization of signs and symbols. As Crook et al. (1992: 35) put it:

> the progressive differentiation of culture, society and personality characteristic of modernity involutes so that the very idea of an independent, purely social structural realm no longer makes sense. Rather, "society" must be understood in terms of "culture" as patterns of signs and symbols penetrate and erode structural boundaries. The power of the large-scale social phenomena of modernity including states, monopolistic economic organizations, ecclesia, military forces and scientific establishments is attenuated as cultural currents propagate and sweep the globe, intersecting in indeterminate ways.

In politics, Crook et al. (1992) apparently also see processes of hyperdifferentiation and de-differentiation. They emphasize the role of "new" social movements, which they see as more important than the structurally determined forms of class politics that were prominent in the corporatist state of advanced modernity. Social movements are hyperdifferentiated in that they all embody a diversity of political processes: "more open organizational structures, more diverse elites, more fluid and fragmented alliances and loyalties, and more complex networks of communication" (1992: 163–4). However, they foresee the possibility of their "normalization" as social movement organizations are absorbed into the formal political process. This is, for example, the fate of the green party in Germany, which is now moving toward a more conventional hierarchical form (1992: 162–3). This does not, however, inevitably mean the co-option of radical politics. They see old political parties as changing their agendas and opening up routes of recruitment as a result of the challenges of social movements. In this respect, they suggest that the hyperdifferentiation of social movements has made a lasting impact by breaking up the modern forms of class politics and enabling the representation of a wider variety of concerns and views in the formal political process. Furthermore, they apparently see de-differentiation in the shift from interest-based class politics to the more moral concerns of "new" social movements. This is, however, rather dubious. While some movements, such as the green movement, are recognizably oriented toward changing morality, in the citizenship politics of social movements, constituents' interests clearly do play an important role.

It is not clear that the direction of hyperdifferentiation and de-differentiation that Crook and his colleagues trace for politics is consistent with their own understanding of postmodernization as a radicalization of modernity. The view that social movements are inevitably "normalized" within political parties seems rather to return politics to its modern form, in which it was centered on the institution which specialized in the production of power, the nation-state. It would be more reasonable to suppose, on the basis of Crook and colleagues' own theory of de-differentiation, that rather than becoming centered on the state, politics would become part of *every* social unit; that attempts to generate power would be made in every aspect of social life. From this point of view, the expansion of culture they see as resulting from de-differentiation would also be seen rather differently. If the "cultural currents sweeping the globe" were thought of as the sites of cultural politics, they would be less readily described in terms of quasi-natural forces. It is a prerequisite of exercising any degree of control over the unstable and indeterminate processes of postmodernization that they should be seen as controllable. An understanding of cultural politics as an inherent possibility in all aspects of social life contributes to such a view.[3]

Laclau and Mouffe's theory of radical democracy

There are three main reasons for taking Laclau and Mouffe as representative theorists of democracy in postmodern conditions, despite the fact that they do not themselves theorize postmodernity. First, and most importantly, from the point of view of their theory of radical democracy, the expansion of culture theorized by sociologists of postmodernity must be seen as offering possibilities for democratization, rather than as undermining radical politics. While Laclau and Mouffe agree with theorists of postmodernity, and also, indeed, with theorists of complexity like Offe and Habermas, that society is fragmented and social solidarity is problematic, they see this neither as cause for celebration, nor for despair, but as an opportunity for constructing more egalitarian and pluralist political associations.

Secondly, although their commitment to liberal democracy as a condition of radical democracy is in some sense a commitment to modernity, the way in which they understand it is thoroughly postmodern. Like all those associated with postmodernism, Laclau and Mouffe, actually reject the term, preferring the term "post-Marxist" since their work has emerged from a deconstruction of the Marxist tradition. Nevertheless, an absolute rejection of the title "postmodern" is difficult to sustain in so far as this deconstruction resulted in anti-foundationalism, anti-essentialism and the commitment to discourse characteristic of the "postmodern turn" (see pp. 32–43). Particularly important here is the way in which Laclau and Mouffe see social reality as discursively constructed. Discourse is what makes perception, thought, and understanding possible on this account. For Laclau and Mouffe, it is a fact of human existence that our perceptions of reality are necessarily mediated in discourse, not a historically specific feature of postmodernity. Nevertheless, from the point of view of sociologists of postmodernity, to the extent that discourse theory recognizes no claims to objectivity and sees all statements as an interpretation from a particular perspective, its prominence in contemporary thought is itself a feature of postmodernity. Laclau and Mouffe do not analyze the expansion of culture in postmodernity in an objective fashion, as Bauman, for example, claims to do. They take the view that there is nothing outside interpretation, and propose that an adequate theory of democratic politics must take this into account.

Finally, there is the rather negative point that Laclau and Mouffe are rare in comparison with other post-structuralist theorists of democracy in that they are relatively oriented toward concrete sociological issues. For the most part, post-structuralist democratic theory has been developed in philosophy rather than sociology (see, for example, Young, 1990; Connolly, 1991; Rorty, 1991).

For Laclau and Mouffe, the problem of radical democracy is how to avoid the totalitarianism associated with the modern certainty of absolute truth and value, on one hand, and the fragmentation and disintegration of solidarity associated with postmodern "language-games," on the other. In fact, they tend to see modernity in terms which are close to the way in which Lyotard sees postmodernity. Following Claude Lefort, they see modern societies as those in which the center of power has been emptied. In pre-modern societies, the monarch embodied knowledge, legitimacy, and power, but in modernity, with the ending of absolute monarchy, absolute certainty is also at an end. This removal of the sovereign has provided the conditions of possibility for democracy, in which truth, value, and power can always be contested. But it also allows totalitarianism, the attempt to fully re-occupy the center with a vision of what is true and good for the people (Laclau and Mouffe, 1985: 186–8). Laclau and Mouffe see the only way of safeguarding pluralism against totalitarianism, and also the possibility of constructing a more egalitarian and inclusive political community, in the radicalization of liberal democracy.

It is the way in which Laclau and Mouffe see liberal democracy as viable which means that they keep a foot in both camps, the modern and the postmodern. First, liberal democracy is modern, based on the Enlightenment ideal of the human capacity for reason as the basis of social justice. However, the way in which Laclau and Mouffe understand liberal democracy is postmodern. That is, they see its viability as founded on nothing more than the way in which it is embedded in the institutions of the West and justified in contemporary political rhetoric; it is not founded on any extra-discursive basis, such as natural human rights, as it was for Enlightenment thinkers. Secondly, the way in which they see society as unified around acceptance of the legitimacy of liberal democracy again seems to make them more modern than postmodern. However, in postmodern fashion, they see this acceptance as pluralist, interpreted differently from different perspectives and, based on the indeterminacy of meaning, as inherently unstable.

For Laclau and Mouffe, the liberal democratic tradition is, like every other aspect of social reality, discursive. The liberal democratic terms "liberty" and "equality" are seen as the "grammar" of modern societies (Mouffe, 1993: 65). They are signs, and like all signs, they have no necessary referent (see pp. 28–30). They are, therefore, articulated in different ways according to the practices within which they are situated. Society is unified around the "universals" of liberty and equality, but they do not produce homogeneity and order since there may be as many different interpretations of these signs as there are forms of citizenship (Mouffe, 1993: 71). Laclau and Mouffe ask us to compare, for example, the discourse of the New Right with that of democratic socialists. Whereas for neo-liberals "liberty" means "non-interference," especially with rights to private property, for social democrats it means the positive capacity to realize life-chances (Laclau and Mouffe, 1985: 171–2).

The prospects for radical democracy are never hopeless, therefore, since the meanings of the liberal democratic discourse can never be finally fixed. However, the concrete possibility of its success depends on particular social and political conditions rather than on the universal potential of political signs. According to Laclau and Mouffe, the politics of social movements both enact and provide the grounds for a further radicalization of liberal democracy. In contesting inequality, they extend the application of "equality" into new domains and provide the conditions for it to be extended still further. At the same time, the struggles of social movements are radically plural since they involve a multiplicity of identities and political sites; in this way they also militate for the extension of "liberty" to new groups of citizens (Mouffe, 1988).

However, in order to consolidate the greater equality and freedom that social movements have achieved in Laclau and Mouffe's view, they argue that they need to join together in a hegemonic project. This is necessary because powerful groups already exercise hegemony over subordinate groups so that to succeed it is necessary to contest and reverse the influence of their perspective on the world. In particular, Laclau and Mouffe see groups benefiting from the hegemony of capitalism as powerful so that a radical democratic project must be anti-capitalist, at least in so far as it is committed to a mixed economy and welfare state rather than to the dominance of markets (Smith, 1998: 19–23).

It is somewhat surprising that Laclau and Mouffe have given so little attention to the state in this respect. It is clearly important to their project of radical democracy, both as it is related to liberal democracy and the rule of law and to socialism, with its emphasis on the redistribution of wealth. It is, however, difficult to combine a commitment to social pluralism and a strong commitment to equality, since the structures designed to promote the latter tend to impose constraints on the former. Laclau and Mouffe recognize the constant tension in radical democracy in so far as the institutionalization of democratic rights requires collective organization which is always at odds with the autonomy of individuals and groups (Laclau and Mouffe, 1985: 83–5). However, they do not discuss how this tension should be negotiated in order to achieve radical, rather than simply liberal, democracy (Nash, 1998b: 55).

What is clear is that radical democracy as a hegemonic project is far from democracy based on rational consensus as Habermas sees it. Although it does require different social identities to link together around common causes, such agreement is seen as pragmatic and strategic. Laclau and Mouffe privilege contestation over consensus, so that, they argue, each movement within the coalition should maintain its autonomy and differences from the others as far as this is compatible with the common project. In so far as consensus involves the attempt to fill the "empty place of power" in contemporary societies, like Lyotard, they see it as "terroristic," achieved by the exclusion of projects opposed to those within the constructed community (Mouffe, 1993: 69). For them, democracy is not possible without power; power is inherent in every social situation in so far as alternative practices have been excluded from it (Laclau, 1990: 33–6). It is not, however, thereby totalitarian. On the contrary, democracy depends on power in that it is necessary to create the conditions within which individuals may take control of their lives. As William Connolly (1991: 212–13) puts it:

> A radical democratic hegemony obtains when the perspective of an identifiable constellation attains predominance in several areas of public debate, resisting factions remain effective in publicly articulating the terms of their opposition and compelling compromises on some of these fronts, the news media, judiciary and electoral system function to keep the terms of contestation among coalitions reasonably open and to protect elemental rights to life, a significant degree of personal self-governance, freedom of expression and full citizenship in a representative government. (Connolly, 1991: 212–13)

Criticism of Laclau and Mouffe's project of radical democracy tends to fall into three main areas. First, from a materialist perspective, it is argued that their analysis gives insufficient emphasis to the constraints of social structures and institutions. Their radical constructivism means that they are unable to give sufficient weight to the material conditions within which articulations between political terms are made and which have important effects on the success of particular hegemonic projects. They are unable, in other words, to explain why it is that some articulations are effective, while others are not (Smith, 1998: 55–6). Laclau and Mouffe do analyze the conditions for radical democracy, seeing them as particularly propitious in contemporary society. They argue that social movements have become a political force, to a greater extent than the traditional "carrier" of the socialist revolution, the working class, because of developments in capitalism itself. From a similar point of view to that of Crook et al. (1992), they argue that commodification, bureaucratization, and the media have thoroughly penetrated what was previously the private sphere of the community and family. In opposition to Habermas, they see the encroachment of the state and economy as opening up possibilities for political contestation and mobilization. The commodification of social needs, state intervention in the form of the welfare state, and the destruction of traditional values in the home have created new relations of subordination and at the same time they have provoked a range of resistances in the form of social movements (Laclau and Mouffe, 1985: 160–4).

In another sense, however, it is true that, in so far as Laclau and Mouffe do not have a general theory of social structures and institutions, it is not possible to make theoretical statements concerning what makes some articulations succeed where others fail. In fact, they are resistant to such theories, on the grounds that there are no necessary links between particular social structures and identities so that an a priori theory of society would inevitably neglect its historical specificity. The advantage they claim for the theory of hegemony is that it does not understand social life in terms of ahistorical "essences," but rather sensitizes us to the particularities of identity formation and complex structural positionings. Anna Marie Smith (1998) argues that it is nevertheless possible to construct more general accounts using the theoretical tools developed by Laclau and Mouffe through comparative studies which pick out differences and similarities across social contexts. She argues that we should see political articulations as successful where they have some continuity, or "family resemblance," with established discourses (Smith, 1998: 159–61).

Secondly, from a Habermasian point of view, it is argued that a model of democracy in which the outcome is based on power means that it is not legitimate. Laclau and Mouffe's model of democracy is of the type sometimes called "agonistic." It is a model in which a central place is given to the claim that there are no fixed certainties on which to depend, neither scientific nor moral, and no final authority to settle contentious issues; there is only the shifting contestation of multiple interpretations through which political identities and positions are formed. While post-structuralists see agonism as democratic because it does not close off any political possibilities in advance of their articulation and contestation, for rationalists the problem is that, without a final adjudication of the outcome of political struggle, it is impossible to be sure that it is "good and just" rather than "unjust, racist, fickle, and capricious" (Benhabib, 1996: 8).

This point is complicated by the fact that, as we have seen, Laclau and Mouffe actually see the radical democratic imaginary as dependent, not on the outcome of an "ideal-speech situation," but on the traditions of Western liberal democracy. Although its terms are essentially contestable in their view, nevertheless they see that tradition as limiting the principles which should be adopted by the radical democratic community. There are no guarantees concerning the outcome of agonistic democracy, but radicalized liberal democracy does require that citizens treat each other as free and equal, and that institutions of representative democracy, the rule of law and the separation of the public and the private are safeguarded (Mouffe, 1993: 128–33).

However, their commitment to Western political traditions leads to a third criticism of Laclau and Mouffe's work, that the "radical democratic imaginary" is therefore limited in a multi-cultural society. It is important to be clear about the ways in which their model of democracy may be seen as Eurocentric. As Laclau has argued, radical democracy supposes that the Western tradition itself must be brought to account where it has involved false claims to universalism and the unrecognized exclusion of minorities by supposedly common ideals (Smith, 1998: 188–9). However, in so far as they see the outcomes of radical democracy as limited by the Western political tradition, Laclau and Mouffe's model of pluralism is insufficient. In a globalizing world, it is also important to recognize, respect, and negotiate with those who do not see themselves as "Western." Thinking of the Rushdie affair, in which Islam is opposed to the liberalized Christian West (see pp. 76–7), Mouffe argues that Islam poses a threat to democratic pluralism because it does not recognize the Western distinction between religious and secular law on which pluralism depends. Western modernity is, as Muslims have shown, based on Christianity in so far as it recognizes secular society as a separate domain, something Islam does not do (Mouffe, 1993: 132). Although Mouffe is correct to argue that difficult questions are raised by the Rushdie case, it is nevertheless more useful from the point of view of political dialogue to think of Muslim identities as multiple, relational, and unfixed, crossed by intra-cultural and trans-cultural antagonisms, as Laclau and Mouffe think in anti-essentialist terms of Western "Christian" identities, rather than as in some way expressive of cultural norms. It is certainly the case, as Mouffe argues, that the paradox of democracy is that it can only be maintained by repression of the undemocratic. There must be limits on pluralism. However, repression should clearly be a last resort, when discussion is no longer possible; there should be no a priori judgments of traditions as necessarily undemocratic.

Arguably, with respect to their ultimately limited view of pluralism, Laclau and Mouffe's theory of radical democracy remains too culturally specific. As we have seen, Habermas's model of deliberative democracy is also limited by its cultural specificity. The emphasis he gives to reason is potentially exclusionary of those who do not easily fit the norms of communication by rational argument. In this respect, although both Laclau and Mouffe's model of radical democracy and Habermas's model of deliberative democracy attempt to reconcile respect for differences in a progressive political community, ultimately both show insufficient "responsibility toward Otherness." While Laclau and Mouffe's understanding of democracy is postmodern, it remains too much within the modern tradition where pluralism should not be limited to those who identify as Western. This is particularly serious with regard to the democratization of globalization and the importance of enabling international and transnational political dialogue across cultural traditions.

5.3 DEMOCRATIZING GLOBALIZATION

By far the most prominent consideration of the sociological implications of globalization for democratization is that of David Held.[4]
His theory of cosmopolitan democratic governance is an important
attempt to develop a sociological understanding of the potential for
the democratization of political institutions beyond the nation-state.
Habermas has given some consideration to the need for a Europe-
wide public sphere now that citizenship is being re-made at the
supranational level in the European Union (Habermas, 1992). Along
radical democratic lines, William Connolly has argued for a post-
national understanding of claims for recognition on the part of those
previously excluded from full citizenship (Connolly, 1996). It remains the case, however, that the issue of globalization has received
very little attention from theorists in these traditions. Held is sometimes seen as a theorist of deliberative democracy, and he does understand cosmopolitan democratic governance to involve deliberation.
However, this aspect of his theory is only very loosely related to
Habermas's model. Held is critical of Habermas's idea that the
impetus toward consensus is built in to all speech acts, and also that
it is necessary to democracy. By deliberative democracy, he apparently means something much more general: that legitimate decisions
follow only from deliberation by the people, who must be self-
determining. Democracy does not require even the ideal of consensus as it does for Habermas; majority decisions are to be considered
binding (Held, 1980: 396–8; Held, 1991: 229).

As we shall see in the following section, the most serious problem
for the theory of cosmopolitan democratic governance is that it does
not develop an understanding of the importance of cultural politics
to global democratization. Held rather neglects the question of how
cosmopolitan democracy might be brought about, although he is
concerned to identify its potential in contemporary global processes.
In so far as it is agreed that what is required is the reconstruction of
the current world (dis)order, involving the contestation and transformation of existing, undemocratic identities and practices, then
cultural politics must be seen as important. Indeed, Held is himself
engaged in cultural politics since he argues that global democracy is
possible, against the skeptical view that, because democratization is
not in the short-term interests of the most powerful nations, it will

never happen. As McGrew (1997) points out, advocates of global democracy take the view that ideas can make a difference, that the world is more susceptible to agency and less immutable than skeptics admit, and it is on this basis that they put forward their proposals. In this way, they may contribute themselves to the possibility of a more democratic global governance.

Cosmopolitan democratic governance

Held's model of global democracy is principally concerned with the reconstruction of already existing formal political institutions at the international and transnational levels, both to make them more globally oriented and also more democratic. He usefully summarizes the problem as follows:

> the meaning and place of democratic politics have to be rethought in relation to a series of overlapping local, regional and global processes. Three features of the latter [must be] emphasized: first, the way processes of economic, political, legal, military and cultural interconnectedness are changing the nature, scope and capacity of the sovereign state from above, as its "regulatory" ability is challenged and reduced in some spheres; secondly, the way regional and global interconnectedness creates chains of interlocking political decisions and outcomes among states and their citizens, altering the nature and dynamics of national political systems themselves; and, thirdly, the way local groups, movements and nationalisms are questioning the nation-state from below as a representative and accountable power system. (Held, 1995a: 267)

Globalization has clear implications for representative democracy, linked as it is to the sovereignty and autonomy of the nation-state. The main principle of democracy, however limited in the theories and practices of "really existing" liberal democracies, is that the people should be self-determining: they should govern the conditions of their own lives. There is a clear spatial dimension to this ideal of self-determination: the institutions of representative democracy by which "the people" rules itself are those of the nation-state, and popular sovereignty is considered to be the same as state sovereignty. If the autonomy and sovereignty of the nation-state are diminished by globalization, then so too is liberal democracy. It is also clear that there is no immediate possibility of simply enlarging liberal democratic institutions to encompass more extensive terri-torial claims, no possibility of a "world government" writ large. Held's project is rather to think about how already existing prac-tices, institutions, and organizations might be developed in order to realize the model of cosmopolitan democracy he proposes (Held 1995a, b).

The starting point is, then, that the autonomy of the nation-state is now severely limited by global processes, while at the same time its sovereignty is divided between national, regional, and interna-tional agencies and limited by this plurality. Cosmopolitan gover-nance would redistribute power between these different levels in order to increase the overall accountability of agencies responsible for governance and also to provide a framework of law which would ensure democratic rights for all. In this way, it would further what Held calls the "principle of autonomy" which is at the heart of democracy:

> persons should enjoy equal rights (and, accordingly, equal obligations) in the framework which generates and limits the opportunities avail-able to them; that is, they should be free and equal in the determina-tion of the conditions of their own lives, so long as they do not deploy this framework to negate the rights of others. (Held, 1991: 228; cf. Held, 1987: 270–1)

Democracy therefore involves both rights to democratic delib-eration to enable participation in directing collective life and also the protection of individual rights to freedom over one's own life.

As we saw in chapter 4 (section 4.5), international law has already made us citizens of the world in so far as human rights law is increas-ingly effective. Similarly, there are well-established international political institutions, notably the UN and its associated bodies, the World Bank, the IMF, and so on, which to some extent already reg-ulate world military and economic affairs. Held proposes that these institutions should be extended in order to realize cosmopolitan democratic governance.

In the short term, Held argues that to increase democratic accountability and ensure democratic rights, the UN must be reformed and made to live up to the terms of its Charter, especially with regard to implementing human rights conventions and the famous promise "to save succeeding generations from the scourge of war" (quoted in Falk, 1995: 174). Democratic rights, including civil, political, social, and economic rights should be embodied in constitutions at national and international level to ensure that global democracy is substantive rather than merely formal and that it enables individual autonomy. In the long term, the UN Charter could be extended to make the General Assembly more like a global parliament, able to make international law on matters which fall under the UN rubric, and to ensure their enforcement, by military means if necessary. However, in order to provide the maximum degree of accountability on specifically global issues, such as the regulation of markets and environmental issues, there should also be an increase in regional power – as there has been in the case of the European Union – especially in Latin America and Africa where individual nation-states are weakest in international terms. Held's model is based on the principle of "subsidiarity" enacted by the European Union: decisions should be made as locally as possible to maximize accountability and the participation of those concerned by particular issues. In addition, he suggests the possibility of transnational referendums where the issues require them.

It is important to note that the nation-state is not ignored or bypassed as a political center in Held's model. It is rather that it is displaced to become one, very powerful, political player among others in global politics. Furthermore, the political bodies with which it shares its sovereignty are those to which it initially transferred power in order to gain a greater degree of control over affairs within and without its borders. The nation-state actually gains power in this way by participating in international negotiations and agreements to regulate global processes over which it would otherwise have very little control.

However, one of the major criticisms of Held's model of cosmopolitan global governance is that he does not give enough attention to the continuing power of nation-states. It is argued that they simply cannot be made subject to international law in the way Held proposes since, without a global state, there is no global peacekeeping force beyond that which they provide. As long as political institutions are international rather than supranational, they depend on nation-states, or rather on those with the greatest economic and military power. As the international relations school known as "realism" sees it, in a politically turbulent world, it is only rational to anticipate danger from other states and to be prepared for conflict where necessary. This increases the danger for all so that, in the absence of a secure over-arching state, international co-operation will always fail. In particular, a powerful nation like the USA, which spends as much on defence as the next ten states combined, has no interest in a more democratic regime of global governance in which it would certainly have less power as a state (McGrew, 1997: 254–7).

A further criticism of Held's model, along similar lines, is that he does not show how global capitalism might be subject to more stringent controls than at present, without which democratic rights will be largely irrelevant for many people (McGrew, 1997: 253). This issue is particularly pressing. In 1999, after ten years of neo-liberal hegemony over world markets, following the collapse of the East Asian and Russian economies, there was speculation concerning the possibility of a worldwide depression if greater regulation of financial markets were not achieved. In fact, it is not that there is no regulation of the global "free market;" it is only possible because of regulation which permits global financial flows, provides the legal backing which secures loans, fixes rates of exchange, and so on. The national "deregulation," or ending of protectionism, which made globalization possible, and which has now significantly reduced the control of nation-states over domestic economies, is nevertheless underpinned by various forms of international regulation (Altvater and Mahnkopf, 1997). What Held proposes is a widening of international agreements to control multinationals, requiring them to pay minimum wages, respect the health and safety of workers, operate equal opportunity policies, and so on. As he rightly points out, where multinationals are free to base production in any country, it is only at the international level that such agreements can be made effective (Held, 1995a: ch. 11).

What both criticisms indicate, however, is that, although Held has identified the potential for democratic cosmopolitan governance in existing political organizations and institutions, he has not given enough consideration to how it might be realized in conditions where the leaders of some nation-states and multinational corporations cannot be compelled to bind themselves by democratic principles.

Although Held is actually *engaged* in cultural politics to a limited extent in putting forward his model of democracy to be debated and, it is hoped, instituted, the model itself has little scope for consideration of the *processes* by which the elements which make up his definition of democracy might come to be accepted, instituted, modified, resisted, or refused. This must be a very important aspect of the project in so far as it is supposed to be realistic rather than simply utopian. Without underestimating the problem, in the next section we will look at aspects of cultural politics which might contribute to its solution.

Global democracy and cultural politics

If the potential for cosmopolitan democratic governance identified by Held is to be realized, the importance of cultural politics must be understood. Widespread and radical changes are needed in perceived interests and definitions of what is possible. There are currently opportunities for such significant changes to be made given that it is now widely acknowledged by economists and state leaders that global capitalism requires closer management if crisis is to be avoided, global risks are widely felt and, following the ending of the Cold War in 1989, the formal political institutions of the new world (dis)order are yet to be stabilized. These opportunities are, however, to be set against the widespread lack of interest in international affairs of most people in advanced liberal democracies. Without an active engagement in the processes of establishing more democratic global institutions on the part of these citizens, it is unlikely that they will be realized.

The most hopeful prospects for the future in this respect lie in the emergence of a global civil society. At the same time, however, the state cannot be ignored as a site of democratic politics. While it has been displaced, as we have seen throughout this book, as the center of political activity, what is now better described as the *internationalized* state rather than the nation-state remains significant as a powerful player in the global political order. It is particularly important in terms of democratization because elected governments are susceptible to the influence of citizens using democratic political rights. Finally, international law, which already plays a role in the lives of citizens of liberal democracies through human rights, must be democratized if cosmopolitan democratic governance is to be genuinely inclusive.

GLOBAL CIVIL SOCIETY AND GLOBAL SOCIAL MOVEMENTS The term "global civil society" is a broad one, embracing organizations, associations, and movements which exist "above the individual and below the state, but across national boundaries" (Wapner, quoted in McGrew, 1997: 13). The most effective transnational organizations are International Non-governmental Organizations (INGOs) such as the Red Cross, Médicins sans Frontières, Save the Children, Oxfam, Greenpeace, and Amnesty International. The number of these organizations has grown enormously: in 1909 there were 176 INGOs compared to 4,624 in 1989 (Held, 1995a: 108). Not all such organizations and movements can be seen as democratizing; many are not themselves run democratically and some have authoritarian projects. Nevertheless, the recent growth of the global civil society in which such organizations play a prominent role does offer some hope for the realization of cosmopolitan democratic governance.

Since there is no global legal body to enforce democracy, it is only by putting pressure on existing political institutions that global democracy may be realized: existing states have to be deprived of powers which they use against their own citizens or to block greater transnational co-operation in their own immediate interests as a first step toward creating a new world order (Falk, 1994a; Archibugi and Held, 1995). There are precedents for the success of such a strategy, though they can only be identified from within the terms of a sociology in which institutions are seen as produced in social action, rather than by large-scale socio-economic structures and organizations; in other words, a sociology in which cultural politics is taken seriously as effectively structuring social life. As James Rosenau writes of the "Velvet Revolution" in Eastern Europe after 1989:

> Put empirically, too many of the squares of the world's cities have late been filled with large crowds who make a wide variety of demands, who return again and again even in the face of brutal governmental efforts to repress them, who thus escalate conflicts and solidify stalemates with a frequency indicating contagious effects that are transforming problems of domestic order into processes of global order

... to ignore the possibility that the micro level is a source as well as a consequence of global change. (Rosenau, 1992: 273–4)

Although Held sees the notion of global civil society as "premature" (Held, 1995a: 125), others see it as potentially democratizing political institutions and global processes "from the bottom up," using all the weapons of the weak, including public protests, consumer power, the withdrawal of labor, sabotage, the mobilization of public opinion in the global mass media, and so on.

Organizations and individuals in civil society may contribute directly to the internationalization of nation-states and the strengthening of global political institutions. As we have seen, this is most marked in Europe, where citizens increasingly have recourse to the European Court of Justice to over-ride perceived injustices of national law, but it is also the case on every occasion when citizens put pressure on their own governments to modify action with a global impact, or on other governments to modify actions with a national or global impact. Economic sanctions against South Africa, although not supported by powerful nations like Britain and the US, almost certainly contributed to bringing about the end of apartheid, for example. Furthermore, through their involvement in INGOs, directly petitioning the UN on such matters as human rights and the environment, individuals and groups may also affect political institutions with a wider international remit (Alger, 1994).

In so far as democracy involves more than the institutions of representative democracy, global civil society also offers the potential for the realization of more egalitarian and participatory relations in every aspect of social life. Democratization in this sense is closely linked to the activities of social movements and to the politicization of everyday life they bring about. In so far as new social movements are at least as concerned with resistance and transformation at the level of everyday life, interpersonal, and community relations as with politics at the level of the nation-state, they are peculiarly well placed to engage in the transnational politics appropriate to globalization. The environmental organization Friends of the Earth, for example, embodies the link between the global and the local as each local group is fully autonomous, dealing only with issues relevant to its immediate area, while at the same time it links those concerns to the national and international campaigns waged by the organization as a whole (Washbourne, 1999). Similarly, the women's movement has linked women across the world to politicize issues of women's work, family relations and poverty at a global level – particularly since the Beijing Conference of 1995 – while all these issues are at the same time tackled by local groups and individual women in their everyday lives (Dickenson, 1997).

Of course, as we noted in chapter 3, it is not that they are uninterested in working through the structures of the state: one of the platforms of the global feminist movement, for example, is that women should be better represented in the procedures of liberal democracy. Because of the way in which political parties have been so dominated by the representation of classes, however, social movements tend to be relatively unintegrated into the political structures of nation-states. It may be, therefore, that, in contradiction to the usual supposition that globalization undermines democracy, because new social movements are developing extensive networks, communications, and campaigns to complement their global understanding of the issues with which they are concerned, they are actually in a better position to influence the institutions of global governance than old-style parties and organizations which direct their attentions to the nation-state. It may be that the "global community of fate" which supersedes the "national community of fate" of modernity will actually prove more democratic for social movements both with respect to the formation of a global civil society and also in terms of the influence they are able to exert over the more formal institutions of global governance.

Transnational social movements can undoubtedly have some effect on the activities of multinationals which are difficult to control through the politics of the nation-state. They do so by influencing individual decisions over consumption choices and ethical investment, and by exerting moral pressure through the media. For example, following protests and widespread boycotting of its products when the oil company Shell proposed to dispose of the Brent Spar oil rig by sinking it, there have been significant changes in its practices. In 1997 Shell set up a Social Responsibility Unit to monitor the policies and conduct of its various businesses, and in 1998 the company published a substantial report outlining its newly adopted corporate responsibility for environmental and human rights (Giddens, 1998: 49–50). In this case, environmental protest in civil society was a good deal more effective than politicians working through government regulation.

Finally, as we have noted, one of the most important aspects of the politics of social movements is the formation of collective identities: subordinated groups must change how they see themselves and how they are seen by others. Clearly, if greater global co-operation is to become possible, it will be necessary to redefine identities and to reconceive what are currently perceived as opposed interests. It is necessary, therefore, to see them as constructed and taken for granted as such as a result of the "politics of interpretation," rather than objectively given. How is it, for example, that the environmental risks produced in the developing world are seen as more threatening than the over-production of the developed North (see Yearley, 1996: 84)? Who is to be included as "European" now that the old Cold War blocs have broken up? The problems with which global governance must deal cannot be addressed in terms of already existing short-term interests since many of them require deep-rooted changes in lifestyle in which privileges and comforts to which many are attached, or to which they aspire, must be abandoned. To some extent social movements have succeeded, if not in transforming perceived interests, at least in putting such questions on the agenda, destroying the taken-for-granted "reality" of what they might be. The environmental movement, for example, has brought the dangers of an ever growing economy to the world's attention, and the limitations on production and consumption required if environmental reform is to be effective. If more equitable global co-operation on such issues is to be realized, the construction of opposing interests which leads to the systematic, but perhaps short-term, advantage of the wealthier nations and citizens must be challenged and reconstructed along new, more inclusive and democratic lines.

INTERNATIONALIZED STATE The state will continue to be important in global democracy for the foreseeable future. As Paul Hirst (1997) notes, ultimately it is only those political leaders who have been democratically elected who have legitimacy in a democratic system and, with the partial exception of the European Union (see pp. 208–11), it is only at the level of the nation-state that this takes place. Furthermore, it is only states which have the power to establish law and to distribute wealth collected as taxes according to non-profit-making criteria. Their wealth, and the power they exercise over military capacity, means that the representatives of nation-states will undoubtedly be major players in any new forms of global democracy. The democratic accountability of elected governments at this level and the responsibility of states to enact and protect democratic rights make them central to cosmopolitan democratic governance.

It is, however, misleading to think of "the state," as if it were a singular, integrated, and fully formed agent which is now taking on a new role on the world stage. A state is better seen as a fluid grouping of institutions with unstable boundaries, all of which are constantly engaged in negotiating their tasks and capacities, both internally, with other state actors, and externally, with representatives of other social and economic groups. In other words, "the state" is always an unstable and temporary outcome – however long a particular formation may last – of ongoing cultural politics. As such, it is always open to contestation and reformation as more or less enabling of democratic participation and the protection of democratic rights.

In contemporary society, what we shall continue to call "the state" for the sake of convenience is currently undergoing transformation. It is, in fact, becoming more clearly disaggregated in practice in comparison with the sovereign nation-state of 50 years ago. At the same time, it is also becoming internationalized. Following Bob Jessop (1997), three main trajectories of change in the form of the state may be identified.

First, there is the denationalization of the state. The capacities of nation-states are being "hollowed out," with old and new capacities being reorganized "upwards," "sideways," and "downwards" (Jessop, 1997: 573). The best example of the "upwards" movement is the way in which state sovereignty is now shared within the European Union. As we have noted elsewhere, the EU is exceptional as a supranational state. In other cases, however, power has also been transferred upwards, where states are committed to co-operation with other states and so to decisions which compromise their sovereignty. This is the case, for example, where they agree to respect international law on human rights. Clearly, some states lose capacities for independent action in such situations while others gain; nevertheless, all forfeit a degree of sovereignty. At the same time, European states have also all been engaged in devolving power "downwards" to the subnational level, to local regions. This has often been combined with shifts of power "sideways" to regions which cut across the territories of nation-states. Barcelona is, for example, the center of a region which includes parts of Spain and France (Giddens, 1998: 32). "Downwards" and "sideways" processes of denationalization are the effects of EU policies encouraging economic growth at the local and regional level, and also because of demands for a greater degree of autonomy from the nation-state within regions themselves (Anderson and Goodman, 1995).

Secondly, Jessop notes a trend toward the de-statization of the political system, a shift from government to governance. This principally involves the movement away from the state as the major sponsor and director of economic and social projects, to the state as co-operating with para-governmental and non-governmental organizations to realize its objectives. This shift is very evident in Britain, a product of neo-liberalist reorganization of relations between the state and the market. There has, for example, been some privatization of branches of the British state, with semi-autonomous agencies taking over many of the functions of civil service departments (Crook et al., 1992: 97). Tasks such as prison security and assessing social security benefit claims are now carried out by contracted firms. While governments have always relied on other agencies and organizations to realize state objectives, and while they continue to set the framework within which services and goods are provided in the name of the state, they are now more likely to do so in negotiation with influential partners on whom they rely to a greater extent than was previously the case (Jessop, 1997: 575).

Thirdly, there is a trend toward the internationalization of policy regimes. The international context of domestic state action now enters much more significantly into domestic policy itself (1997: 575–6). In fact, it is not always easy to make a sharp distinction between the two in a world in which: "IBM is Japan's largest computer exporter, and Sony is the largest exporter of television sets from the United States" (J. Ruggie, quoted in Anderson and Goodman, 1995: 605–6). Furthermore, each branch of the domestic bureaucracy now takes on an international dimension. This results in transgovernmental coalitions of bureaucrats around particular policy aims. The state does not appear on the international stage as a unified whole but as a coalition of bureaucratic agencies each pursuing its own agenda, sometimes with minimal direction (McGrew, 1992).

While the internationalized state has a central role in global governance, then, it should not be seen as acting in a unified fashion. On the contrary, the ongoing disaggregation of state institutions and practices and the redefinition of its capacities and boundaries are continually being negotiated by different state and non-state actors. Within internationalized state bureaucracies themselves, there is no agreement about the precise division of sovereignty between states and international political institutions. There is continual conflict between different layers of authority in the EU, for example, concerning where the remit of the European institutions runs out and that of member states begins. The cultural politics of such intra-state contestation is decidedly undemocratic. It takes place largely behind closed doors and is usually conducted by non-elected representatives of governments. In this respect, it is quite unlike the politics of global civil society which are conducted openly and which depend on the formation of public opinion. Nevertheless, the fact that such issues are so highly contested does mean opportunities for more democratized political structures. In particular, where the appointed representatives of states are accountable in their own countries, governments ultimately have to satisfy the electorate that transferences of sovereignty and the setting up of international and supranational political institutions are in their best interests. This returns us to the cultural politics of civil society and the contestation and reframing of interests carried out by social movements. The form of the internationalized state, the extent to which it is democratically accountable and oriented toward instituting and protecting democratic rights, depends to a large extent on what is acceptable to the citizens of advanced capitalist liberal democracies.

Similarly, at its interface with other agencies and organizations in governance, the form of the state is also highly contested. As we have seen, international and supranational political institutions are in part a product of the neo-liberal politics of free markets which involved the lifting of national restrictions on economic activity and re-regulation at the international level. However, as Leslie Sklair (1997) points out, although it may seem that transnational corporations have gained undisputed legitimacy and global mobility as a result, this is not at all how it is seen by members of the emerging global elite. On the contrary, the executives of global companies and certain globalizing bureaucrats, politicians, and professionals are very concerned to convince governments and their citizens that, in Sklair's apposite phrase, "the business of society is business." They aim to create a climate of opinion in which opposition to that tenet is seen as nothing more than sectional interests, while business groups are taken to be working in the common interest (Sklair, 1997: 526). To a large extent they have been successful. Multinational corporations and states tend to be mutually supportive since politicians and citizens see their role as promoting economic growth to generate and maintain high levels of employment, wages, and national wealth. This tendency is reinforced rather than undermined in the internationalized state, since the rationale for international co-operation has been made largely in terms of improving national economies.

However, multinational corporations are far from invulnerable. In particular, they are vulnerable to the transnational power of consumers, as we have seen in the case of Shell. Furthermore, the interests of transnational corporations are not themselves wholly unified. Where a company like Shell has adopted more socially and environmentally responsible practices, it may form alliances with other groups to put pressure on those transnational corporations which have not done so in order to avoid being disadvantaged in the marketplace. Since the onset of the crisis in global capitalism at the close of the century, moreover, the way in which economic growth is best managed is now in question. The hegemony of neo-liberalism has been challenged, with influential capitalists and economists in the IMF and World Bank speculating about how global capitalism might be saved with new forms of Keynesianism and a new type of Bretton Woods agreement (see pp. 95–6). In this respect, the role of the internationalized state in relation to multinational corporations is highly contested, and again the institutions which emerge will depend to a large extent on what can be made acceptable to the citizens of advanced capitalist countries.

DEMOCRATIZED INTERNATIONAL LAW The most important aspect of international law from the point of view of cosmopolitan global governance is human rights agreements. They are all, broadly speaking, based on the articles of the Universal Declaration of

Human Rights passed by the UN General Assembly in 1948. These include the rights to life, to be free from slavery and torture, to be treated equally before the law, to own property, to freedom of thought and religion, to work and fair pay. It is widely accepted that they are liberal democratic rights with a strong Western bias (Evans, 1997: 126).

The most prominent disagreements over rights, even among those who have signed up to the various human rights conventions and covenants of international law since 1948, now concern this Western bias. It is argued by the representatives of developing countries that human rights law is actually imposed by the West. The issue is complicated, not least because there are justified suspicions of ulterior motives on both sides. Developing countries, for example, accuse the West of using human rights as a way of opening up the economies of poorer countries to exploitation. Given that funds granted by the IMF require economic liberalization, this suspicion is not unfounded. On the other hand, it may be suspected that the rejection of international law as culturally specific and biased toward Western norms and values is related to the fact that violations of human rights by Third World states, including imprisonment without trial, torture, and unlawful killing, are quite common, as recorded by such INGOs as Amnesty International.

Held sees the democratization of human rights as an genuine issue. He argues that there would be less resistance to the discourse of human rights as Western if post-colonial nations had a more equal, participatory role in the framing of global governance. Rights would no longer be seen simply as a means of gaining socio-economic dominance and they would therefore have universal legitimacy (Held, 1995b: 115). The democratic rights which Held sees as necessary to global democratic governance are actually more substantial than those of the UN Declaration. They include rights to health, welfare, freedom of cultural expression, freedom of association and information, to a guaranteed minimum income, to physical security, and to participation in public deliberation and elections (Held, 1995a: 192-3). They do touch on issues which are particularly of concern to those in the Third World; the availability of clean water, for example, is included as a matter of the right to health. They are also very wide ranging: economic rights include the rights to have access to productive and financial resources which would require a significantly more egalitarian social organization of economic resources than is currently the case. Although it is not entirely clear what this would involve in practice, the enactment of such rights would seem to extend liberal democracy into socialism.

However, they are also undoubtedly culturally specific. Held, rightly or not, lays out definitions of human rights as the rights of individuals. This definition is contested by African and Asian perspectives on human rights. The African Charter of Human and People's Rights (1981), for example, emphasizes the collective rights of peoples and individual responsibilities and duties over the individual human rights of Western conventions. Individuals are, for example, seen as having duties of service to the national community, a duty to foster a sense of social and national solidarity, to promote African unity, and to strengthen positive African cultural values (Evans, 1997: 131). Western definitions of human rights may still be seen as culturally relativist even if they are not immediately linked to economic and political dominance. The issue of universal human rights is extremely complicated, but if it is possible to establish a single set of democratic rights worldwide – and if it were not, global governance as such would seem to be impossible – the form of those rights can only be established through democratic discussion.

The only possible means of arriving at a set of universal human rights which would be acceptable to all would seem to be discussion with representatives from all significantly differing perspectives. This means taking seriously the cultural relativism of Western definitions of universal human rights. It also means understanding the importance of cultural politics: particular definitions of universal human rights must be articulated, defended, and modified in the light of inclusive public debate. Human rights cannot be established monologically by Western theorists. Held's list, interesting and well thought out as it is, is no more than a contribution to a possible democratic discussion of human rights; it cannot be taken as established.

Finally, the institution of a more democratic form of human rights will undoubtedly require a transformation of identity: we will all have to become more cosmopolitan. In an interesting discussion of "cosmopolitans" and "locals," Ulf Hannerz defines cosmopolitanism as:

first of all an orientation, a willingness to engage with the Other . . .
There is the aspect of a state of readiness, a personal ability to make
one's way into other cultures, through listening, looking, intuiting and
reflecting. And there is cultural competence in the stricter sense of the
term, a built-up skill in manoeuvring more or less expertly with a particular system of meanings and meaningful forms. (Hannerz, 1990:
239)

As Hannerz (1990) points out, the growth of global culture makes
locals – those for whom home is entirely obvious, natural, and necessary – much rarer than they once were: in global culture, the local
is itself entwined with the global in processes of "glocalization" (pp.
84–8). The most important conclusion to be drawn from his observations in relation to global governance, however, is surely that cosmopolitanism is an orientation which should be actively cultivated
and encouraged in order to counteract discourses of cultural essentialism and to facilitate global democratic participation.

Cultural politics is central to the ongoing realization of cosmopolitan democratic governance. The contestation and transformation of existing identities and institutionalized practices is intrinsic
to democratization, not just in the more obviously cultural issues of
global civil society but also in the sites of formal politics, the internationalizing state and international law. In so far as global governance is reflexively created, it is not just ideas of political theory
which may contribute to the reconstruction of democracy. The
understandings of social actors engaged in the contestation of existing practices and the development of new, more egalitarian ways of
life in both formal and informal political institutions are most important to the realization of the potential for more democratic global
politics.

5.4 DEMOCRACY AND CULTURAL POLITICS

Throughout this book we have been looking at the oppositional cultural politics of social movements from within the framework of the
"postmodern turn" in new political sociology. In particular, we have
taken up several themes related to the cultural politics of contemporary social life: individualization and changes in civil society, both
at the local and the global level and including the way in which they
are now intertwined to an unprecedented degree; globalization and

changes in political structures; and citizenship and the new forms of egalitarian pluralism advocated by social movements. We have taken seriously the idea that significant changes are taking place in contemporary societies which mean that the nation-state is being displaced as the center of political activity. The state remains important, but it is now *one* site of the political among others, privileged in some respects, but far from being the exclusive holder of power as it was for traditional political sociology. Furthermore, as we have seen, the state is itself an object of cultural politics in so far as it is now being reformed as the internationalized state.

Other sites of contestation and transformation in civil society are also important, both because they are themselves the sites of subordination and exclusion and also because it is there that the far-reaching and deep-rooted changes in perspective, the redefining of interests, and the reconfiguration of social relations take place. This is nowhere more evident than in the effects of the women's movement. It has had comparatively little direct effect on state policies in Western liberal democracies, but it has transformed social life to the point where the state is now forced to respond to changing conditions. Although it is hard to pin down precisely what effects the women's movement has had, as distinct from the other changes in society which have impacted on our lives, it is only necessary to look at films, books, and TV programs from the 1960s – and to remember that the presentation of relations between the sexes there is generally not intended to be ironic – to realize that the definition of what it is to be a woman in contemporary society has completely changed. It is no longer assumed that women will sacrifice their individual desires in the name of being a good wife and mother, living vicariously through their husbands and children; nor that they will defer to men in public in exchange for men's protection and chivalry. Such changes are almost imperceptible over the long term, but they are nevertheless very real. It is incontrovertible that the way in which representations of women, women's subjectivity, and the details of relations between the sexes have been contested as a result of the women's movement has resulted in profound changes in all these aspects of our lives. The expression "I'm not a feminist, but . . ." followed by a statement which would have been unthinkable before the emergence of the women's movement in the 1960s is a well-documented feature of contemporary life.

Other social movements have not been effective to the same degree. Nevertheless, they are similarly engaged in cultural politics in civil society, opening up sites of contestation at work, at home, in the media, and so on. In so far as the environmental movement has had an impact on our perspectives on global damage and the possibilities of sustainable development, for example, it requires that we think about what we consume, what modes of transport we use, the extent to which we support how national economies are oriented toward growth, our relationship with animals and the countryside, and so on. Although, as in the case of the women's movement, there are no uncontroversial answers to any of the problems posed by these issues, the very fact that they are now issues is in itself of political importance. They are not problems which can simply be solved by states, or even by international regulation. They require a complete transformation in our understanding of how life should be lived. In this respect, politics at the level of the state follows from such fundamental understandings; their transformation is effected at this more wide-ranging and deep-rooted level.

Cultural politics in civil society is inherently democratizing in so far as it opens up questions concerning how to live which were previously settled or taken for granted; it makes discussion of the issues possible across different groups and in different social contexts. Clearly, the media play an important role in shaping these debates as they are extended across time and space. However, the issues are also raised in social interactions which are less controlled. There are certain issues around which each individual must organize his or her life, and, in so far as this is the case, everyone participates in the ongoing consideration of how fundamental questions might be resolved. In this respect, the questions raised by cultural politics are necessarily democratically contested, even if it is the case that some individuals are more articulate or better placed to make their definitions of the issues acceptable.

Cultural politics in liberal democracies also tends to lead to a greater degree of pluralism. The most effective social movements in the West are sympathetic to left-wing politics and inclined toward libertarianism and equality. The effects of the cultural politics in which they are engaged has been to open up sites of contestation and to resist their closure except where considerations of equality override those of individual freedom. Again, the women's movement is exemplary. Despite fears of "political correctness," a wide range of personal and professional life choices are now acceptable for both men and women. At the same time, the issue of equality between the sexes is a recurring one in the media and in relation to policy-making and the law. The cultural politics of the women's movement has been broadly democratizing, then, as it has tended to be identified with claims that individuals should have the right to choose their own way of life and that women should enjoy the same conditions and rewards as men.

It is important to note, however, that cultural politics is not necessarily democratizing in this respect. Right-wing social movements are neglected in political sociology, and we have followed this tendency in this book. They include nationalist, racist movements like the National Front in Britain, the White Supremacy movement in the US, and those which are now so prominent in Europe. All those movements which militate for a return to the pre-1960s morality of the "permissive society" are also to be included in this category. Far from advocating libertarian and egalitarian practices, such movements are concerned to homogenize society around the values of "the moral majority" claimed by movements in the US, and to re-institute what they see as the traditional ways of white societies. Such movements engage in cultural politics, though they attempt to close down rather than to open up the contestation of fundamental questions. The paradox, of course, is that, in order to do so, they have to engage in constructing new identities and transforming ongoing social practices. Arguably, it is for this reason that such movements cannot ultimately succeed. The fact that they have to engage in cultural politics to bring about a re-traditionalization of society makes their very project self-defeating. Nevertheless, the way in which right-wing social movements engage in cultural politics to limit individual freedom and equality makes it evident that, although cultural politics is inherently democratic in promoting contestation, it is not necessarily democratic in terms of aims, nor, possibly, of effects.

The emphasis of the "postmodern turn" of new political sociology has been on cultural politics in civil society. This is an important corrective to the old political sociology which was only concerned with politics at the level of the nation-state. But it is also important that the state should not be neglected as a site of politics. Disaffection with party politics and cynicism concerning representative democracy, the way in which processes of globalization problematize the autonomy and sovereignty of the old model of the nation-state, and the importance of transnational politics to global democracy notwithstanding, as we have seen, the internationalizing state is vital to the realization of more democratic global governance. In fact, the democratization of civil society and of the state are closely linked. Tolerance of diversity and respect for the contestation of fundamental issues depend, in part, on the rule of law enforced by states. In the dramatic case of the "Velvet Revolution" referred to above, for example, while it was undoubtedly protests in civil society which brought down the totalitarian regimes of Eastern Europe, this would not have been possible if the government of the USSR had not withdrawn the military support which would otherwise have crushed them.

Furthermore, the model of cultural politics we have been using in this book need not be seen as applying only to politics in civil society. The new state formations developing at the international and supranational level necessarily involve cultural politics. Fundamental questions of state power, how it is to be shared and how it is to be used, are now open to contestation. The practices which are instituted depend on how such questions are resolved, both in the short and longer term. In this respect, the current period offers opportunities for a more democratic cosmopolitan governance to which political sociology should be both a response and a resource.

Notes

1   There is also great interest in democracy elsewhere in the world, especially in the recently democratizing countries of Eastern Europe and South Africa. Quite different issues are raised in these cases, with the introduction of markets and the growth of ethno-nationalist groups demanding sovereignty in Eastern Europe and the dismantling of apartheid in the case of South Africa. In this book, however, we are focusing on Western liberal democracies and such questions will be dealt with only so far as they are relevant to these, already established, political regimes. For a good overview of democratization across the world, see Potter et al. (1997).

2   A third prominent model is that of reflexive democracy, elaborated in the work of Ulrich Beck and Anthony Giddens. However, much of this work has already been dealt with in chapter 2. While both have written quite extensively on democracy, this work has been mainly addressed to a popular audience and has tended to deal with topical debates in

contemporary politics. As a theory of democracy, it remains underdeveloped in comparison with their ideas on reflexivity and globalization (see Giddens, 1994, 1998; Beck, 1997, 1998).

3   All the theories of postmodernity outlined here share a major difficulty, that of the tense in which they are written. It is often not clear whether the writer is analyzing changes which have already taken place or are now taking place, anticipating changes which may come about or predicting changes which will come about. In many cases they seem to involve a mixture of all of these. The issue is an important one because, in the case of the more empirical theories, those of post-industrialism and post-Fordism, the evidence does not support the sweeping changes they propose. It is, however, sufficient to identify *tendencies*. Then it is a matter of judging, to borrow Kumar's phrase, "whether the glass is half-empty or half-full." For example, there is undoubtedly evidence that changes in production, such as flexible specialization, are being introduced. However, the extent to which they will dominate production in the future is difficult to predict. See Kumar's excellent discussion of the evidence in *From Post-industrial to Postmodern Society* (1995).

4   There are other models of global governance. McGrew details, for example, the "liberal-internationalist" and the "radical communitarianist" (see McGrew, 1997: ch. 10). They have not been outlined here, however, because they tend to be more normative than sociological. Although Held's theory has normative elements, he proposes the most sociologically sensitive model of global democracy.

GLOSSARY

civil society: as an ideal of liberal democracy, it is the sphere of private institutions, organizations, associations, and individuals protected by, but outside the scope of, state intervention.

complex societies: associated with systems theory, the term refers to contemporary societies following modernization. They have a highly differentiated division of labor in which social tasks are carried out in highly specialized and functionally interdependent subsystems; a lack of social solidarity as a result of rapidly changing, fragmented socio-economic formations and detraditionalizing culture; and "weak states" undermined by lack of social solidarity and processes of globalization (Zolo, 1992; Offe, 1996). See also *post-Fordism*; *post-industrialism*; *postmodernity*.

cultural politics: there are at least four ways in which the term is used:

1   The politics of cultural representations: for example, Stuart Hall charts the shift from a politics of "the relations of representation" to a politics of "representation itself" (Hall, 1992b: 253).
2   The politics of cultural production, the way in which it is organized, promoted, or suppressed in, for example, education, broadcasting, and trade policy (Street, 1997b).

3 The politics of what counts as culture and who is marginalized or excluded from its production (Jordan and Weedon, 1995: 7).
4 The politics of signifying practices through which identities, social relations, and rules are contested, subverted, and may be transformed. This is the sense with which this book is predominantly concerned.

See also *culture*.

culture: the best analysis of the term is still that of Raymond Williams. It is used in at least four different ways:

1 "A general process of intellectual, spiritual, and aesthetic development" as in "she is a cultured person."
2 "A particular way of life, whether of a people, a period or a group" as used by anthropologists to describe different cultures.
3 "The works and practices of intellectual and especially artistic activity:" music, literature, painting, and sculpture, sometimes including works of popular culture too.
4 "The signifying order through which necessarily . . . a social order is communicated, reproduced, experienced and explored:" the post-structuralist understanding of culture as material practices in which identities, objects, and social rules are constituted (quoted in Jordan and Weedon, 1995: 6–8).

discourse: the meaningful field which provides the conditions of possibility for experience, thought, and action. Ernesto Laclau (1993) distinguishes two main traditions:

1 That emerging from a critique of the structural linguistics of Saussure (for example, in the work of Roland Barthes and Jacques Derrida) in which relations between signifiers (the sound or image of words) are what create meaning; the distinction between signifier and signified (mental concept) is dropped, reality as we perceive it is taken to be created by words since there is nothing meaningful outside language, and, similarly, so are the intentions, thoughts, and feelings of speakers and writers.

2   That developed in the work of Michel Foucault in which
    discourse is made up of statements contingently linked in a
    "regularity of dispersion" which does not obey any essential
    principle of structuration.

A major issue in discourse theory is the status of the
extra-discursive: for the first tradition it is a logical impossibility;
for Foucault, at least in his genealogical studies, the extra-discursive
provides the institutional basis for discourse; for Laclau
and Mouffe, it is also a logical impossibility and social reality
is nothing but discourses embedded in social practices (Laclau,
1993).

essentialism: Diana Fuss (1989) gives a very subtle analysis of essentialism in contemporary debates in *Essentially Speaking*. Following
Locke, she distinguishes between:

1   "Real essences:" "the Aristotelian understanding of essence as
    that which is most irreducible and unchanging about a thing;"
    it is discovered in nature by close observation.
2   "Nominal essence:" "merely a linguistic convenience, a
    classificatory fiction we need to categorize and label;" it is
    assigned or produced in language through the arbitrary
    naming of objects.

To use an example Fuss gives to sum up the difference between
them: for a real essentialist, a rose by any other name would still be
a rose; for a nominal essentialist, it would be something quite different (Fuss, 1989: 4–5). Challenges to essentialism have been particularly important in feminist and queer theory and also in debates
on racism and cultural differences. "Essentialism" is invariably used
as a pejorative term in such debates.

governance: the effective regulation of social activity without the
formal authority of government.

globalization: Martin Albrow (1996) gives an extremely comprehensive and precise definition, according to which globalization
involves:

1 Making or being made global:
   (a) in individual instances
      (i)   by the active dissemination of practices, values, technology, and other human products throughout the globe;
      (ii) when global products and so on exercise an increasing influence over people's lives;
      (iii) when the globe serves as a focus for, or a premise in shaping, human activities;
      (iv) in the incremental change occasioned by the interaction of any such instances;
   (b) seen as the generality of such instances;
   (c) such instances being viewed abstractly.
2 A process of making or being made global in any or all of the senses in (1).
3 The historical transformation constituted by the sum or particular forms and instances of (1). (Albrow, 1996: 88)

international: referring to the relations between nation-states. See also *transnational*.

internationalized state: the form of the state currently developing as an aspect of global governance. It shares sovereignty as a result of its participation in international agreements, especially those which bring its citizens under international law. See also *nation-state*.

nation-state: a historically specific form of the state, developed initially in Europe and the US from the seventeenth to the nineteenth centuries and spread to the rest of the world with decolonization in the twentieth century. The modern state is sovereign over a nation, the members of which are taken to form a community or common culture. See also *internationalized state*; *state*.

post-Fordism: a mode of production involving forms of socio-economic organization which differ from that of the mass production, corporatism, and class relations of Fordism. It includes the following changes: globalization problematizes national economies; flexible specialization for niche markets displaces mass production and consumption; a workforce organized more clearly in terms of core and periphery than as a hierarchical class structure; long-term structural unemployment; the decline of class politics and corporatism and the rise of social movements and "networks;" increased individualism and pluralism of lifestyles, particularly in relation to consumption patterns (Kumar, 1995: 52)

post-industrialism: a stage of society after industrial society in which knowledge is the key organizing principle rather than the production of goods. Daniel Bell (1976) emphasizes the benefits, including a highly skilled workforce and rational planning. Alain Touraine (1971) emphasizes conflicts over knowledge between dominant and subordinate groups. More recently, Alberto Melucci (1989) has added globalization and individualization as features of post-industrial society.

postmodernity: includes the changes listed above under post-Fordism. It emphasizes the increased importance of culture with the growth of information, media, and consumer culture; of signs and meaning; the fluidity and depthlessness of cultural forms; shifting identities and the continual undermining of traditional grounds for social practices. (Note: the importance of culture in postmodernity makes an absolute distinction between postmodernity and postmodernism unsustainable: Kumar, 1995: 112–21).

postmodernism: used in two main ways in sociology:

1 *The culture of postmodernity*: involves fragmentation, self-referentiality, intertextuality, irony, pastiche, montage, juxtaposition of forms, for example in postmodern architecture (Bauman, 1992); incredulity toward meta-narratives of science and progress; the relativization and pluralization of the dominant definition of Western culture as universal in its themes and implications.

2 *The philosophical movement*: includes the work of post-structuralists (see *post-structuralism*); also that of Jean-François Lyotard for whom it involves incredulity toward meta-narratives, i.e. the end of the belief in historical progress as the application of reason and science; and also the work of Richard Rorty (the only one not to reject the term) for whom

it involves anti-foundationalism: the abandonment of the
modern search for the rational grounds of knowledge and
morality in reality and in human nature.

post-structuralism: used to describe the theories in the later work
of Barthes, those of Lacan, Foucault, Derrida, Laclau and Mouffe
and others. It involves the following elements: anti-foundationalism
– the abandonment of the modern search for the rational
grounds of knowledge and morality; anti-humanism – concern
with the ongoing construction of subjectivity; emphasis on the construction of meaning and rhetoric in philosophical texts (especially
Derrida); concern with the relations between knowledge and
power (especially Foucault). The work of these theorists is known
as post-structuralism because they have all been concerned with
the historicization and de-totalization of structures, especially
the universal structures theorized by Levi-Strauss as underpinning
all human societies, and including "society" as a structured
totality as it was theorized by Althusser. Post-structuralism as a
movement in philosophy, social, and political theory is included
in the category "postmodernism" which has wider cultural
and social resonances (Best and Kellner, 1991: 25). See also
postmodernism.

reflexivity: as Beck (1994) points out, in a very useful article on this
concept, it is used by himself, Giddens and Lash and Urry in slightly
different ways. In Giddens's work it refers to the way in which
"expert knowledges" produce reflection on the foundations of social
action, including the production of knowledge itself, so contributing
to the continual revisability of social structures in "high modernity"
(Giddens, 1991). Lash's understanding, and that of his collaborator
Urry, is similar in that reflexivity concerns reflection on knowledge,
but Lash and Urry are critical of what they see as Giddens's exces-
sive concern with *cognitive* reflexivity, drawing attention particularly
to the importance of *aesthetic* reflexivity in contemporary society in
which identities are constructed through consumption (Lash and
Urry, 1994). In contrast, Beck's notion of reflexivity concerns, he
says, not knowledge, but *unawarene*ss. For him, reflexive modernization refers to a type of society beyond "simple modernity" in
which there is an acknowledgement of the impossibility of knowing
the unintended consequences produced by modernization and

attempts to respond to this which result in social re-structuring (Beck, 1998, ch. 7; see also Beck et al., 1994).

state: Hall and Ikenberry (1989: 1–2) give the following definition:

1   It is a set of institutions, the most important of which are those of violence and coercion.
2   It is at the center of a geographically bounded territory, a society.
3   It monopolizes rule-making within its territory which tends to create a common political culture shared by its citizens.

See also *internationalized state*.

supranational: above the nation-state; a political institution with powers which have been transferred from the nation-state and with which it must share sovereignty, for example, the European Parliament.

transnational: referring to relations or processes which cross national boundaries, by-passing the nation-state. See also *international*.

REFERENCES

Akbar, A. 1992: *Postmodernism and Islam: Predicament and Promise.* Routledge: London.

Albrow, M. 1996: *The Global Age: State and Society beyond Modernity.* Polity Press: Cambridge.

Alger, C. 1994: "Citizens and the UN System in a Changing World," in Y. Sakamoto (ed.), *Global Transformation: Challenges to the State System.* United Nations University Press: Tokyo.

Althusser, L. 1971: "Ideology and Ideological State Apparatuses," in *Lenin and Philosophy and Other Essays*, trans. B. Brewster. New Left Books: London.

Altvater, E. and Mahnkopf, B. "The World Market Unbound," in A. Scott (ed.), *The Limits of Globalization: Cases and Arguments.* Routledge: London.

Amin, A. 1997: "Placing Globalization," *Theory, Culture and Society*, 14 (2).

Anderson, B. 1983: *Imagined Communities: Reflections on the Origin and Spread of Nationalism.* Verso: London.

Anderson, J. and Goodman, J. 1995: "Regions, States and the European Union: Modernist Reaction or Postmodern Adaptation," *Review of International Political Economy*, 2 (4).

Appadurai, A. 1990: "Disjuncture and Difference in the Global Cultural Economy," in M. Featherstone (ed.), *Global Culture: Nationalism, Globalization and Modernity.* Sage: London.

Archibugi, D. and Held, D. (eds) 1995: *Cosmopolitan Democracy: an Agenda for a New World Order.* Polity Press: Cambridge.

Ashley, D. 1997: *History without a Subject: the Postmodern Condition.* Westview Press: Boulder, Colorado.

Bacchi, C. 1990: *Same Difference: Feminism and Sexual Difference*. Allen and Unwin: London.

Balakrishnan, G. 1996: "The National Imagination," in G. Balakrishnan (ed.), *Mapping the Nation*. Verso: London.

Barbalet, J. 1988: *Citizenship*. Open University Press: Milton Keynes.

Barker, M. 1981: *The New Racism*. Junction Books: London.

Barrett, M. 1991: *The Politics of Truth*. Polity Press: Cambridge.

Barrett. M. 1992: "Words and Things," in M. Barrett and A. Phillips (eds), *Destabilizing Theory: Contemporary Feminist Debates*. Polity Press: Cambridge.

Baudrillard, J. 1983: *In the Shadow of the Silent Majorities*. Semiotext(e): New York.

Baudrillard, J. 1987: *Forget Foucault*. Semiotext(e): New York.

Bauman, Z. 1987: *Legislators and Interpreters: on Modernity, Postmodernity and Intellectuals*. Polity Press: Cambridge.

Bauman, Z. 1992: *Intimations of Postmodernity*. Routledge: London.

Beck, U. 1992: *Risk Society: Towards a New Modernity*. Sage: London.

Beck, U. 1994: "Self-dissolution and Self-endangerment of Industrial Society: What Does it Mean?," in U. Beck, A. Giddens, and S. Lash (eds), *Reflexive Modernization: Politics, Tradition and Aesthetics in the Modern Social Order*. Polity Press: Cambridge.

Beck, U. 1996: "World Risk Society as Cosmopolitan Society?," *Theory, Culture and Society*, 13 (4).

Beck, U. 1997: *The Reinvention of Politics: Rethinking Modernity in the Global Social Order*. Polity Press: Cambridge.

Beck, U. 1998: *Democracy without Enemies*. Polity Press: Cambridge.

Beck, U., Giddens, A., and Lash, S. (eds) 1994: *Reflexive Modernization: Politics, Tradition and Aesthetics in the Modern Social Order*. Polity Press: Cambridge.

Bell, D. 1976: *The Coming of Post-industrial Society: a Venture in Social Forecasting*. Peregrine Books: London.

Benhabib, S. 1996: "Introduction" to *Democracy and Difference: Contesting the Boundaries of the Political*. Princeton University Press: Princeton, New Jersey.

Benton, T. 1994: *The Rise and Fall of Structural Marxism*. Macmillan: London.

Bertens, H. 1995: *The Idea of the Postmodern: a History*. Routledge: London.

Best, S. and Kellner, D. 1991: *Postmodern Theory: Critical Investigations*. Guilford Press: New York and London.

Best, S. and Kellner, D. 1997: *The Postmodern Turn*. Guilford Press: New York and London.

Bottomore, T. 1964: *Elites and Society*. Penguin: Harmondsworth.

Bottomore, T. 1993: *Political Sociology*, 2nd edn. Pluto Press: London.

Brah, A. 1992: "Difference, Diversity and Differentiation," in J. Donald and A. Rattansi (eds), *"Race," Culture and Difference*. Sage: London.

Brubaker, R. 1992: *Citizenship and Nationhood in France and Germany*. Harvard University Press: Cambridge, Massachussetts.

Butler, J. 1990: *Gender Trouble: Feminism and the Subversion of Identity*. Routledge: London.

Butler, J. 1993: *Bodies that Matter: on the Discursive Limits of Sex*. Routledge: London.

Calhoun, C. (ed.) 1992: *Habermas and the Public Sphere*. MIT Press: Cambridge, Massachusetts.

Calhoun, C. 1995: "'New Social Movements' of the Early Nineteenth Century," in M. Traugott (ed.), *Repertoires and Cycles of Collective Action*. Duke University Press: Durham.

Castles, S. 1993: "Migrations and Minorities in Europe. Perspectives for the 1990s: Eleven Hypotheses," in J. Solomos and J. Wrench (eds), *Racism and Migration in Western Europe*. Berg: Oxford.

Christoff, P. 1996: "Ecological Citizens and Ecologically Guided Democracy," in B. Doherty and M. de Geus (eds), *Democracy and Green Political Thought: Sustainability, Rights and Citizenship*. Routledge: London.

Connolly, W. 1991: *Identity/Difference: Democratic Negotiations of Political Paradox*. Cornell University Press: Ithaca, New York.

Connolly, W. 1996: "Pluralism, Multiculturalism and the Nation-state: Rethinking the Connections," *Journal of Political Ideologies*, 1 (1).

Cox, R. 1997: "Democracy in Hard Times: Economic Globalization and the Limits to Liberal Democracy," in A. McGrew (ed.), *The Transformation of Democracy? Globalization and Territorial Democracy*. Polity Press: Cambridge.

Crook, S., Pakulski, J., and Waters, M. 1992: *Postmodernization: Change in Advanced Society*. Sage: London.

Cross, M. 1993: "Migration, Employment and Social Change in the New Europe," in R. King (ed.), *The New Geography of European Migrations*. Belhaven Press: London.

Culler, J. 1976: *Saussure*. Harvester Press: Brighton.

Dahl, R. 1956: *A Preface to Democratic Theory*. University of Chicago Press: Chicago.

Dalton, R. J. and Kuechler, M. 1990: *Challenging the Political Order: New Social and Political Movements in Western Democracies*. Polity Press: Cambridge.

Della Porta, D. and Kriesi, H. forthcoming: "Introduction" to D. Rucht, D. Della Porta, and H. Kriesi (eds), *Social Movements in a Globalizing World*. Blackwell: Oxford.

Derrida, J. 1978: "Structure, Sign, Play," in *Writing and Difference*, trans. A. Bass. Routledge and Kegan Paul: London.

Derrida, J. 1982: "Différance," in *Margins of Philosophy*, trans. A. Bass. Harvester Wheatsheaf: Hemel Hempstead, Hertfordshire.

Derrida, J. 1996: "Remarks on Deconstruction and Pragmatism," in C. Mouffe (ed.), *Deconstruction and Pragmatism*. Routledge: London.

Descombes, V. 1980: *Modern French Philosophy*. Cambridge University Press: Cambridge.

Dews, P. 1984: "Power and Subjectivity in Foucault," *New Left Review*, 144: 72–95.

Dews, P. 1986: *Autonomy and Solidarity: Interviews with Jürgen Habermas*. Verso: London.

Diani, M. 1992: "The Concept of Social Movement," *Sociological Review*, 40 (1).

Dickenson, D. 1997: "Counting Women in: Globalization, Democratization and the Women's Movement," in A. McGrew (ed.), *The Transformation of Democracy? Globalization and Territorial Democracy*. Polity Press: Cambridge.

Dowse, R. and Hughes, J. 1972: *Political Sociology*. John Wiley and Sons: London.

Dunleavy, P. and O'Leary, B. 1987: *Theories of the State: the Politics of Liberal Democracy*. Macmillan: London.

Eagleton, T. 1991: *Ideology: an Introduction*. Verso: London.

Edwards, T. 1994: *Erotics and Politics: Gay Male Sexuality, Masculinity and Feminism*. Routledge: London.

Evans, D. 1993: *Sexual Citizenship: the Material Construction of Sexualities*. Routledge: London.

Evans, T. 1997: "Democratization and Human Rights," in A. McGrew (ed.), *The Transformation of Democracy? Globalization and Territorial Democracy*. Polity Press: Cambridge.

Fainstein, N. 1996: "A Note on Interpreting American Poverty," in E. Mingione (ed.), *Urban Poverty and the Underclass*. Blackwell: Oxford.

Falk, R. 1994a: "Democratizing, Internationalizing, and Globalizing," in Y. Sakamoto (ed.), *Global Transformation: Challenges to the State System*. United Nations University Press: Tokyo.

Falk, R. 1994b: "The Making of Global Citizenship," in B. van Steenbergen (ed.), *The Condition of Citizenship*. Sage: London.

Falk, R. 1995a: *On Humane Governance: Toward a New Global Politics*. Polity Press: Cambridge.

Falk, R. 1995b: "The World Order between Inter-state Law and the Law of Humanity: the Role of Civil Society Institutions," in D. Archibugi and D. Held (eds), *Cosmopolitan Democracy: an Agenda for a New World Order*. Polity Press: Cambridge.

Featherstone, M. 1988: "In Pursuit of the Postmodern," *Theory, Culture and Society*, 5: 195–215.

Featherstone, M. (ed.), 1990: *Global Culture: Nationalism, Globalization and Modernity*. Sage: London.

Featherstone, M. 1995: *Undoing Culture: Globalization, Postmodernism and Identity*. Sage: London.

Featherstone, M., Lash, S., and Robertson, R. (eds) 1995: *Global Modernities*. Sage: London.

Fiske, J. 1987: *Television Culture*. Routledge: London.

Foucault, M. 1972: *The Archaeology of Knowledge*, trans. A. Sheridan. Tavistock: London.

Foucault, M. 1979: *Discipline and Punish: the Birth of the Prison*, trans. A. Sheridan. Penguin: Harmondsworth.

Foucault, M. 1980a: "Two Lectures," in C. Gordon (ed.), *Power/Knowledge: Selected Interviews and Other Writings 1972–1977*. Harvester: Brighton.

Foucault, M. 1980b: "Truth and Power," in C. Gordon (ed.), *Power/Knowledge: Selected Interviews and Other Writings 1972–1977*. Harvester: Brighton.

Foucault, M. 1982: "The Subject and Power," in H. Dreyfus and P. Rabinow (eds), *Michel Foucault: Beyond Structuralism and Hermeneutics*. Harvester Wheatsheaf: Brighton.

Foucault, M. 1984a: "Politics and Ethics: an Interview," in P. Rabinow (ed.), *The Foucault Reader*. Penguin: Harmondsworth.

Foucault, M. 1984b: *The History of Sexuality: an Introduction*, trans. R. Hurley. Penguin: Harmondsworth.

Foucault, M. 1984c: "The Ethic of Care for the Self as a Practice of Freedom," in J. Bernauer and D. Rasmussen (eds), *The Final Foucault*. MIT Press: Cambridge, Massachusetts.

Foucault, M. 1984d: "Nietzsche, Genealogy, History," in P. Rabinow (ed.), *The Foucault Reader*. Penguin: Harmondsworth.

Foucault, M. 1991: "Governmentality," in G. Burchell, C. Gordon, and P. Miller (eds), *The Foucault Effect: Studies in Governmentality*: Harvester Wheatsheaf: London.

Fraser, N. 1989: "Foucault on Modern Power: Empirical Insights and Normative Confusions," in *Unruly Practices: Power, Discourse and Gender in Contemporary Social Theory*. Polity Press: Cambridge.

Frazer, E. and Lacey, N. 1993: *The Politics of Community: a Feminist Critique of the Liberal-Communitarian Debate*. Harvester Wheatsheaf: London.

Friedman, J. 1990: "Being in the World: Globalization and Localization," in M. Featherstone (ed.), *Global Culture: Nationalism, Globalization and Modernity*. Sage: London.

Friedman, J. 1995: "Global System, Globalization and the Parameters of Modernity," in M. Featherstone, S. Lash, and R. Robertson (eds), *Global Modernities*. Sage: London.

Fukuyama, F. 1992: *The End of History and the Last Man*. Free Press: New York.

Fuss, D. 1989: *Essentially Speaking: Feminism, Nature and Difference*. Routledge: London.

Gamson, J. 1996: "Must Identity Movements Self-Destruct?," in S. Seidman (ed.), *Queer Theory/Sociology*. Blackwell: Oxford.

Gamson, W. 1992: "The Social Psychology of Collective Action," in A. Morris and C. Mueller (eds), *Frontiers in Social Movement Theory*. Yale University Press: New Haven and London.

Gamson, W. and Meyer, D. 1996: "Framing Political Opportunity," in D. McAdam, J. McCarthy, and M. Zald (eds), *Comparative Perspectives on Social Movements: Political Opportunities, Mobilizing Structures, and Cultural Framings*. Cambridge University Press: Cambridge.

Giddens, A. 1972: *Politics and Sociology in the Thought of Max Weber*. Macmillan: Houndmills, Basingstoke.

Giddens, A. 1979: *Central Problems in Social Theory: Action, Structure and Contradiction in Social Analysis*. Macmillan: Basingstoke, Hampshire.

Giddens, A. 1982: "Class Division, Class Conflict and Citizenship Rights," in *Profiles and Critiques in Social Theory*. Macmillan: Basingstoke, Hampshire.

Giddens, A. 1984: *The Constitution of Society: Outline of the Theory of Structuration*. Polity Press: Cambridge.

Giddens, A. 1990: *The Consequences of Modernity*. Polity Press: Cambridge.

Giddens, A. 1991: *Modernity and Self-identity: Self and Society in the Late Modern Age*. Polity Press: Cambridge.

Giddens, A. 1994: *Beyond Left and Right: the Future of Radical Politics*. Polity Press: Cambridge.

Giddens, A. 1998: *The Third Way: the Renewal of Social Democracy*. Polity Press: Cambridge.

Gilligan, C. 1993: *In a Different Voice: Psychological Theory and Women's Development*. Harvard University Press: Cambridge, Massachusetts and London.

Gilroy, P. 1992: *There Ain't No Black in the Union Jack: the Cultural Politics of Race and Nation*. Routledge: London.

Gilroy, P. 1993a: *The Black Atlantic: Modernity and Double Consciousness*. Verso: London.

Gilroy, P. 1993b: *Small Acts; Thoughts on the Politics of Black Cultures*. Serpent's Tail: London.

Goldblatt, D. 1997: "Liberal Democracy and the Globalization of Environmental Risks," in A. McGrew (ed.), *The Transformation of Democracy? Globalization and Territorial Democracy*. Polity Press: Cambridge.

Goodman, J. 1997: "The European Union: Reconstituting Democracy Beyond the Nation-state," in A. McGrew (ed.), *The Transformation of Democracy? Globalization and Territorial Democracy*. Polity Press: Cambridge.

Gould, C. 1996: "Diversity and Democracy: Representing Differences," in S. Benhabib (ed.), *Democracy and Difference: Contesting the Boundaries of the Political*. Princeton University Press: Princeton, New Jersey.

Gramsci, A. 1971: *Selections from Prison Notebooks*, ed. Q. Hoare and G. Nowell Smith. Lawrence and Wishart: London.

Guibernau, M. 1996: *Nationalisms: the Nation-state and Nationalism in the Twentieth Century*. Polity Press: Cambridge.

Guild, E. 1996: "The Legal Framework of Citizenship of the European Union," in D. Cesarani and M. Fullbrook (eds), *Citizenship, Nationality and Migration in Europe*. Routledge: London.

Gutting, G. 1994: "Michel Foucault: a User's Manual," in G. Gutting (ed.), *The Cambridge Companion to Foucault*. Cambridge University Press: Cambridge.

Habermas, J. 1981: "Modernity versus Postmodernity," *New German Critique*, 2 (1).

Habermas, J. 1987a: *The Theory of Communicative Action*, vol. I, trans. T. McCarthy. Polity Press: Cambridge.

Habermas. J. 1987b: *The Theory of Communicative Action*, vol. II, trans. T. McCarthy. Polity Press: Cambridge.

Habermas, J. 1987c: *The Philosophical Discourse of Modernity*. Polity Press: Cambridge.

Habermas, J. 1988: *Legitimation Crisis*, trans. T. McCarthy. Polity Press: Cambridge.

Habermas, J. 1989: *The Structural Transformation of the Public Sphere*, trans. T. Burger. Polity Press: Cambridge.

Habermas, J. 1990: *Moral Consciousness and Communicative Action*. Polity Press: Cambridge.

Habermas, J. 1992: "Citizenship and National Identity: Some Reflections on the Future of Europe," *Praxis International*, 12 (1).

Habermas. J. 1996: *Between Facts and Norms*. Polity Press: Cambridge.

Hall, J. and Ikenberry, G. 1989: *The State*. Open University Press: Milton Keynes.

Hall, S. 1990: "Cultural Identity and Diaspora," in J. Rutherford (ed.), *Identity: Community, Culture, Difference*. Lawrence and Wishart: London.

Hall, S. 1991a: "Old and New Identities, Old and New Ethnicities," in A. D. King (ed.), *Culture, Globalisation and the World System: Contemporary Conditions for the Representation of Identity.* Macmillan: London.

Hall, S. 1991b: "The Local and the Global: Globalisation and Ethnicity," in A. D. King (ed.), 1991: *Culture, Globalisation and the World System: Contemporary Conditions for the Representation of Identity.* Macmillan: London.

Hall, S. 1992a: "The Question of Cultural Identity," in S. Hall, D. Held, and A. McGrew (eds), *Modernity and its Futures.* Polity Press: Cambridge.

Hall, S. 1992b: "New Ethnicities," in J. Donald and A. Rattansi (eds), *"Race," Culture and Difference.* Sage: London.

Hall, S. and Jacques, M. 1989: *New Times: the Changing Face of Politics in the 1990s.* Lawrence and Wishart: London.

Hammar, T. 1990: *Democracy and the Nation-State: Aliens, Denizens and Citizens.* Avebury Press: Aldershot, Hants.

Hannerz, U. 1990: "Cosmopolitans and Locals in World Culture," in M. Featherstone (ed.), *Global Culture: Nationalism, Globalization and Modernity.* Sage: London.

Harvey, D. 1989: *The Condition of Postmodernity.* Blackwell: Oxford.

Harvey, D. 1993: "Class Relations, Social Justice and the Politics of Difference," in J. Squires (ed.), *Principled Positions: Postmodernism and the Rediscovery of Value.* Lawrence and Wishart: London.

Held, D. 1980: *Introduction to Critical Theory: Horkheimer to Habermas.* Hutchinson: London.

Held, D. 1987: *Models of Democracy.* Polity Press: Cambridge.

Held, D. 1991: "Democracy, the Nation-State and the Global System," in D. Held (ed.), *Political Theory Today.* Polity Press: Cambridge.

Held, D. 1995a: *Democracy and Global Order: from the Modern State to Cosmopolitan Governance.* Polity Press: Cambridge.

Held, D. 1995b: "Democracy and the New International Order," in D. Archibugi and D. Held (eds), *Cosmopolitan Democracy: an Agenda for a New World Order.* Polity Press: Cambridge.

Herman, D. 1993: "The Politics of Law Reform: Lesbian and Gay Rights Struggles into the 1990s," in J. Bristow and A. Wilson (eds), *Activating Theory: Lesbian, Gay, Bisexual Politics.* Lawrence and Wishart: London.

Hernes, H. 1984: "Women and the Welfare State: the Transition from Private to Public Dependence," in H. Holter (ed.), *Patriarchy in a Welfare State.* Universitetsforlaget: Oslo.

Hindess, B. 1996: *Discourses of Power: from Hobbes to Foucault.* Blackwell: Oxford.

Hirst, P. 1979: *On Law and Ideology.* Macmillan: London.

Hirst, P. 1997: "Why the National Still Matters," in *From Statism to Pluralism.* UCL Press: London.

Hirst, P. and Thompson, G. 1996: *Globalization in Question: the International Economy and the Possibilities of Governance.* Polity Press: Cambridge.

Inglehart, R. 1990: "Values, Ideology and Cognitive Mobilisation in New Social Movements," in R. J. Dalton and M. Kuechler (eds), *Challenging the Political Order: New Social and Political Movements in Western Democracies.* Polity Press: Cambridge.

Jacobson, D. 1996: *Rights across Borders: Immigration and the Decline of Citizenship.* Johns Hopkins University Press: Baltimore and London.

Jameson, F. 1984: "Postmodernism, or the Cultural Logic of Late Capitalism," *New Left Review,* 146.

Jessop, B. 1997: "Capitalism and its Future: Remarks on Regulation, Government and Governance," *Review of International Political Economy,* 4 (3).

Joas, H. 1991: "The Unhappy Marriage of Hermeneutics and Functionalism," in A. Honneth and H. Joas (eds), *Communicative Action: Essays on Jürgen Habermas's "The Theory of Communicative Action,"* trans. J. Gaines and D. L. Jones. Polity Press: Cambridge.

Johnston, H. and Klandermans, B. (eds) 1995: *Social Movements and Culture.* UCL Press: London.

Jordan, G. and Weedon, C. 1995: *Cultural Politics: Class, Gender, Race and the Postmodern World.* Blackwell: Oxford.

Katz, E. and Liebes, T. 1984: "Once Upon a Time in Dallas," *Intermedia,* 12 (3).

Kellner, D. 1989: *Jean Baudrillard: from Marxism to Postmodernism and Beyond.* Polity Press: Cambridge.

Kellner, D. 1995: *Media Culture: Cultural Studies, Identity and Politics between the Modern and the Postmodern.* Routledge: London.

King, D. 1991: "Citizenship as Obligation in the United States: Title II of the Family Support Act of 1988," in U. Vogel and M. Moran (eds), *The Frontiers of Citizenship.* Macmillan: London.

Klandermans, B., Kriesi, H., and Tarrow, S. (eds) 1988: *From Structure to Action: Social Movement Research across Different Cultures.* JAI Press: Greenwich, Connecticut and London.

Kuhn, T. 1970: *The Structure of Scientific Revolution.* University of Chicago Press: Chicago.

Kumar, K. 1978: *Prophecy and Progress: the Sociology of Industrial and Post-industrial Society.* Penguin: Harmondsworth, Middlesex.

Kumar, K. 1995: *From Post-industrial to Postmodern Society: New Theories of the Contemporary World.* Blackwell: Oxford.

Kymlicka, W. 1995: *Multi-cultural Citizenship: a Liberal Theory of Minority Rights*. Oxford University Press: Oxford.

Laclau, E. 1990: *New Reflections on the Revolution of our Time*. Verso: London.

Laclau, E. 1993: "Discourse," in R. Goodin and P. Pettit (eds), *The Blackwell Companion to Political Philosophy*. Blackwell: Oxford.

Laclau, E. and Mouffe, C. 1985: *Hegemony and Socialist Strategy: Towards a Radical Democratic Politics*. Verso: London.

Lash, S. and Urry, J. 1987: *The End of Organized Capitalism*. Polity Press: Cambridge.

Lash, S. and Urry, J. 1994: *Economies of Signs and Space*. Sage: London.

Layton-Henry, Z. 1992: *The Politics of Immigration: Immigration, "Race" and "Race Relations" in Post-war Britain*. Blackwell: Oxford.

Lister, R. 1996: *Charles Murray and the Underclass: the Developing Debate*. IEA Health and Welfare Unit: London.

Lloyd, C. and Waters, H. 1991: "France: One Culture, One Nation?," *Race and Class*, 32 (3).

Lukes, S. 1974: *Power: a Radical View*. Macmillan: London.

Lull, J. 1995: *Media, Communication, Culture: a Global Approach*. Polity Press: Cambridge.

Lyon, D. 1994: *Postmodernity*. Open University Press: Buckingham.

Lyotard, J-F. 1984: *The Postmodern Condition: a Report on Knowledge*, trans. G. Bennington and B. Massumi. Manchester University Press: Manchester.

McAdam, D. 1996: "Conceptual Origins, Current Problems, Future Directions," in D. McAdam, J. McCarthy, and M. Zald (eds), *Comparative Perspectives on Social Movements: Political Opportunities, Mobilizing Structures, and Cultural Framings*. Cambridge University Press: Cambridge.

McAdam, D., McCarthy, J., and Zald, M. (eds) 1996: *Comparative Perspectives on Social Movements: Political Opportunities, Mobilizing Structures, and Cultural Framings*. Cambridge University Press: Cambridge.

McCarthy, J., Smith, J., and Zald, M. 1996: "Accessing Public, Media, Electoral and Governmental Agendas," in D. McAdam, J. McCarthy, and M. Zald (eds), *Comparative Perspectives on Social Movements: Political Opportunities, Mobilizing Structures, and Cultural Framings*. Cambridge University Press: Cambridge.

McCarthy, T. 1991: "Complexity and Democracy: or the Seducements of Systems Theory," in A. Honneth and H. Joas (eds), *Communicative Action: Essays on Jürgen Habermas's "The Theory of Communicative Action,"* trans. J. Gaines and D. L. Jones. Polity Press: Cambridge.

McClure, K. 1992: "On the Subject of Rights: Pluralism, Plurality and Political Identity," in C. Mouffe (ed.), *Dimensions of Radical Democracy: Pluralism, Citizenship, Community*. Verso: London.

McGrew, A. 1992: "A Global Society?," in S. Hall, D. Held, and A. McGrew (eds), *Modernity and its Futures*. Polity Press: Cambridge.

McGrew, A. 1995: "World Order and Political Space," in J. Anderson, C. Brook, and A. Cochrane (eds), *A Global World? Re-ordering Political Space*. Oxford University Press: Oxford.

McGrew, A. 1997: "Democracy beyond Borders," in A. McGrew (ed.), *The Transformation of Democracy? Globalization and Territorial Democracy*. Polity Press: Cambridge.

McNay, L. 1994: *Foucault: a Critical Introduction*. Polity Press: Cambridge.

Mann, M. 1996: "Ruling Class Strategies and Citizenship," in M. Bulmer and A. Rees (eds), *Citizenship Today: the Contemporary Relevance of T. H. Marshall*. UCL Press: London.

Marsh, D. 1995: "The Convergence between Theories of the State," in D. Marsh and G. Stoker (eds), *Theory and Methods in Political Science*. Macmillan: London.

Marshall, G. (ed.), 1994: *The Concise Oxford Dictionary of Sociology*. Oxford University Press: Oxford.

Marshall, T. H. 1992: *Citizenship and Social Class*, ed. T. Bottomore. Pluto Press: London.

Marx, K. 1977: *Selected Writings*, ed. D. McLellan. Oxford University Press: Oxford.

Marx, K. 1992: "The Eighteenth Brumaire of Louis Bonaparte," in *Surveys from Exile: Political Writings*, vol. 2, ed. D. Fernbach. Penguin: London.

Mason, D. 1995: *Race and Ethnicity in Modern Britain*. Oxford University Press: Oxford.

Mead, L. 1986: *Beyond Entitlement: the Social Obligations of Citizenship*. Free Press: New York.

Meehan, E. 1997: "Political Pluralism and European Citizenship," in P. Lehning and A. Weale (eds), *Citizenship, Democracy and Justice in the New Europe*. Routledge: London.

Melucci, A. 1988: "Getting Involved: Identity and Mobilization in Social Movements," in B. Klandermans, H. Kriesi, and S. Tarrow (eds), *From Structure to Action: Comparing Social Movement Research across Cultures*. JAI Press: Greenwich, Connecticut.

Melucci, A. 1989: *Nomads of the Present: Social Movements and Individual Needs in Contemporary Society*, ed. J. Keane and P. Mier. Hutchinson Radius: London.

Melucci, A. 1995a: "The New Social Movements Revisited: Reflections on a Sociological Misunderstanding," in L. Maheu (ed.), *Social Movements and Social Classes: the Future of Collective Action.* Sage: London.

Melucci, A. 1995b: "The Process of Collective Action," in H. Johnston and B. Klandermans (eds), *Social Movements and Culture.* UCL Press: London.

Melucci, A. 1996: *The Playing Self: Person and Meaning in the Planetary Society.* Cambridge University Press: Cambridge.

Merkl, P. 1995: "Radical Right Parties in Europe and Anti-foreign Violence: a Comparative Essay," in T. Bjørgo (ed.), *Terror from the Extreme Right.* Frank Cass: London.

Michels, R. 1962: *Political Parties.* Free Press: New York.

Miles, R. 1993: *Racism after "Race Relations."* Routledge: London.

Miliband, R. 1969: *The State in Capitalist Society.* Weidenfeld and Nicolson: London.

Mills, C. W. 1956: *The Power Elite.* Oxford University Press: Oxford.

Mitchell, M. and Russell, R. 1996: "Immigration, Citizenship and the Nation-state in the New Europe," in B. Jenkins and S. Sofos (eds), *Nation and Identity in Contemporary Europe.* Routledge: London.

Morris, A. 1993: "Cultures of Black Protest: its Significance for America and the World," in H. Hill and J. E. Jones Jr (eds), *Race in America: the Struggle for Equality.* University of Wisconsin Press: Madison, Wisconsin.

Morris, A. and Mueller, C. (eds) 1992: *Frontiers in Social Movement Theory.* Yale University Press: London.

Morris, L. 1996: "Dangerous Classes: Neglected Aspects of the Underclass Debate," in E. Mingione (ed.), *Urban Poverty and the Underclass.* Blackwell: Oxford.

Morris, M. 1992: "The Man in the Mirror: David Harvey's 'Condition of Postmodernity'," in M. Featherstone (ed.), *Cultural Theory and Cultural Change.* Sage: London.

Morrison, T. 1992: *Playing in the Dark: Whiteness and the Literary Imagination.* Picador: London.

Mort, F. 1994: "Essentialism Revisited? Identity Politics and Late Twentieth Century Discourse of Homosexuality," in J. Weeks (ed.), *The Lesser Evil and the Greater Good: the Theory and Politics of Social Diversity.* Rivers Oram Press: London.

Mouffe, C. 1988: "Hegemony and New Political Subjects: Towards a New Concept of Democracy," in C. Nelson and L. Grossberg (eds), *Marxism and the Interpretation of Culture.* Macmillan: Basingstoke, Hampshire.

Mouffe, C. 1993: *The Return of the Political.* Verso: London.

Nash, K. 1997: "A 'Politics of Ideas' and Women's Citizenship," *Acta Philosophica*, 2.

Nash, K. 1998a: *Universal Difference: Feminism and the Liberal Undecidability of "Women."* Macmillan: London.

Nash, K. 1998b: "Beyond Liberalism: Feminist Theories of Democracy," in V. Randall and G. Waylen (eds), *Gender, Politics and the State.* Routledge: London.

Newman, M. 1996: *Democracy, Sovereignty and the European Union.* Hurst and Co: London.

Nicholson, L. 1983: "Women, Morality and History," *Social Research*, 50 (3).

Oberschall, A. 1973: *Social Conflict and Social Movements.* Prentice-Hall: Englewood Cliffs, New Jersey.

Offe, C. 1987: "Challenging the Boundaries of Institutional Politics: Social Movements since the 1960s," in C. S. Maier (ed.), *Changing Boundaries of the Political: Essays on the Evolving Balance between the State and Society, Public and Private in Europe.* Cambridge University Press: Cambridge.

Offe, C. 1996: *Modernity and the State: East, West.* Polity Press: Cambridge.

Offe, C. and Preuss, U. 1991: "Democratic Institutions and Moral Resources," in D. Held (ed.), *Political Theory Today.* Polity Press: Cambridge.

O'Leary, S. 1995: "The Social Dimension of Community Citizenship," in A. Rosas and E. Antola (eds), *A Citizens' Europe: in Search of a New Order.* Sage: London.

Olson, M. 1968: *The Logic of Collective Action: Public Goods and the Theory of Groups.* Schocken Books: New York.

Omi, M. and Winant, H. 1987: *Racial Formation in the United States: from the Sixties to the Eighties.* Routledge: London.

Oommen, T. 1997: *Citizenship, Nationality and Ethnicity.* Polity Press: Cambridge.

Orum, A. 1983: *Introduction to Political Sociology: the Political Anatomy of the Body Politic*, 2nd edn. Prentice-Hall: Englewood Cliffs, New Jersey.

Outhwaite, W. 1994: *Habermas: a Critical Introduction.* Polity Press: Cambridge.

Owen, D. 1994: *Maturity and Modernity: Nietzsche, Weber, Foucault and the Ambivalence of Reason.* Routledge: London.

Owen, D. (ed.) 1997: *Sociology after Postmodernism.* Sage: London.

Pakulski, J. 1995: "Social Movements and Class: the Decline of the Marxist Paradigm," in L. Maheu (ed.), *Social Movements and Social Classes: the Future of Collective Action.* Sage: London.

Pakulski, J. and Waters, M. 1996: *The Death of Class*. Sage: London.

Parekh, B. 1993: "The Cultural Particularity of Liberal Democracy," in D. Held (ed.), *Prospects for Democracy: North, South, East, West*. Polity Press: Cambridge.

Parekh, B. 1995: "Liberalism and Colonialism: a Critique of Locke and Mill," in J. N. Pieterse and B. Parekh (eds), *The Decolonization of Imagination: Culture, Knowledge and Power*. Zed Books: London.

Parry, G. 1969: *Political Elites*. George Allen and Unwin: London.

Pateman, C. 1989: "Feminist Critiques of the Public/Private Dichotomy," in *The Disorder of Women*. Polity Press: Cambridge.

Phillips, A. 1991: *Engendering Democracy*. Polity Press: Cambridge.

Phillips, A. 1995: *The Politics of Presence*. Clarendon Press: Oxford.

Pickvance, C. 1995: "Social Movements in the Transition from State Socialism," in L. Maheu (ed.), *Social Movements and Social Classes: the Future of Collective Action*. Sage: London.

Pierson, C. 1991: *Beyond the Welfare State? The New Political Economy of Welfare*. Polity Press: Cambridge.

Pieterse, J. N. 1995: "Globalization as Hybridization," in M. Featherstone, S. Lash, and R. Robertson (eds), *Global Modernities*. Sage: London.

Potter, D., Goldblatt, D., Kiloh, M., and Lewis, P. (eds) 1997: *Democratization*. Polity Press: Cambridge.

Procacci, G. 1996: "A New Social Contract? Against Exclusion: the Poor and the Social Sciences," European University Institute Working Paper, RSC no. 96/41.

Przeworski, A. 1990: *The State and the Economy under Capitalism*. Harwood Academic Publishers: London.

Pugh, M. 1992: *Women and the Women's Movement in Britain 1914–59*. Macmillan: London.

Rees, A. 1996: "T. H. Marshall and the Progress of Citizenship," in M. Bulmer and A. Rees (eds), *Citizenship Today: the Contemporary Relevance of T. H. Marshall*. UCL Press: London.

Richmond, A. 1994: *Global Apartheid: Refugees, Racism and the New World Order*. Oxford University Press: Oxford.

Riley, D. 1988: *Am I That Name?: Feminism and the Category of "Women" in History*. Macmillan: London.

Robertson, R. 1992: *Globalization: Social Theory and Global Culture*. Sage: London.

Robertson, R. 1995: "Glocalization: Time–Space and Homogeneity–Heterogeneity," in M. Featherstone, S. Lash, and R. Robertson (eds), *Global Modernities*. Sage: London.

Roche, M. 1995: "Rethinking Citizenship and Social Movements: Themes in Contemporary Sociology and Neoconservative Ideology," in L. Maheu (ed.), *Social Movements and Social Classes: the Future of Collective Action*. Sage: London.

Rorty, R. 1991: "Solidarity or Objectivity," in *Objectivity, Relativism, and Truth*. Cambridge University Press: Cambridge.

Rosenau, J. 1992: "Citizenship in a Changing Global Order," in J. Rosenau and E. Czempiel (eds), *Governance without Government: Order and Change in World Politics*. Cambridge University Press: Cambridge.

Roseneil, S. 1997: "The Global Common: the Global, Local and Personal; Dynamics of the Women's Peace Movement in the 1980s," in A. Scott (ed.), *The Limits of Globalization: Cases and Arguments*. Routledge: London.

Said, E. 1979: *Orientalism*. Vintage Books: New York.

Saussure, F. de 1983: *Course in General Linguistics,* ed. C. Bally and A. Sechelaye, with the collaboration of A. Riedlinger, trans. R. Harris. Fontana: London.

Schumpeter, J. 1943: *Capitalism, Socialism and Democracy.* Unwin University Books: London.

Scott, A. 1990: *Ideology and the New Social Movements*. Unwin Hyman: London.

Scott, A. 1996a: "Weber and Michels on Bureaucracy," in R. Bellamy and A. Ross (eds), *A Textual Introduction to Social and Political Theory*. Manchester University Press: Manchester.

Scott, A. 1996b: "Movements of Modernity: Some Questions of Theory, Method and Interpretion," in J. Clark and M. Diani (eds), *Alain Touraine*. Falmer Press: London.

Scott, A. 1997a: "Modernity's Machine Metaphor," *British Journal of Sociology*, 48 (4).

Scott, A. 1997b: "Introduction – Globalization: Social Process or Political Rhetoric," in A. Scott (ed.), *The Limits of Globalization: Cases and Arguments*. Routledge: London.

Scott, J. 1994: *Poverty and Wealth: Citizenship, Deprivation and Privilege*. Longman: Harlow, Essex.

Seidman, S. 1993: "Identity Politics in a 'Postmodern' Gay Culture: Some Historical and Conceptual Notes," in M. Warner (ed.), *Fear of a Queer Planet*. University of Minnesota Press: Minneapolis.

Seidman, S. (ed.) 1994a: *The Postmodern Turn: New Perspectives on Social Theory*. Cambridge University Press: Cambridge.

Seidman, S. 1994b: *Contested Knowledge: Social Theory in the Postmodern Era*. Blackwell: Oxford.

Siim, B. 1988: "Towards a Feminist Rethinking of the Welfare State," in K. Jones and A. Jonasdottir (eds), *The Political Interests of Gender: Developing Theory and Research with a Feminist Face*. Sage: London.

Silver, H. 1996: "Culture, Politics and National Discourses of the New Urban Poverty," in E. Mingione (ed.), *Urban Poverty and the Underclass*. Blackwell: Oxford.

Simon, R. 1982: *Gramsci's Political Thought: an Introduction*. Lawrence and Wishart: London.

Sklair, L. 1997: "Social Movements for Global Capitalism: the Transnational Capitalist Class in Action," *Review of International Political Economy*, 4 (3).

Smart, B. 1993: *Postmodernity*. Routledge: London.

Smith, A. D. 1990: "Towards a Global Culture," in M. Featherstone (ed.), *Global Culture: Nationalism, Globalization and Modernity*. Sage: London.

Smith, A-M. 1998: *Laclau and Mouffe: the Radical Democratic Imaginary*. Routledge: London.

Smith, M. 1995: "Pluralism," in D. Marsh and G. Stoker (eds), *Theory and Methods in Political Science*. Macmillan: London.

Snow, D. and Benford, R. 1988: "Ideology, Frame Resonance, and Participant Mobilization," in B. Klandermans, H. Kriesi, and S. Tarrow (eds), *From Structure to Action: Social Movement Research across Different Cultures*. JAI Press: Greenwich, Connecticut and London.

Snow, D. and Benford, R. 1992: "Master Frames and Cycles of Protest," in A. Morris and C. Mueller (eds), *Frontiers in Social Movement Theory*. Yale University Press: New Haven and London.

Snow, D., Rocheford, E., Worden, S., and Benford, R. 1986: "Frame Alignment Processes, Micromobilization and Movement Participation," *American Sociological Review*, 51: 464–81.

Snow, D., Zurchner, L., and Ekland-Olson, S. 1980: "Social Networks and Social Movements," *American Sociological Review*, 45 (5).

Solomos, J. 1993: *Race and Racism in Britain*, 2nd edn. Macmillan: London.

Soysal, Y. 1994: *Limits of Citizenship: Migrants and Postnational Membership in Europe*. University of Chicago: Chicago.

Spivak, G. 1987: "Subaltern Studies: Deconstructing Historiography," in *In Other Worlds: Essays in Cultural Politics*. Methuen: London.

Steward, F. 1991: "Citizens of Planet Earth," in G. Andrews (ed.), *Citizenship*. Lawrence and Wishart: London.

Street, J. 1997a: "'Across the Universe': the Limits of Global Popular Culture," in A. Scott (ed.), *The Limits of Globalization: Cases and Arguments*. Routledge: London.

Street, J. 1997b: *Politics and Popular Culture*. Polity Press: Cambridge.

Sullivan, A. 1995: *Virtually Normal: an Argument about Homosexuality*. Picador: London.

Tarrow, S. 1989: "Struggle, Politics and Reform: Collective Action, Social Movements and Cycles of Protest," Western Societies paper no. 21. Cornell University: Ithaca, New York.

Tarrow, S. 1992: "Mentalities, Political Cultures, and Collective Action Frames: Constructing Meanings Through Action," in A. Morris and C. Mueller (eds), *Frontiers in Social Movement Theory*. Yale University Press: New Haven and London.

Tarrow, S. 1994: *Power in Movement: Social Movements, Collective Action and Politics*. Cambridge University Press: Cambridge.

Tarrow, S. 1996: "States and Opportunities: the Political Structuring of Social Movements," in D. McAdam, J. McCarthy, and M. Zald (eds), *Comparative Perspectives on Social Movements: Political Opportunities, Mobilizing Structures, and Cultural Framings*. Cambridge University Press, Cambridge.

Tarrow, S. 1998: *Power in Movement: Social Movements and Contentious Politics*. Cambridge University Press: Cambridge.

Taylor, B. 1983: *Eve and the New Jerusalem: Socialism and Feminism in the Nineteenth Century*. Virago: London.

Taylor, G. 1995: "Marxism," in D. Marsh and G. Stoker (eds), *Theory and Methods in Political Science*. Macmillan: London.

Thompson, G. 1997: "Multinational Corporations and Democratic Governance," in A. McGrew (ed.), *The Transformation of Democracy? Globalization and Territoral Democracy*. Polity Press: Cambridge.

Thompson, J. 1995: *The Media and Modernity: a Social Theory of the Media*. Polity Press: Cambridge.

Thrift, N. 1988: "The Geography of International Disorder," in D. Massey and J. Allen (eds), *Uneven Re-development: Cities and Regions in Transition*. Hodder and Stoughton: London.

Tilly, C. 1978: *From Mobilization to Revolution*. Addison-Wesley: Reading, Massachusetts.

Tilly, C. 1984: "Social Movements and National Politics," in C. Bright and S. Harding (eds), *Statemaking and Social Movements: Essays in History and Theory*. University of Michigan Press: Ann Arbor.

Touraine, A. 1971: *The Post-industrial Society: Tomorrow's Social History. Classes, Conflicts and Culture in the Programmed Society*, trans. L. F. X. Mayhew. Wildwood House: London.

Touraine, A. 1981: *The Voice and the Eye: an Analysis of Social Movements*. Cambridge University Press: Cambridge.

Touraine, A. 1983: *Anti-nuclear Protest: the Opposition to Nuclear Energy in France*. Cambridge University Press: Cambridge.

Turner, B. 1986: *Citizenship and Capitalism: the Debate over Reformism*. Allen and Unwin, London.

Van Steenbergen, B. 1994: "Towards a Global Ecological Citizenship," in B. van Steenbergen (ed.), *The Condition of Citizenship*. Sage: London.

Walby, S. 1994: "Is Citizenship Gendered?," *Sociology*, 28 (2).

Walker, R. B. J. 1988: *One World, Many Worlds: Struggles for a Just World Peace*. Lynne Rienner: Boulder, Colorado.

Wallerstein, I. 1979: *The Capitalist World Economy*. Cambridge University Press: Cambridge.

Wallerstein, I. 1990: "Culture as the Ideological Battleground," in M. Featherstone (ed.), *Global Culture: Nationalism, Globalization and Modernity*. Sage: London.

Wallerstein, I. 1991: "The National and the Universal: Can There Be Such a Thing as World Culture?," in A. King (ed.), *Culture, Globalization and the World-System*. Macmillan: London.

Washbourne, N. 1999: "Beyond Iron Laws: Information Technology and Social Transformation in the Global Envirnonmental Movement," unpublished PhD thesis, University of Surrey.

Waters, M. 1995: *Globalization*. Routledge, London.

Weber, M. 1948a: "Class, Status and Party," in H. H. Gerth and C. Wright Mills (eds), *From Max Weber: Essays in Sociology*. Routledge and Kegan Paul: London.

Weber, M. 1948b "Science as a Vocation," in H. H. Gerth and C. Wright Mills (eds), *From Max Weber: Essays in Sociology*. Routledge and Kegan Paul: London.

Weber, M. 1948c "Politics as a Vocation," in H. H. Gerth and C. Wright Mills (eds), *From Max Weber: Essays in Sociology*. Routledge and Kegan Paul: London.

Weeks, J. 1986: *Sexuality*. Routledge: London.

Weeks, J. 1989: *Sex, Politics and Society: the Regulation of Sexuality since 1800*. Routledge: London.

Weeks, J. 1993a: *Sexuality and its Discontents*. Routledge: London.

Weeks, J. 1993b "Rediscovering Values," in J. Squires (ed.), *Principled Positions: Postmodernism and the Rediscovery of Value*. Lawrence and Wishart: London.

Wheeler, M. 1997: *Politics and the Mass Media*. Blackwell: Oxford.

White, S. 1991: *Political Theory and Postmodernism*. Cambridge University Press: Cambridge.

Wieviorka, M. 1993: "Tendencies to Racism in Europe: Does France Represent a Unique Case, or is it Representative of a Trend?," in J. Solomos and J. Wrench (eds), *Racism and Migration in Western Europe*. Berg: Oxford.

Williams, F. 1989: *Social Policy: a Critical Introduction*. Polity Press: Cambridge.

Williams, R. 1976: *Keywords*. Fontana: London.

Williams, R. 1981: *Culture*. Fontana: Glasgow.

Wilpert, C. 1993: "The Ideological and Institutional Foundations of Racism in the Federal Republic of Germany," in J. Solomos and J. Wrench (eds), *Racism and Migration in Western Europe*. Berg: Oxford.

Wilson, W. J. 1987: *The Truly Disadvantaged: the Inner City, the Underclass and Public Policy*. University of Chicago Press: Chicago.

Wrench, J. and Solomos, J. 1993: "The Politics and Processes of Racial Discrimination in Britain," in J. Solomos and J. Wrench (eds), *Racism and Migration in Western Europe*. Berg: Oxford.

Yearley, S. 1996: *Sociology, Environmentalism, Globalization*. Sage: London.

Young, I. 1990: *Justice and the Politics of Difference*. Harvard University Press: Cambridge, Massachusetts.

Young, I. 1996: "Communication and the Other: Beyond Deliberative Democracy," in S. Benhabib (ed.), *Democracy and Difference: Contesting the Boundaries of the Political*. Princeton University Press: Princeton, New Jersey.

Yuval-Davies, N. 1991: "The Citizenship Debate: Women, Ethnic Process and the State," *Feminist Review*, 39.

Zald, M. 1996: "Culture, Ideology and Strategic Framing," in D. McAdam, J. McCarthy, and M. Zald (eds), *Comparative Perspectives on Social Movements: Political Opportunities, Mobilizing Structures, and Cultural Framings*. Cambridge University Press: Cambridge.

Zald, M. and McCarthy, J. (eds) 1987: *Social Movements in an Organizational Society: Collected Essays*. Transaction Books: New Brunswick.

Zald, M. and McCarthy, J. (eds) 1988: *The Dynamics of Social Movements: Resource Mobilization, Social Control, and Tactics*. University Press of America: Lanham, Boston and London.

Zolo, D. 1992: *Complexity and Democracy: a Realist Approach*, trans. D. McKie. Polity Press, Cambridge.

INDEX